KU-028-172

A Month by the Sea

Encounters in Gaza

DERVLA MURPHY

ELAND

First published by Eland in 2013
61 Exmouth Market, London EC1R 4QL.
This paperback edition first published in 2015

Foreword © Avi Shlaim
Text © Dervla Murphy 2013

ISBN 978 1 78060 067 3

Dervla Murphy has asserted her right under the
Copyright, Designs and Patents Act 1988 to be
identified as the author of this work

This publication may not be reproduced, stored in
a retrieval system or transmitted in any form or by
any means, electronic, mechanical, photocopying,
recording, or otherwise, without permission
in writing from the publishers

Cover Image: *12th Century AD,
Walls of Gaza II* (1994) by Laila Shawa
© Laila Shawa, courtesy of October Gallery
and Janet Rady Fine Art.
Photograph © Jonathan Greet

Text set by Antony Gray
Printed and bound in Spain by
GraphyCems, Navarra

To the many Gazans whose helpfulness
and hospitality made this book possible

Contents

A MONTH BY THE SEA
page 1

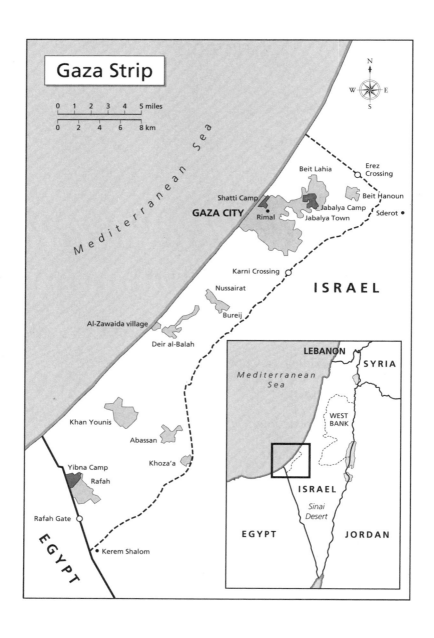

Foreword

Home to 1.6 million Palestinians, the Gaza Strip is one of the poorest, most densely populated, isolated and embattled places on earth. Israel's control of access by land, sea and air, coupled with the illegal blockade it imposed in 2007, have effectively turned this tiny sliver of land, 330 square kilometres, into an open-air prison. As a result of Israel's restrictions, Gaza receives few foreign visitors and only limited coverage in the Western press.

It is against this background of far from benign neglect that Dervla Murphy's new book should be evaluated. The book gives a much-needed description of life inside the prison. Based, as are all her books, on first-hand experience, it sheds a great deal of light on all aspects of daily life and on the dire conditions in this dark corner of the Palestinian Occupied Territories.

The title of the book carries more than a modicum of irony. *A Month by the Sea* conjures up images of a relaxing holiday with buckets and spades, ice creams and sun-kissed beaches. This image could not be further removed from reality. Dervla spent only a month in Gaza in June 2011. But what an intense, eventful and eye-opening month that was!

As Dervla explains in the prologue, the section on Gaza was originally intended as only two chapters of a longer account of the life of the Palestinians under Israeli occupation. In 2008–10, she spent three months in Israel and five months on the West Bank. On the West Bank, she lived in the Balata refugee camp near Nablus. On reflection, she decided to write two separate books. The 'month by the sea' provided ample material for a separate book on Gaza. Hopefully this will be followed up in due course by another volume on the land-locked West Bank.

ix

The inhabitants of Gaza, like their fellow citizens on the West Bank and in the Diaspora, are victims of the cruel geopolitics of the region. The modern history of this region is punctuated by Arab–Israeli wars, starting with the war for Palestine in 1948 and culminating in the attack on Gaza (known by the Israelis as Operation Cast Lead) in 2008–9. In the course of the first Arab–Israeli war, the Egyptian army captured and retained the Gaza Strip. From 1949 until 1967, the strip was under Egyptian military rule. During the Six Day War of June 1967, the Israel Defence Forces (IDF) captured the Gaza Strip and the entire Sinai Peninsula from Egypt, the West Bank from Jordan, and the Golan Heights from Syria. In 1979 Israel relinquished Sinai in return for a peace treaty with Egypt but retained the Gaza area up to the old international border. The 1993 Oslo Accord raised the hope of, but failed to deliver, an independent Palestinian state alongside Israel with a capital in East Jerusalem.

The essential framework for understanding the conflict between Israelis and Palestinians is that of colonialism. Although there are cultural, ideological and religious dimensions to the conflict, at its core is the appropriation of land and the domination of a weaker by a stronger power. The Oslo peace process was used by Israel not to end but to repackage the occupation. Under the guise of Oslo, Israel continued to pursue its aggressive agenda in the Palestinian Occupied Territories. The colonial exploitation was especially egregious in Gaza. At the time of Israel's unilateral disengagement from Gaza in 2005, 1.4 million Palestinians and 8,000 Israeli settlers lived in the Strip. The 8,000 settlers controlled 25 per cent of the territory, 40 per cent of the arable land and the lion's share of the desperately scarce water resources. Even after Israel's withdrawal, under international law it remained the occupying power with responsibilities towards the civilian population, responsibilities it has flouted with complete impunity.

Israeli propaganda portrays the people of Gaza as a bunch of

Muslim fanatics, and terrorists to boot, who are implacably opposed to a Jewish state in any part of Palestine. What this book shows is that ordinary people in Gaza crave the same things as ordinary people anywhere: a normal life, freedom, democracy, respect for human rights, economic opportunity, social justice, independence and national dignity. There is certainly widespread hostility and even deep hatred towards Israel, but what Israelis tend to overlook is the part that they themselves have played in planting hatred in the hearts of Palestinians.

Another argument frequently advanced by Israeli spokesmen is that real peace is not possible because of the Palestinians' alleged addiction to authoritarianism. This too is a gross distortion. With the possible exception of Lebanon, the Palestinians have achieved the only genuine democracy in the Arab world. And they achieved it before the Arab Spring began to sweep through the area from the Atlantic to the Persian Gulf in early 2011. This achievement is all the more remarkable given that they had to operate within the constraints imposed by the Israeli occupation. In January 2006, Hamas, the Islamic resistance movement, won a fair and free election and proceeded to form a government. Israel refused to recognise this democratically elected government and resorted to economic warfare to undermine it. The United States and the twenty-seven members of the European Union followed Israel's lead by refusing to deal with the Hamas-led government. In March 2007, Hamas and Fatah formed a national unity government with the declared aim of sharing power and negotiating a long-term ceasefire with Israel. Israel refused to negotiate, denouncing Hamas as a terrorist organisation. Behind the scenes, Israel conspired with Fatah, the Americans and the Egyptians to isolate, weaken and topple Hamas.

To preempt a Fatah coup, Hamas violently seized power in Gaza in June 2007. Israel responded by imposing a blockade of Gaza and denying free passage between Gaza and the West Bank.

A blockade is a form of collective punishment which is proscribed by international law. Israel justified the blockade as a measure of self-defence, a means of preventing Hamas from importing arms. The blockade, however, was not limited to arms; it also restricted the flow of food, fuel and medical supplies, inflicting heavy economic losses and serious hardship on the civilian population. Another consequence was to prompt Islamic militants to escalate their rocket attacks on cities in southern Israel.

In June 2008, Egypt brokered a ceasefire between Israel and Hamas. The ceasefire worked reasonably well until 4 November when the IDF launched a raid into Gaza, killing six Hamas fighters. Hamas was willing to renew the ceasefire on a basis of reciprocity. Shunning negotiations, Israel launched a devastating military attack on Gaza, Operation Cast Lead, at the end of December. Dervla recalls Noam Chomsky's reference, as 'Cast Lead' was ending, to the Israelis' 'desperate fear of diplomacy'. She also quotes the comment of Norman Finkelstein, another prominent American-Jewish critic of Israel, that 'Israel had to fend off the latest threat posed by Palestinian moderation and eliminate Hamas as a legitimate negotiating partner'.

The encounters described so vividly in this book took place in the shadow of Cast Lead. They were with people from all walks of life, including moderates and militants from a baffling array of political factions, and senior Hamas officials. Accustomed as they are to being ignored by the outside world, many of Dervla's interlocutors warmed to her and opened their hearts. They spoke with touching frankness about personal as well as political matters to this feisty eighty-year-old woman who cares so passionately about justice. Her official escorts were puzzled by her lack of journalistic equipment: no camera, no tape recorder, not even a notebook and pencil. 'I don't like interviewing people,' she explained, 'I just like talking with them.'

All the qualities that make Dervla Murphy such an outstanding travel writer are on display in this wonderful little book: her love of people, her descriptive powers, her honesty, her unswerving dedication to social justice and her dislike of any kind of religious fanaticism, especially when hitched to nationalist bandwagons. One puts the book down with disturbing thoughts about the Israelis and their addiction to violence and collective punishment and with renewed respect for the Palestinians – for their resilience, tenacity and quiet dignity. It is these qualities which shine through Dervla Murphy's fascinating encounters by the sea. They provide a ray of hope in what is otherwise a thoroughly bleak and shaming story.

Avi Shlaim
Oxford, July 2012

Prologue

In 1976, during the worst of 'the Troubles', I first visited Northern Ireland. Distrusting most media interpretations, I wanted to see for myself how things were, day by day, among the ordinary people on both sides. My book about that experience ended on a pessimistic note; there was no light, then, at the end of Northern Ireland's tunnel. Yet now the region is at peace, with a power-sharing administration. Neither side has 'won'. Both sides have accepted an honourable compromise.

Also in the 1970s, Nelson Mandela and his comrades were labelled 'terrorists' and anyone predicting a black president within a generation would have been derided. Yet by 1993–5 South Africa was inspiring me to write a book about the transition from Apartheid.

In many ways the Israeli/Palestinian problem is utterly unlike the Northern Irish and South African conflicts. But for me the resolutions in those places have sown a tiny, frail seed of hope. When a 'problem' reaches a certain stage – seeming insoluble and ever more threatening, inducing despair – something can shift and by default the unthinkable becomes thinkable. Possibly even doable – eventually . . .

Over the past decade or more realistic observers have come to the conclusion that an independent Palestine is unattainable. Most of those who accept the need for compromise, as an escape from the trap both Palestinians and Israelis presently find themselves in, advocate the one-state solution. I am unlikely to live long enough to see this in place, but my travels have led me to the same conclusion – that only a secular, binational democracy, based on one-person-one-vote for all Arabs and Israelis, can bring peace with justice.

*   *   *

Between November 2008 and December 2010 I spent three months in Israel and five months on the West Bank. During Operation Cast Lead, Israel's 22-day attack on the defenceless Gaza Strip in December 2008–January 2009, I was living in Balata refugee camp near Nablus on the West Bank. It was not until two and a half years later, in June 2011, that I was able to see for myself many of the durable results of that war crime (let's give up calling spades agricultural implements).

My Gazan month in the summer of 2011 was planned to provide the last two chapters of an account of those eight other months in Israel and on the West Bank. On returning home I decided to write them at once, while the material was fresh in my mind. Then Gaza grew – and grew – and became nine chapters, having taken on a life of its own. So here it is.

Acknowledgements

Gwyn and Avi Shlaim provided invaluable moral support and practical advice.

Oliver McTernan kindly read the first draft and corrected a few errors which, had they got into print, would have made me look like somebody's stooge.

Rose Baring and Rachel Murphy patiently polished the final draft.

Lovena Jernaill Wilson did all that was necessary to transform the unkempt twentieth-century typescript of a computer-illiterate author into something acceptable to a twenty-first-century printer.

Five other people, who have chosen to remain nameless, provided crucially important introductions and background information.

To all, my heartfelt gratitude.

Author's Note

Many personal and place names have been changed to protect privacy. The exceptions are public figures and people whose experiences are already in the public record.

A timeline of the Middle East conflict can be found at the end of the book, along with a glossary and a list of abbreviations.

A Month by the Sea

Encounters in Gaza

'For the West to concern itself with the lived experience of the Palestinians would be to challenge an Israeli psyche in part held together by its refusal to acknowledge those realities . . . The issue is not the unavailability of data concerning the conditions of life for Palestinians under Israeli control – international bodies produce detailed reports providing the relevant information. It is the apparent inconsequentiality of such reporting that presents us with a paradox.'

Martin Kemp, 2011

One

For years it seemed that I would never get into Gaza. I made my first approach to the Israeli press office in Jerusalem in November 2008, bearing a letter from the editor of the *Irish Times* and requesting a one-month residence permit. Such a request, from a freelance non-journalist, provoked only scorn. Subsequently I made other less direct attempts to gain access, but without a sponsor (i.e. some insurance cover lest I might be killed by the Israel Defence Forces (IDF)) no one would help me.

Since September 2005, when Israel had finally withdrawn the last of its settlers and soldiers from Gaza after a 38-year occupation, the Rafah Gate into Egypt had been the Strip's only exit to the outside world. The IDF had bombed and bulldozed Gaza's new airport in 2000 when the Second Intifada began, and the rest of the 70-mile perimeter was tightly sealed by Israeli land and sea forces. The European Union Border Assistance Mission (EUBAM) had remained on duty at the Gate, sharing control with Egyptian officials. But the 2005 US-brokered Access and Movement Arrangement (AMA) had restricted crossings to a few diplomats, foreign investors, international NGO employees – and a very few Gazans, holding Israel-issued ID cards (an awkward anomaly, inconsistent with Israel's 'withdrawal'). By the end of 2006 events had rendered the AMA obsolete and the Gate was rarely unlocked after June 2007.

However hopes rose among Palestinians and their friends when Mubarak was deposed in February 2011 and Egypt's Foreign Minister announced that the Rafah Gate was soon to open. Immediately I swung into action and with the help of a Gazan friend living in Ireland, and the Irish Embassy in Cairo, it took only a fortnight to obtain an Egyptian permit to enter the Strip through Rafah.

*   *   *

I rarely travel anywhere by taxi – never mind from Cairo to Gaza – but a friend familiar with the post-Mubarak Sinai had advised me that finding a bus could take at least a day, perhaps two days. And my Rafah entry permit stipulated that I must cross between 9.00 am and 5.30 pm on Saturday 4 June. Moreover, Gaza-bound buses – assumed to be laden with valuable cargo – were often robbed by Bedouin highwaymen. These have been busy over the last few millennia on all desert trade routes; they may have served as role models for our most successful twenty-first-century financiers. My friend therefore gave me the name of his trusty Cairo taxi-driver.

So it came about that on 2 June, in a sunny, flowerful north Oxford garden, an eminent historian was telephoning Abdallah on my behalf. Avi hadn't spoken Arabic for years and Abdallah seemed to find him hard to understand, especially when it came to my name. I recommended an accurate description: old white-haired woman, semi-toothless, slightly stooped, wearing black slacks and T-shirt, with hand-luggage only. In response Abdallah described himself: small, elderly, grey-haired, clean-shaven with a big stomach, wearing brown trousers and a blue shirt – which description must fit several hundred Cairo taxi-drivers. We arranged that as I emerged from 'Arrivals', we would each be holding aloft a placard. Abdallah planned to drive me to a hotel on the appropriate side of Cairo and at dawn we would set off on our 250-mile journey.

It's my habit to arrive at airports too early, so it didn't matter that British Midland had transferred me to an Air Egypt flight with a check-in desk at the far end of Terminal 3, twenty minutes' walk away. The travelling public's twitchiness meant a tourist-free

2

boarding queue and an 80 per cent empty Jumbo. Its centre aisles were given over to gleeful Arab children, their play admirably civilised – shoes off, decibels under control.

That evening I noted in my diary:

Vile food, surly cabin staff, sensationally bumpy landing for lack of ballast. No visa queue but closed desks meant a tedious immigration wait. Easy to find Abdallah: a brother accompanied him speaking basic English. Tomorrow morning the hotel staff must be told he's driving me to the airport, not to Gaza. Did I understand? For Abdallah this was *very* important. Of course I didn't understand but mine not to reason why. The Middle East is in transition . . .

Smog blurred the rising sun as we left Cairo's rush hour behind. Abdallah's informal taxi was small and old with one broken door handle and no air-conditioning. It did however have a radio and beyond the industrial zone Abdallah fumbled experimentally with various buttons, then beamed in triumph – we were hearing an English language news bulletin, including obits of regional interest. Sami Ofer had died the day before, in Tel Aviv, aged eighty-nine, leaving 14 billion euros to prove that he was Israel's richest citizen, which sufficiently explains why he was an honorary KBE. The Mossad agents who assassinated Mahmoud al-Mabhuh, a Hamas leader, in his Dubai hotel room are said to have left Dubai on an Ofer ship. Recently the US had punished the Ofer Brothers conglomerate for selling an oil tanker to Iran. In the past they had naughtily leased many tankers to that putative nuke-hatchery, just as Israel was loudly demanding increased international sanctions.

Of more relevance was the next item. Under US pressure, the Lebanese government had dissuaded a group named 'The Third Intifada' from leading a march on Israel's borders to mark 5 June 1967, Naksa Day – when Palestinians remember Israel's seizure of the West Bank from Jordan, the Golan Heights from Syria, and the Sinai Peninsula from Egypt. A month earlier, inspired by events in Egypt, thousands of refugees had marked Nakba Day, which commemorates the earlier dispossession of the Palestinians, by marching on Israel's borders from Syria and Lebanon – and the IDF had killed 13 unarmed men. Then we heard Netanyahu warning that new mines had been laid along Gaza's fence and the IDF had been ordered to use live fire if anyone attempted border crossing.

After the bulletin, as Abdallah put on a rollicking Arab tape, I wished we could converse. (Later I learned that that tape was an anti-Mubarak ballad.) We were now surrounded by wide mango orchards, vivid fields of leafy vegetables, colonies of plastic tunnels, wayside spurts of bougainvillaea and groves of date palms. Momentarily I was puzzled by an optical illusion: motor vehicles seemed to be flying through the air. In fact they were crossing a very long bridge spanning a delta on high stilts. Beyond that flourish of hi-tech engineering we escaped from the Port Said traffic and were down on the desert where Bedouin homes – windowless concrete cubes no bigger than bus shelters – huddle amidst untidy vegetable patches. Most men were wearing *galabiyas*, all women were enshrouded and many carried head loads. For the rest of the way donkey-carts far outnumbered motor vehicles; the donkey was first domesticated hereabouts, some 3,000 years ago. Thrice we passed mothers with small children, trudging through heat and dust to distant towns, but Abdallah wouldn't stop. (Insurance? Or contempt for Bedouin? Or both?) When all cultivated areas had been left behind we were on the coast road along which General Moshe Dayan's victorious troops advanced into Egypt on 7 June 1967.

That chanced to be the date of my return from Ethiopia and I remembered staring down at the Sinai desert as our pilot reassured us that the war was confined to ground level, that the Egyptian airforce had been destroyed by the Israelis. Beside me sat a young

Englishman who had been tutoring two of the Emperor Haile Selassie's grandchildren. Excitedly he suggested that the third world war might soon begin – if Israel invaded Syria and the USSR decided to protect its precious protégé. Everyone then believed that Israel had attacked Egypt only because Egypt was about to attack Israel. In fact Zionist expansionism prompted the Six Day War, which owed its brevity to some fifteen years of meticulous preparation.

Along the roadside, among many rusting relics of past conflicts, there loomed ambiguous tanks which might or might not be usable. Army checkpoints were numerous but uninterested in an aged foreign taxi passenger. As we passed, Abdallah waved cheerfully at the young soldiers who grinned cheerfully in response. Thinking back to the West Bank's checkpoints, I couldn't recall even one exchange of smiles.

Nothing was stirring in el-Arish, the Sinai's tourist capital – an agreeable enough place, as mass developments go. In the old, paint-thirsty town Abdallah pointed to traces of the British army's occupation in December 1916 when Sir Archibald Murray's troops were preparing for their attack on Gaza three months later. Twice they failed to take the Strip from Turkish troops under German commanders, then General Allenby assumed command. Those three battles devastated many of Gaza's ancient monuments and in 1926 an earthquake destroyed most of what remained.

Half an hour after el-Arish, Rafah Gate's formidable superstructure rose above the desert's bleached flatness. Having been thwarted for so long, it suddenly seemed incredible that I was about to enter Gaza. Our journey time pleased Abdallah: four and a half hours including a twenty-minute P&T stop.

I had expected a crowded scene but at 11.45 no vehicles were queuing. A pole-barrier stopped us some 150 yards from the Gate; only VIPs could drive through, we must park behind the three empty buses. My documents were merely glanced at before a policeman waved us on saying laconically, 'Today is problems.'

As we followed the wide unpaved road, its verges merging into the rock-strewn Sinai, an excited young man rushed towards us. He was small, slim and designer-dressed with a gold Rolex and an engaging smile. Seizing my hand he said, 'Welcome to Gaza! You are from where? From *Ireland* – then more welcomes to Gaza! In Ireland is Gerry Adams and many, many good friends for Palestine! I want to show you my country. After nine years in Cairo today I go home – now a doctor! You have paper for my name and number? Atef the name. Give me a number and tomorrow we make plans, I want to talk English to go to America for work.' As he scribbled his details, and mine, I noted Abdallah's disapproval.

Atef raced ahead of us to overtake his luggage, loaded on a donkey-cart. For him a side-gate was opened at once and he had vanished by the time we joined an angry crowd of 100 or so, all shouting and jostling around the iron double gate – high, wide and heavy, embedded in concrete fortifications. Everyone knew there was a problem, most likely Egypt-generated and evidently complicated but never to be clearly defined. The benign afterglow of Egypt's revolution had, one sensed, faded in relation to the Palestinians. Who and where were the decision-makers? There was no obvious individual in charge. Many rough young men in civvies were on power trips, seeming to make decisions and ordering people around in a frenetic way – until uniformed characters appeared briefly, to worsen the tension and distress by cancelling their orders. I was clutching my essential documents (passport, letter of invitation from a Gazan resident, exit chit from an Egyptian government department) but could see no office or kiosk at which to present them. Occasionally the side-gate opened – just wide enough to admit one person. Why was there no crowd within agitating to get out? (I had a lot to learn about Rafah and one day I'd learn it all the hard way.)

When I turned to Abdallah and urged him not to wait, to get home before dark, he refused to move until I was safely through.

At that point the Gate was opened to admit twenty, summoned by an obese bureaucrat reading names from a long list. Hastily Abdallah took my passport, grabbed a passing policeman and thrust it into his hand with an impassioned plea. The policeman looked bemused, then gave it to the bureaucrat who scowled at me and snapped in English, 'Two hours' wait.' Uneasily I watched him sauntering away, shoving my passport into his shirt pocket.

While Abdallah was seeking sustenance in a lean-to café (Rafah's only 'facility') I sat on my luggage and counted my blessings – all two of them. Were I required to produce a different sort of permit, Abdallah's touching loyalty would help. And the weather was tolerable, a strong breeze coming off the invisible Mediterranean to temper the midday sun. Distant dust clouds indicated the arrival of two more buses. The passengers' heavy luggage was immediately heaved onto home-made carts drawn by dainty white donkeys driven by fully veiled women, only their eyes visible. They unloaded beside me, seeming young and strong, able to lift heavy trunks, crates, sacks and unwieldy cardboard cartons. None of the luggage owners, or the many youths idling nearby, thought it necessary to help them. Returning to the barrier, those well-fed donkeys trotted faster, on their spindly legs, than I've ever before seen donkeys moving.

The newcomers were Gulf State workers; some had not seen their families since the Second Intifada (2000–5) and they thanked Allah for Rafah's reopening. (Did they blame Allah a month later when many found it impossible to get exit chits in time to return to precious jobs?) At Cairo airport, police had conducted them to 'prison buses' (their phrase) which they were forbidden to leave, without a police escort, until arriving at Rafah. Now they pressed against the Gate, some silently tense, some angrily shouting at the Egyptians strolling from office to office on the far side. Mourid Barghouti was not exaggerating when he wrote: 'The Rafah crossing point on the Gaza–Egypt border is the ugliest embodiment of the ruthlessness of Egyptian official policy and the cruelty with which the regime treats the ordinary Palestinian citizen.'

I withdrew from this unhappy throng to sit with Abdallah under the café's awning, assembled from shreds of UN-blue tenting. Two other foreigners, hitherto unobserved, were slumped in a far corner. The lanky blond American, severely sunburnt, wanted to settle in Gaza for a year while learning Arabic and was being querulous in an old-mannish way because no one had told him he needed an Egyptian chit. Hearing of the Gate's reopening, he had assumed anyone could walk through unhindered. His companion in distress was an ersatz foreigner, a Canadian passport-holder born in Gaza whose grandmother was dying. He had been told he must show a permit from the Hamas representative in Cairo – a document furiously spurned by Rafah's Egyptians. According to the Canadian Consul in Cairo, it would take at least a month to obtain the acceptable permit, and granny was dying fast. He rang his uncle in Toronto, the sponsor for his Canadian citizenship, and was advised to tunnel in. But he couldn't afford to; no one would take him through for less than US$800. He didn't know any Hamas operators – 'My family is Fatah by orientation.'

As I tried to think of some comforting comment Abdallah, who had ambled back to the Gate, suddenly yelled and beckoned. I sprinted to join him. He was laughing and clapping and repeating 'OK! OK!' Hastily we shook hands before I made to step through the main Gate, being held slightly open for me by a man waving my passport. But then someone slammed the heavy mass of iron against my breasts (very painful) and I was locked out – by my old enemy, he who first said 'No!', the senior officer with the white uniform, lavishly gold-braided. I pointed out that the blue-uniformed man, holding my passport, had invited me in. Whereupon his senior snatched the passport and gave it to a man in civvies who drove out of sight in a shiny new limousine. He wasn't seen again for one hour and forty minutes, during which time I'd no idea whether or not I'd get in. Was this a bribing situation? If so, I didn't feel like giving a present to any of these uncommonly nasty men. Now more busloads were arriving and all was in such flux one felt officials were making it up as they went along. Later we heard that high-level confusion had prevailed throughout the day as Egyptians and Israelis quarrelled over how best to deal with Naksa Day border demos, should they happen. Then some policy shift or softening of bureaucratic hearts allowed a dozen Gazans to trickle through. When Gulf State returnees pushed smallish bags under the side-gate these were quickly appropriated and loaded onto porters' trolleys by un-uniformed louts who rushed them into a nearby building – and perhaps held them to ransom.

Meanwhile one-person dramas – like my own – were being played out on the edges of the throng. For hours I had been aware of an anxious young man – shabbily dressed, his holdall held together with string – who clung doggedly to the Gate and diffidently attempted to argue his case whenever an official came within earshot. Now his wife appeared on the other side, holding a toddler son who squealed joyously on recognising father. Moments later a junior policeman strode towards them with bad news. Father's application to enter had been decisively rejected and mother had no right to be in this space near the Gate. Again the young man kissed his son through Rafah's iron bars, then sobbed goodbye to his weeping wife who quickly walked away – the toddler looking over her shoulder, his arms outstretched towards his father. As the young man picked up his holdall and turned back to the pole-barrier, tears were flowing and I wanted to hug him. But such bodily contact with a female (however octogenarian) would have been inappropriate.

Back at the café, craving a strong drink, I had to choose between Coca-Cola and Nescafé made with dodgy water. The American was again being querulous, this time about his sunburn; he seemed to think the sun itself, as a hostile entity, was to blame. He planned to return to Cairo with Abdallah. The Canadian citizen had gone, having met someone offering a cut-price tunnel walk. Everyone was hungry, the café was foodless. Abdallah remained smiley and optimistic; all my documents were in order, eventually they'd let me in. But I couldn't persuade him to go home *before* they did so.

I pondered the true significance of those documents. Only my passport seemed of interest; the Egyptian exit permit, in theory so important, was being perversely ignored. As was the formal letter of invitation from Nabil al-Helou. Nabil and Nermeen were an elderly couple whose youngest son (a Cork University student) I had met in May at a Dublin pro-Palestine rally. Hearing of my plan to rent a room in Gaza, as I had done in Balata, he promoted his family's spare flat and promptly made all necessary arrangements by email. Abdallah had tried to ring Nabil soon after our arrival at the Gate, hoping a foreigner's Gazan host might be able to cut Rafah's Gordian knot, but his cell phone wouldn't talk to a Gaza phone.

At 3.15 a youth came running towards us waving his arms and making strange sounds which might have been 'Dervla Murphy' in Arabic. This time we didn't allow ourselves to become over-excited – yet it was true, I really could enter through the side-gate. Having given Abdallah a grateful embrace and a very large tip I passed between two brown-uniformed men and was in Gaza – or so I thought.

With difficulty I evaded three competing trolley louts and hurried across a wide empty plaza between grassy borders, stubby palms and lines of whitewashed one-storey offices. The Gaza City bus stop must surely be close . . . Then the plaza narrowed and I swore and ground my few remaining teeth. A sprawling edifice, guarded by Egyptian soldiers and labelled TRAVEL HOUSE in high yellow letters, completely blocked the way ahead. I was still in Egypt, now at the mercy of immigration officers, policemen, currency clerks, customs inspectors, exit fee collectors and truculent army officers. (Those last because of Naksa Day.)

In 'Passport Control', a vast concourse, scores of travellers sat on a phalanx of metal chairs in the centre of the floor – from where they could watch their luggage, piled against the walls. I saw some familiar faces and several Gulf Staters were lamenting 'lost' bags. Small children slept in corners; their older siblings romped tirelessly and were the only jolly people in sight. Of course being *inside* made this a different sort of ordeal, exhausting yet free of suspense. Here everything was organised – moving very, very slowly but one could discern a pattern. The Immigration Officers processed passports in bulk, a bus-load at a time. Then names were shouted, owners went to the counter, handed over a stamp costing two Egyptian pounds (about 50 US cents) and watched it being stuck to the relevant page. I stood alone at the 20-foot-long counter and slid my passport under high brass bars, smiling ingratiatingly at an officer with a bulbous skull, a sharply pointed chin and rotten teeth. As a solo traveller, perhaps I could have my passport stamped without delay. But alas! my being a brazen lone woman obviously irritated this officer. Glancing at me spitefully, he placed the foreign passport *under* a pile of 44 Gulf-State travel documents. It was then 3.50. Ten minutes later another clerk neatly stacked all those IDs on a wire tray and took them upstairs. At 4.40 they reappeared and a third clerk spread them on a desk in a far corner and carefully copied all details into a massive Victorian-era ledger.

Meanwhile I'd been having a currency crisis. The stamp-seller (a policeman wearing a distinctive arm-band) rejected a US one-dollar bill. He could accept only Egyptian money – I *must* change – but not here because the currency clerk had just gone off duty. I stared at him in silent dismay, foreseeing a long night on the Travel House floor. Suddenly he relented, gave me my stamp and sent a trolley boy to wherever irregular currency changes happen. I didn't even register that the Egyptian state now owed me fifty US cents. It was quite a moving experience to be handed two Egyptian pounds, half an hour later, by the trolley boy.

Reunited with my passport, I hurried through a long wide corridor where in the old days luggage was x-rayed. Free at last? No, not quite – at the far end, barring the exit, three men in civvies sat on a wooden bench beside a new-looking notice saying DEPARTURE FEE. No amount was specified; those officers demanded what they estimated they could get – EP 120 in my case. Another currency crisis, another youth sent off to – wherever . . . Now at last I could see The Border, an enormous wooden gate where a soldier glanced at IDs before passengers boarded a luxury coach, with laden trailer attached. This takes one a few miles to the EUBAM building. It surprised me that nobody cheered as we passed beneath a colourful archway saying 'Welcome to Palestine!' and flying the Palestinian flag.

Here all was simple and swift. A tall, polite, English-speaking PA official, his precise status unclear, took charge of the one foreign arrival, led me past the customs queue, paused for two minutes to register my passport on a computer, rang Nabil and requested a communal taxi (a *serveece*) driver to leave me on the al-Helou doorstep. My fellow-passengers spoke no English, seemed ill at ease with the lone woman and ignored me. I sat in the back between two fortyish clean-shaven men who argued incessantly with the short-bearded driver and his young friend in the front seat – long-bearded and long-robed, his turban untidy and his gesticulations uncontrolled. He was not a typical Gazan.

What little I could see of the Strip from a speeding taxi was as expected: depressing. Time has been unkind to the region. In 1500 BC, according to a Karnak inscription, Gaza was flourishing, renowned for its rich soil and deep-water harbour. Thereafter the usual suspects came and went: Egyptians, Philistines, Canaanites, Israelites, Persians, Greeks, Romans, Byzantines, Crusaders, Mamluks, Ottomans, British. Ironically, now-isolated Gaza ranked for centuries among the Near East's most cosmopolitan cities, where travellers met en route to or from Egypt, Central Asia, East Africa,

Arabia. Always there was much fighting, trading and building; not until the twentieth century did the Strip lose its cultural and commercial significance. In the spring of 1917 the Royal Flying Corps sent SE5s to help Allenby's troops by dropping so many 250-pound bombs that most Gazans fled. (One forgets that until 1940 Britain's cavalry and airforce coexisted.)

The Strip's population was less than 35,000 in 1948; after partition it rose, within months, to 170,000. In 1996 Gaza City, towards which we were now travelling, became the PA's administrative centre, sometimes wrongly described as its 'seat of government'. (The 1993–5 Oslo Accords did not allow Palestinians to govern themselves.) Now 'Gaza' has become synonymous with 'blockade-as-punishment' and by 2011 more than 75 per cent of families were wholly or partly dependent on food aid.

Throughout the Strip small ragged dark-green flags hang from electricity poles or are strung as bunting across busy streets – reminders that Hamas Rules OK. The IDF have left many speed bumps on the reasonably well-maintained roads. These explain a low accident rate despite the popular Palestinian belief that if Allah doesn't want you to die you can get away with breaking all the rules. In Gaza City the dominant continuous sound is of motors hooting, loudly and continuously; private car ownership is rare, yet a Gazan conviction that vehicles won't move unless fingers are kept on horns gives an aural impression of heavy traffic.

The driver's excitable friend got off near Bureij camp, the others were delivered to apartment blocks near my destination – Rimal district, which retains many traces of poshness. Because the kind driver had been busy on his mobile, the whole adult al-Helou family stood smiling on the pavement outside their front door: Nabil and Nermeen, their married son Khalil and his wife Amal, their unmarried son Mehat. (Two other married sons have long been settled in Europe.) The al-Helous are 'native' Gazans, rooted on the Strip for uncountable generations. Their four-storey family home, pleasingly Ottoman-influenced, has been divided into flats and everyone escorted me to the top floor, roomy enough for a family of six – at the other end of the comfort scale from my Balata squat on the West Bank. Astonishment was expressed because I wouldn't be using the microwave, the washing machine or the iron. Also some relief: electricity cuts wouldn't bother me too much. However, as in many otherwise luxurious non-Western homes, the most important mod con was missing: a bedside light.

In the elders' flat a 'Welcome to Gaza' meal awaited me and at the time seemed almost embarrassingly lavish. I was to discover that all Nermeen's meals are equally lavish and memorable. Cooking, she explained, is her main hobby. Whereupon Nabil corrected her, preferring to describe his wife's dishes as works of art.

I was asleep before dark; it had been quite a gruelling day.

*   *   *

Waking at dawn, for a moment I fancied myself back in Cuba. The only sound was the brisk clip-clopping of horse traffic as farmers drove their produce to market. My bedroom window overlooked a mature olive grove and a small, surprisingly green lawn with flowery borders. Next door lived a Christian family, also 'natives' and lifelong friends of the al-Helous. 'It's sad,' Nabil had said, 'that by now most Christians have left Gaza.'

Soon after my return from a walk in the cool of the morning, through dreary littered streets, Atef rang – oddly, this being his first day at home. 'Is OK I show you Gaza now? Only today I have. My father goes for long treatment to al-Shifa hospital – kidney cleaning. I leave him there, then find you living near it. At 9.30 is OK?'

By 9.30 I was waiting on the pavement, chatting to Khalil and two of his friends who chanced to be passing. When Atef flung his arms around me and kissed me on both cheeks all three young men hastily turned away before I could do introductions. (Khalil later commented that it's easy to forget how to behave during a long exile in Westernised Cairo.) Unaware of his solecism, Atef led me around the corner to father's car, a new Volvo imported though a tunnel and looking aggressively affluent in contrast to Gaza's average vehicle. I would not have chosen to glean my first impressions from the cool comfort of a walnut-panelled limousine but I do believe in 'letting things happen'. And our tour proved illuminating. My companion, home for the first time since 2002, reacted with mixed and sometimes disconcerting emotions to the many profound changes. Politically he seemed a babe in arms and when I provided current facts and figures, based on my recent homework, they didn't really interest him.

Before switching on the engine Atef switched on a gadget displaying numerous pictures of his daughter Mira, then aged seven months and one week. She had, it seemed, been photographed several times a day since birth. Skirting Beach/Shatti camp we drove along wide, dismal al-Nasser Street where Israel's blockade has killed businesses that were still alive – if only just – before the Second Intifada began in 2000. Mingling with the motor vehicles were scores of horse- and donkey-carts, most animals well-fed, the more shapely Arab horses groomed to a glossiness not usually associated with draught animals in poor communities. Atef looked puzzled when I admired the cart-drivers' skill, and their animals' remarkable adaptability, and the motorists' intelligent coping with these equine rivals for space. He glared at a horse's ear, three inches from his window, and said, 'Soon I hope we ban these carts. They are uncivilised and wrong in a modern city. On the West Bank you don't see this.' He ignored my riposte that, given polar ice-caps in meltdown, animal transport is the only sensible way forward, its waste fertilising the earth instead of polluting the air.

This was a day of blurred vignettes – mere glimpses of camp-slums where malnourished children swarm, of unexpected stretches of empty golden beaches (why were the children not frolicking there?) and of war-degraded fields where women labour in the midday heat wearing garments prescribed by fundamentalist bullies.

Arriving at the far end of the Strip from Rafah, we paused near the closed Erez crossing to survey the site of Gaza's vast Ottoman-era government building, one of Operation Cast Lead's earliest targets. There I noted Asef's (self-protective?) detachment from his birthplace. As a boy he had often visited those offices with his father. Now he seemed to view that shockingly empty bomb site almost as a tourist attraction.

Before the First Intifada in 1987, Israel officially employed some 45,000 Gazan day-workers and an estimated 10,000 more who, lacking permits, could be extra-severely exploited. At least 30 per cent of those 'illegals' were adolescents. Permit holders received approximately one-third of the Israelis' minimum wage. Before the Second Intifada, 30,000 or so workers crossed every day at Erez, a number reduced to 2,000 or less by July 2005, the date of the 'withdrawal'. Since June 2007 only Israeli-approved VIPs and NGO employees and some urgent medical cases (with the right connections) have been allowed through.

Erez's grimly militaristic infrastructure includes one passageway for labourers and petty traders and another for the elite. Those neglected buildings and their IDF-ravaged environs seem to symbolise the cruel futility of 'collective punishment'. At a pole-barrier two semi-uniformed, short-bearded Hamas policemen spurned Atef's attempt to engage them in friendly conversation. Gesturing angrily, they shouted something my companion declined to translate. As he hastily backed, turned and jolted away on a tank-torn surface, I could see figures moving within an IDF watchtower sporting outsize Israeli flags.

Soon we were passing a cluster of abandoned factories, once attached to an Israeli settlement and employing more than 3,000 from nearby camps. Then, briefly, we got lost in territory that would have been forbidden to Palestinians before the 'withdrawal'.

Our rough rocky track traversed a desolation of sand dunes and war rubble and smouldering mounds of household garbage. Here the most destitute of all Gazans somehow survive, unnoticed, amidst low, dusty bushes that half-hide ragged tents and clumsily contrived shelters – sheets of rusty tin propping each other up, with plastic sacking doors. We overtook a small skinny boy on a cantering donkey – riding bareback along the sandy verge, urging his steed on with his heels, singing loudly, a smile on his face.

'See him!' exclaimed Atef. 'He's happy! These Negev people don't expect much, they're OK in their tents.'

I had to protest. 'You're forgetting something – in Gaza they can't replace their tents or run their herds.'

Atef wasn't listening. Beyond a long sand dune the border fence had appeared, less than 200 yards ahead, and an IDF jeep had halted to address us through a loudhailer. Atef, looking tense, stated the obvious: 'We must go back.' He couldn't understand the message but it was either a landmine warning or a threat to shoot us if we drove on. All along the fence Gazans are forbidden to use their sparse dunums (1000 square metres) of cultivable land, appropriated by the IDF as a 'security zone' – another of its many Orwellian phrases.

Turning towards the coast, we detoured around sand dunes to avoid a Volvo-endangering stretch of track abused by tank traffic. Here were a few shelled ruins, two-storey dwellings semi-encircled by fire-blasted fig and lemon trees. Near one, the family was living in tents donated by the United Nations Relief and Works Agency for Palestine Refugees in the Near East (UNWRA). Olive saplings, newly planted on their tiny patch of land – overlooked by an IDF patrol road – could not thrive for lack of water but seemed a magnificently defiant flourish. Ten days later I returned to this area on foot, with a new friend from Jabalya camp, and was shown two poisoned wells. The IDF had thrown dead dogs and cats into this more-precious-than-gold water.

As Atef remarked, one can't readily distinguish between Jabalya town and Jabalya camp (population about 130,000). Both look like places that shouldn't exist in the twenty-first century. Yet the multitudinous children seemed cheerful enough, as did the old men sitting chatting in their doorways (another reminder of Cuba). However, the generations of men in between – the hopeless jobless, silently slumped wherever there was space to sit – gave off another sort of vibe. These of course were superficial impressions; Atef didn't like my suggestion that we stop to talk and buy tea from a peripatetic chai-seller aged about ten. 'They'll beg if we stop,' he objected. On my future visits to Jabalya, as a pedestrian, no one ever begged and several people bought me tea.

'Gazan people make the best of things,' continued Atef. 'They go on living like they were in a normal country. They have weddings, play with kites, go to the beach, pretend it's OK. Israel bombed our electricity plant in '06 when the World Cup started. My father told me everyone invented different ways to watch – *many* ways! Same with tunnels, through so much dangerous sand. Gazans are good for inventing things.'

Jabalya camp is famed for its militancy and boasts (a contested claim) that the First Intifada began here, on 9 December 1987, following the deaths of several workers in a collision with an Israeli driver near Erez. Within a day the uprising had spread throughout the OPT and it continued for more than six years. A memorial to the crash victims in a local cemetery is said to be worth seeing but Atef jibbed at trying to find the way, inching through streets blocked by carts and traders' stalls.

Instead we drove towards the Karni crossing, another militaristic monument visible from the Strip's central road and approached across treeless farmland strewn with war litter. At this crucial crossing all goods entering Gaza from Israel, whatever their origin, must be inspected by Israelis. No imports are allowed by air or sea or through the Rafah Gate. Therefore Karni's closure or malfunctioning leaves

Gaza economically paralysed – not that it can ever be nimble. After the 2005 'withdrawal', Karni was open for 222 days but on 166 of those only a quarter of the truck lanes functioned for limited hours. From June 2007 closure was total for a year, until the ceasefire brought about intermittent openings. Meeting no traffic, we assumed a closure – this, after all, was Naksa Day. Soon we passed a few more recently shelled houses; in the smallest, two men were struggling to repair a shattered gable end. Noticing us, they paused to shout advice. We would do well to keep away from Karni, the squad now on patrol were looking for trouble.

'We go to Rafah town,' decided Atef.

Back on the coast road – the sea dancing brightly a few yards away, the sandy roadside vegetable fields densely green – I marvelled at the absence of any building. That evening Nabil explained: an acute shortage of fresh food made it essential to protect this fertile stretch where native Gazans maintain an ancient tradition of using morning dew to supplement an ever-dwindling water supply. Those few miles reminded us that Gaza, when normally populated, had its own sort of tranquil beauty.

Turning inland, we drove through a few camps on the wide bisecting roads built to Sharon's orders, causing the destruction of some 2,000 homes – mere shacks, of course, but to their occupants they were homes. In 1971 the Zionists were keen to abolish 'refugee' status and they rented land compulsorily from Palestinian landlords for 99 years. Then they offered the minimum of basic construction materials to any family willing to build themselves new homes and surrender their UNRWA card. I was to visit some of those families during the weeks ahead. By now many thousands have left the camps.

Around Deir al-Balah groves and avenues of tall palms soften the camp's bleakness. Then a dirt track winds through Israeli settlement remains, tons of weed-fringed rubble interspersed with rows of white plastic tunnels.

'When I left,' said Atef, 'Palestinians walking here got shot.' He remembered regularly driving past on the Area B road to visit his grandparents in Khan Younis. The settlers' sapphire swimming pools, emerald lawns and spreading shade trees were clearly visible to thousands of their water-rationed neighbours (as is now the case on the West Bank). If Gaza has indeed become a 'hotbed of fanatics', why be surprised?

Initially Israelis hesitated to move into the Strip; wherever they built, camps would be close. Then, in 1978, the Zionists, calculating that a settler presence would be useful, began to unofficially encourage (illegal) settlement. They could help to keep the maritime border with Egypt under surveillance and to disrupt inter-camp communications, thus frustrating any attempt to establish a Palestinian state on the Strip. By 2005 8,000 settlers lived in twenty farming and military units; Israel had appropriated 25 per cent of the territory of Gaza and 40 per cent of the arable land. The disproportionate cost of that occupation provided one motive for the 'withdrawal' – soon to be followed by the planting of 30,000 new settlers on the West Bank.

In Rafah as in Jabalya, city and camp have, to the outsider's eye, merged into one homogeneous deprived mass. The combined population is around 100,000 and the Volvo could advance only jerkily along broken streets heaving with people. The majority were children or adolescents, statistics come alive. Rafah has a reputation for 'militancy' and UNRWA records that since the beginning of the Second Intifada the IDF have demolished more than 1,700 Rafah houses, forcing 17,300 people to 're-locate' – but to where . . . ? Atef didn't know and was shocked by this information. He now admitted that many Gazans studying abroad are unaware of – even indifferent to – events back home.

During the '90s Atef's father held a business permit and took his eldest son on several trips to Israel and the West Bank, places beyond the reach of most Gazans. Atef remembered Nablus as 'a great city, very old and famous with many rich men'. He mentioned the name of his father's closest Nablus associate, a man reviled throughout the Casbah and Balata for selling cement to the Apartheid Barrier builders. 'We stayed with that family,' Atef recalled, 'in a big new house high on a mountain. They liked all Oslo plans but they didn't like Arafat. I think now they're liking Mr Fayyad [PM of the PA]. It would be good if he could come to help Gaza.'

Atef had his own positive memories of the Oslo period when the Strip's cities and camps were freed of IDF patrols and at last Gazans were allowed to build and his father's construction company prospered. But such uncontrolled expansion leads away from shared prosperity, a lesson Ireland has recently learned. The Second Intifada ended this boom and abruptly destitution threatened the majority, even before Israel's blockade caused complete economic collapse.

In 1998 Atef had attended the ceremonial opening of Gaza's Yasser Arafat International Airport, an Oslo spin-off on the out-skirts of Rafah. His father had been lucratively involved and preened himself when the foreign press described it as 'state of the art'. Four years later Israel bombed it 'back to the stone age' and Atef felt curious about the site's present use. Predictably, a pole-barrier thwarted us and its pair of policemen, sitting under a fig tree munching falafel, forbade us access to this 'restricted industrial zone'. We could see only a few bombed houses and low sand dunes extending to both borders – Israel and Egypt. Atef looked startled when I surmised that the 'industry' in question was arms related. Most tunnel-transported goods come above ground in public in broad daylight. But there are exceptions.

Atef then announced, 'I want to make a statistic.' By this he meant that we would drive non-stop from Rafah Gate to Erez and see how long it took. From my point of view that frivolity was almost worthwhile. Hearing that the Strip measures 140 square miles doesn't have the same impact as being driven its full length in one hour and fifteen minutes while realising that at its widest point one could *walk* from sea to fence in less than two hours.

All morning Atef's mother and wife had been phoning him – both in argumentative mood, judging by the length of the conversations and the controlled impatience with which he replied. However, during our drive north he talked affectionately of his family, originally from Jaffa (now in Israel) and slowly being dispersed throughout the Arab world. He was the twenty-eight-year-old eldest of eight. Next came a sister who had just graduated as a dentist and was to marry in September; she would then migrate to Abu Dhabi leaving grief-stricken parents behind. In Abu Dhabi she must work unpaid for a year while gaining experience (no doubt treating hand-picked patients) and this her father bitterly resented. A twenty-five-year-old engineer brother, as yet jobless, was to marry a month hence and Atef invited me to the wedding. It would cost about 40,000 shekels though the guest list had been pared down to 300: not excessive, given the size of Palestinian extended families. A twenty-three-year-old sister, a fledgling psychiatrist, was to be married the following year when her fiancé graduated from medical school; she would be migrating to Alexandria. Atef quoted his father: 'Daughters are guests, must be well treated because soon they're gone forever!' (to my ears an ambivalent sentiment, tying in too neatly with the concept of 'female as property'). Two brothers attended a private university in the Yemen where courses had recently been suspended until the fighting stopped. A brother and a 'baby sister', aged eleven, were still at school. Both would be sent to foreign universities; father reckoned Gazan degrees are now of questionable value, so severe and various are the restrictions imposed on the Strip's four universities.

Atef himself had married the daughter of another Gazan tycoon. 'It was half arranged,' he chuckled. 'Our parents arranged four parties in Cairo to make us meet. Like they hoped, we then fell in love. They didn't know about my Canadian girl, teaching at the

American University – very clever but against religions. She wanted marriage and it became sad. She couldn't see why a Muslim can't marry a woman not converted. She thought I'd stopped loving her and that wasn't true. She cried when I said her sort of Western love can't come first. It would anger all my big family – so many people angry and upset if I'm selfish! This is not the way good Muslims live.'

Although Atef had by then been based in Cairo for seven years, his wife's residence permit cost (unofficially) US$1500. He was adamant that she must never again work though before Mira's birth she had practised as a physiotherapist. 'To be a mother,' he declared earnestly, 'is for women the *most* important! But for us, two is enough – maybe three if my wife wants it. Some women feel shame not to have many. That's why we got a baby sister – some women feel old if not pregnant!' It bothered Atef that father considered nine or ten to be the correct contribution, given demography's increasing significance on the political scene. I was beginning to take an interest in this tycoon and gladly accepted an invitation to lunch on the following Friday. Politically motivated breeding seemed inconsistent with his semi-Westernised attitudes (that half-arranged marriage!) and his dubious business associates outside the Strip.

I wondered then what could have deterred this devoted son from visiting his family between 2002 and 2011, when his parents' connections allowed them to travel freely. Palestinian 'notables' are notorious for family feuding but surely *that* sort of thing can't have persisted into the twenty-first century?

Atef regarded Egypt as his second home but had not been out in Tahrir Square and feared a future without Mubarak. If he couldn't get his US green card he'd try for Saudi Arabia or the Gulf States and on the previous evening he had broken this news to the family. Father then urged him to spend at least a few years in doctor-deprived Gaza. Mother tearfully begged him never again to live abroad. ('Muslim mothers always want sons staying near, giving them respect.') Atef's wife, who dreaded imprisonment on the Strip, vehemently supported her husband. All those cell phone calls had been a continuation of the debate and I now understood Atef's eagerness to take a day trip with his new friend.

At Erez the same policemen were on duty and unamused by our reappearance. Atef waved cheekily before speeding back to the al-Rimal beachfront for lunch in a long-established and grossly expensive seafood restaurant. He was choosing his live fish from a tank by the entrance when the elderly restaurateur came hurrying to welcome him home with embraces and kisses and exclamations of surprised joy. We were escorted down a short flight of worn flagged steps to an agreeable semi-basement (old stone walls and floors, elegantly plain wooden furniture, neatly ironed napery). Only one other table was occupied and an English-speaking waiter lamented, 'Since the blockade, business go slow, slow. Shop food costing more, less for us.' He had worked for several homesick years in a London hotel. Then, 'I saw Arafat returning with Oslo promises and I said everything's fine! And it was until it wasn't! Now I'm feeling a fool, Oslo like a trick to split Palestinians.'

The numerous complex *hors d'oeuvres* came in hand-made clay bowls with an over-supply of oven-fresh Palestinian and French bread – by my standards a substantial meal. Side dishes accompanied the main course and Atef sampled everything but finished nothing. As the table was being cleared – all these delicacies being jumbled together in a dirty basin with fish bones and bread – I asked where leftovers went. Our waiter friend looked perplexed. 'Is garbage,' he said. I controlled a surge of rage; Shatti camp (80,000 plus) is scarcely 100 yards away. And my self-control broke down as Atef sliced a large juicy lemon to clean his fishy hands, ignoring the washbasin in the corner. How many obviously vitamin-deficient children had we just seen, none of whose parents could afford lemons?

Atef looked at his watch; it was time to fetch father from al-Shifa hospital, near my luxury apartment. On the following Friday we would meet at 11 am and paddle in the sea before lunch.

*　　*　　*

When I described our tour to the al-Helous they stared at me for a moment in silence, wide-eyed with horror. Then Khalil asserted that I was lucky to be alive. Atef's father is among Gaza's richest men. His Volvo would have been readily identifiable in such places as Jabalya, Rafah and Khan Younis. Atef, as his son, was the answer to a kidnapper's prayer. I, as an irrelevant passenger, might well have been murdered and dumped by the wayside. Even in 2011 such kidnappings are more common than the outside world realises; Hamas, busy cultivating Gaza's new 'orderly society' image, prefers not to publicise them.

I didn't know how seriously to take all this. Despite the tragic death a few weeks earlier of Vittorio Arrigoni, a long-term Italian resident of Gaza, kidnapping had never occurred to me – though I had been vaguely tempted, in Rafah, to advise Atef to conceal that heavy gold watch which looked so conspicuous (and rather absurd) on his narrow wrist. The Volvo certainly attracted much attention throughout the camps and had we stopped to talk, as I suggested, we might possibly have been at risk. Yet to me, on Day One, Gaza felt much less tense than the West Bank.

Atef rang next morning, sounding confused and embarrassed. We couldn't meet on Friday, there was some complication about his driving licence – of course we must meet again sometime but he couldn't say exactly when. Days later I heard on the grapevine (Gaza's rich class is very small) that his reckless behaviour had earned 'a severe punishment'. I longed to know what that entailed but felt it would be impolite to ask. I've always lacked the essential qualifications for investigative journalism. We never met again.

Two

During the Nakba (the 'Catastrophe') of 1948, following the UN Resolution to partition Palestine between Jews and Arabs, almost a quarter of a million Palestinians took refuge on the Strip and Egypt's King Farouk foresaw them fleeing into his territory should the Zionists grab Gaza. Therefore a boundary was set on 24 February 1949, between two new entities: the State of Israel and the Gaza Strip. To ensure Israel's security, the Arab League (no friend of the Palestinians, then or now) authorised Egypt to install a military administration in Gaza. In contrast, the West Bank was annexed to Jordan. Benny Morris has commented on the various new borders: 'In great measure, and especially around the West Bank and the Gaza Strip, they followed no natural topographical contours. Often they abruptly severed Arabs from their land and kin. A few villages were even cut in two . . . '

Under Egyptian rule, Gaza's modernisation, begun in Mandate times, gained momentum. Newly built cinemas showed the latest Cairo films and traditional home-centred celebrations were replaced by jolly café gatherings, or by music and dancing on the beach. Like their contemporaries in Cairo and Beirut, young Gazans discarded the *galabiya* and the *thobe*. Rich Egyptians swarmed in to enjoy tax-free shopping, safe swimming off a smooth, 20-mile-long beach and seafood restaurants with snob-value. From Egypt's universities hundreds of middle-class students brought back Nasserist dreams and cared nothing for the Muslim Brotherhood's Islamic Revival, then appearing on the Strip but being driven underground by the military administration.

In June 1967 Israel's victory in the Six Day War discredited Nasser's brand of Arab nationalism (socialist and secular). Soon young graduates were coming home from Egypt all fired up by the writings and sermons of leaders of the Muslim Brotherhood, men like Sayyed Qutb – executed in Cairo in the late 1960s for 'preaching sedition'. They could see only one way forward: an unquestioning acceptance of Allah's will, as revealed to his Messenger in the seventh century AD. Modernisation was out. Qutb's successors fixed the 'infidel' label on all leaders, including Arafat, who allowed their followers to be corrupted by Westernisation in any of its insidious forms.

When resistance to the Zionist take-over burgeoned on the Strip, Major-General Ariel Sharon, then CO Southern Command, launched a year-long 'anti-terrorist' operation. In January 1971 hundreds of the refugees' frail, family-built dwellings were levelled to make way for military roads. Sharon used the Druze Border Police as his crack troops; they celebrated their arrival by shooting dead twelve Palestinian civilians rash enough to ignore 'Halt!' commands. Another of the General's favourite units was made up of Arabic-speaking kibbutzniks, disguised as Palestinians, who could mingle with the Gazans and detect 'terrorists'. They were ordered to execute their captives promptly. When Ziad al-Husseini, the Strip's Popular Front for the Liberation of Palestine (PFLP) leader, killed himself on 21 November 1971, Sharon boasted that resistance had been eliminated at a low cost: 100 or so Palestinians killed, 700 or so imprisoned. To an extent, his boast was justified. For several years Gaza remained politically subdued, its activists focusing on religious reform.

In 1973, when a group of young Gazan graduates established al-Mujamma' al-Islami (Mujamma for short), the Israeli military governor on the Strip noted, 'Mujamma is not a problem.' Sheikh Ahmed Yassin led the Mujamma preachers, urging Gazans to join in a 'restorative jihad' to strengthen and purify Islam. The Zionist oppressors were not yet a target; guiding Muslims back to 'the true path of Islam' had to precede liberation. (Or driving them back:

from the outset fanatical offshoots favoured physical intimidation.) The secular Palestine Liberation Organisation (PLO) was then gaining stature, globally, as a guerrilla movement but Mujamma angrily denied its right to exercise political control, either within the Occupied Palestinian Territories (OPT) or throughout al-Shatat (the Palestinian Diaspora). The Islamists also denounced Darwinism, thus siding with the most pernicious Christian fundamentalists. They were not trained theologians – so a venerable philosopher told me, when I visited him in his al-Azhar University office. (Gaza's al-Azhar, not to be confused with Cairo's.) Mujamma's fundamentalism, said my learned friend, might be described not as a movement to reform Islam for the sake of all mankind but as a frustrated protest against a system (Westernisation) seen as belittling Muslim traditions while exploiting Muslim workers. To this extent, as the philosopher observed with a chuckle, Mujamma adherents and PLO leftists had more in common than either was allowed to recognise by their leaders.

On the positive side, Mujamma had inherited from the Brotherhood various Islamic Social Institutions (ISIs) set up in the 1950s, despite Egyptian repression, to help Gaza's disadvantaged. In 1978 the Israel Defence Forces (IDF) administration registered Mujamma as a charity, to the dismay of those Israelis who saw its anti-Westernisation stance as anti-Semitic. From 1979 to 1981 Brigadier General Itshak Segev governed Gaza and commended Sheikh Yassin's tireless work for the poor, who were consistently neglected by the PLO's self-serving representatives. In 1980 Segev arranged a consultation for Yassin with Israel's top surgeons but the Sheikh's spinal injury (caused by a childhood accident) was found to be irreparable.

To cater for Gaza's fast-growing population more than 100 Mujamma-run mosques were built within a decade, funded by Saudi Arabia and Kuwait. These became (and remain) central to the daily life of the poor in most camps, villages and urban districts.

In the run-up to the First Intifada in 1987, when Palestinians rose up to protest at the occupation of their territory by Israel, certain preachers were alarmingly inflammatory and from their Friday prayers youthful mobs emerged to taunt the PLO as 'atheist' and 'Communist'. At the Islamic University of Gaza (IUG), opened in 1978, lecturers who taught evolution were bullied into dropping the subject. They had no one to defend them; by then some 15,000 of the PLO's nationalist/socialist followers had been imprisoned in Israel's remote desert camps. During the early '80s, in defiance of the Mujamma leadership – which prided itself on maintaining order – many mobs ran amok, burning and smashing cafés, video stores, hairdressing salons, cinemas, liquor stores, libraries, billiard clubs, boutiques and bookshops. Meanwhile IDF troops stood around, watching. Israel's tolerance for this anarchy has been likened to US support for Afghanistan's anti-Soviet Mujahedin: another case of what the CIA calls 'blowback'. These rampages shocked most Gazans, whether Mujamma, PLO or unlabelled. Yet the contrast between the PLO's endemic embezzling and the incorruptibility of the ISI's Mujamma officials enabled Islamism to retain the loyalty of Gaza's deprived. Mujamma might lack trained theologians but few of its members ever forgot Allah's views on honesty.

In 1984 Sheikh Yassin was arrested for the first time and charged with demanding an end to the Occupation and setting up a militant cell (Hamas in embryo). His thirteen-year sentence shrank to one year through a prisoner exchange but he was forbidden to resume his chairmanship of Mujamma.

On 9 December 1987 the first Intifada started in Jabalya in Gaza and a fortnight later Hamas was born.

In 1993 Hamas condemned the Oslo Accords as 'a heresy that will lead to the surrender of Muslim lands to Jews'. Edward Said agreed, reproaching Arafat for signing 'the equivalent of the Versailles Treaty' and foretelling the Second Intifada as an inevitable consequence. However the PLO's compromise won international approval and lavishly increased funding. By the mid-'90s most Palestinians, throughout the OPT, had made plain their aversion to any further violence. It was time to put militarism aside, Hamas realised, and concentrate on non-violent community building. As Professor Ali al-Jarbawi of Birzeit University often points out, 'Hamas is a *very* pragmatic political institution.'

By then ISIs had proliferated and were doing much to relieve the Strip's multiple miseries. The unscrupulous Israeli/US-led vilifying of Hamas (shamefully backed up, since Oslo, by the Palestinian Authority (PA)) presents these charities as a 'front for terror'. In 2003 the Israeli Ministry of Foreign Affairs circulated a report entitled 'The Exploitation of Children for Terrorist Purposes'. It claimed:

> In addition to the encouragement of children through the media, the Palestinian educational institutions and summer camps are also involved in brainwashing and indoctrinating Palestinian children and youth. Children are indoctrinated with extreme Islamic ideas, calling for support and encouragement of the Jihad against Israel . . . Pictures of martyrs are hung in every place. In this way, the seeds of hatred towards Israel are planted in the children.

Many outsiders seem unaware of the deep roots, within traditional Islam, of 'social institutions' linked to a Muslim's duty to donate to the needy a fixed percentage of his income. With an obstinate sort of blinkered cynicism, most English-language commentators present all ISIs as an integral part of the 'terror' machine. Yet Hamas' political/military leadership has never had close relations with individual ISIs, though obviously their steady support for the whole system burnishes their image on the Strip – and elsewhere. (The ISIs are so autonomous and diffuse one can't refer to them as a 'network'.)

The best analysis of this contentious issue comes from Sara Roy, a US Jew and senior research fellow at Harvard, whose intimate knowledge of the OPT (especially Gaza) extends over the past twenty-five years. She writes:

Islamic social services organisations typically

- had no (political) ideological criteria as conditions for access to Islamic social services, or for membership in Islamic social organisations;
- evinced no desire or intent to create a strictly Islamic society or to implement any Islamic mode;
- desired greater practical cooperation with the Palestinian government, itself reflecting an openness on the part of the Islamists for better state–society relations and not an attempt to challenge, alienate, or sabotage state authority; and
- prioritised professionalism over ideology.

. . . Hamas's post-Oslo internal shift arguably represented the beginning of a new ethos of civic engagement, a limited pluralism, as it were. It further points to what the scholar Amr Hamzawy calls 'the inner secularisation of the religious discourse' as a means of adapting to existing social, political and economic realities.

*   *   *

On Day Two I walked indirectly to the beach, at first along wide streets carrying light traffic. The pavements were ankle-deep in fine golden sand, many of the office blocks, engineering works, stores and restaurants looked either partially used or abandoned. Years ago normal business life came to a halt and while the blockade continues no one is going to invest in Gaza. An occasional shop offered meagre stocks of Egyptian junk food. Commercial animation was confined to al-Majdal Street's busy roadside stalls, loaded with cheap Chinese goods. I was to discover that a specific item – not seen for weeks – could appear all over the city with sudden abundance when one importer's order had just come through a tunnel.

Most Gazans are monolingual but keen to help a stranger. When I asked the way to the beach by miming swimming two amused men directed me down a long, slightly sloping passageway between tall slummy tenements – the edge of Shatti camp. Then, from a low embankment, I could see Ashkelon's tall factory chimneys smoking a few miles away to the north, in Israel. It was two and a half years since I'd walked along that unwelcoming beach on a cold windy Sabbath morning – I remembered gazing gloomily at Gaza, not believing I could ever clear the bureaucratic barrier.

Here I gave thanks for the relief of a frisky breeze off the Mediterranean. Below me children played on a poisonously littered shore – untreated sewage flowing into the sea, domestic garbage heaped around chunks of people's bombed homes. The municipality tries hard with limited resources but in many districts overpopulation defeats it. Mopping my sweaty face I strolled towards a wannabe café: a bent tin sheet propped on unequal lengths of half-burned spars with three battered plastic tables under two torn beach umbrellas. Five men sat staring at a patrolling gunboat, looking jobless – a look difficult to describe but easy to recognise. Ersatz coffee was served with a glass of water. Stupidly I had neglected to acquire coins and while a youth was seeking change the oldest man insisted on paying my bill. In Gaza 'Where from?' is always the first question and, as in most countries, being Irish is an advantage. Three of those men had had their little boats confiscated and done time in detention for fishing beyond the Israeli-imposed limit.

We were joined by a slim youngish man, an UNRWA teacher who told me in halting yet vivid English how impossible it is to manage fifty 10-year-olds with 'everything not enough' – especially when half a class may be traumatised long-term. He taught at his old school in Shatti camp, his birthplace. He himself had had a good education in the '80s, before UNRWA funding dwindled and pupil numbers soared. In his view, the rich native Gazans think refugees are dirt but don't dare say so. He showed me pictures of his five children (aged two to nine) and advised me, as I went on my way, to buy a sunhat.

A half-hour walk took me back to Rimal, to the shoal of seafront hotels spawned by Oslo: the al-Deira, the Grand Palace, the Adam, the Commodore, the Palestine, all equipped with generators to evade the daily Gazan reality of prolonged power cuts. They survive now on expense-account guests such as UN agency and international NGO delegations, and foreign and Palestinian 'humanitarian' teams who collect statistics to be carefully collated at considerable expense for sponsors powerless to use them. Those visitors' favourite restaurant is the Roots Club, where one meal costs more than a Shatti couple's monthly food supply.

The beach is Gaza's main recreation area – its 20-odd miles free for all to enjoy now the settlers have gone. At 9.00 am quite a few were strolling by the wavelets or swimming, the women walking into the water fully clothed, their long black coats buttoned to the neck, their hijabs firmly tied. Some stood up to their armpits, dunking babies and toddlers, and one swam underwater for a remarkable distance despite her handicap. Probably all had learned to swim at an UNRWA summer camp, during their free pre-puberty years. The school holidays had begun and high-spirited teenage boys were wrestling, leap-frogging, constructing elaborate sand castles or hunting pale brown edible crabs – up to six inches wide – by pouring water down their burrows, then gingerly capturing them as they scuttled away. Meanwhile in waist-deep water their teenage sisters (also fully clothed) played 'Ring-a-ring-a-rosy, all fall *down!*' squealing in mock alarm as they submerged themselves.

Near the port a large café had been improvised by placing tables and chairs under palm fronds supported by lengths of old rope.

Here a young couple sat on their own, husband talking angrily, wife looking sulky. Behind a one-plank stall stood a wizened, white-bearded man selling packets and bottles of unwholesome things. Reluctantly I bought a litre of water; to *pay* for water hurts but on the Strip there really is no alternative. Nabil had warned me never *ever* to drink tap water – or even rinse my mouth, or boil an egg in it. The level of contamination is high enough to penetrate eggshells.

On my way home I called in to the Spartan office of a 'legal rights' Palestinian NGO at the top of a wide shadowy stairway in a dismal semi-ruin – formerly a government department. Two friendly young women offered tea and water and explained that the Director was away at a conference in Rafah but would ring me on his return. They disapproved of my walking around Gaza and gave me the card of a private taxi firm, admonishing me never to stop passing *serveece* cabs – the Strip's substitute for public transport and *much* too risky! All their foreign friends were agreed on that. I didn't argue; yet I couldn't bring myself to use that card. Shared taxis are valuable conversational seedbeds. And Vittorio Arrigoni's was the first abduction of a foreigner since Hamas took control.

*   *   *

Soon I was leading a compartmentalised life, sometimes with my Fatah contacts to whom I had introductions from the West Bank and East Jerusalem, sometimes with my expanding circle of Hamas contacts. There were none of the mixed debates I had often enjoyed in Nablus between Fatah and Hamas supporters and 'neutrals'. My new friends would talk politics only within the security of their own homes – and then often in elliptical terms that might have bemused a visitor not so soaked in 'the Problem'.

All over the Strip small green Hamas flags fluttered high but one saw no signs of macho triumphalism, no heavily armed soldiers patrolling the streets or ostentatiously guarding government offices or banks. Fatah supporters tended to mutter darkly about the entire population being kept under surveillance, day and night, by sinister plainclothes operatives. This may indeed be the case: a foreign visitor wouldn't notice. I was happy to exchange the West Bank's omnipresent hard-faced IDF and PA security forces, their weapons always at the ready, for Gaza's occasional pairs of bearded, vaguely uniformed men who sat chatting and smoking at street corners, their shared weapon on a lap or hanging on the back of a chair.

In 2007 Hamas' rapid restoration of public order confounded its critics. Operation Desert Shield – the Israeli response to the Second Intifada – had left the Fatah-controlled security machine in bits and five lawless years later, when Hamas took over, no one expected the miracle that happened. Since 1987 Hamas had been training and arming its military wing, from which special units were now deployed to uphold the law – often using methods of which house-trained democrats might not approve. For Palestinians the tensions on the Strip are certainly no less than on the West Bank though of a different (in some respects) order. The Hamas/Fatah antagonism, of which I was so aware in Nablus and Hebron, has another sort of flavour where Hamas is in control: a flavour of dictatorship. To me this tasted less unsavoury than the PA's collusion with Israel, which coexists with open IDF support for ever-increasing settler aggression. But then, I was not trapped on the Strip.

Improbably, one government department became my home-from-home, where I could drop in at any hour between 8 am and 3.30 pm to have a stimulating discussion about 'the way ahead', or to refill my water bottle or empty my bladder or seek guidance to some particularly obscure camp address. The Department of Foreign Affairs is housed in an imposing Mandate-era mansion approached through unguarded gates and a well-tended blossom-bright shrubbery. Its large rooms are either empty or staffed by underworked men and a few women – their office of course segregated. The numerous English-speakers were happy to talk with an Irish citizen and my being a compatriot of John Ging, the head of UNRWA during Operation Cast Lead, counted for a lot.

As on the West Bank, comparisons were often made between Britain's reaction to the IRA's illegitimate campaign in Northern Ireland and Israel's reaction to the Palestinians' legitimate armed opposition to the IDF as an occupying force. How would the world have reacted had the British armed forces, seeking to eliminate IRA activists, repeatedly bombed houses in Derry and Belfast, murdering whoever happened to be at home, and bulldozed barns and cottages around the countryside, and killed the livestock and vandalised the crops in areas of rural Northern Ireland frequented by 'terrorists'?

Deeb, my chief Foreign Affairs mentor, ruefully admitted that Palestinians have always neglected to take PR seriously, and have never put enough resources into explaining their case. His colleagues agreed that when given airtime most of their spokespersons have been incoherent and unconvincing – whereas Israel's smoothies keep going with such conviction one suspects them of believing what they are saying. Aysha (a forceful young woman who became a good friend) argued that the world media are so Israel-compliant this doesn't much matter. I saw her point. When Israel sought international sympathy in 2008, as rockets from Gaza began to reach Beersheva, no mainstream commentators pointed out that the IDF regularly attacks Palestinians using US F-16 bombers, Apache attack helicopters, Merkava tanks, naval gunships and made-in-Israel computerised armed drones – these last ranked among the world's most technologically advanced weapons. Why do media interviewers never ask the obvious questions? For instance: 'How many have those rockets killed since the first was fired in October 2001? And how many Palestinians have the IDF killed in the same period?' In December 2008, before Cast Lead, the respective answers were: 14 and more than 4,800. By June 2011 Gazan rockets had killed a total of 23 Israelis and one Thai farm-labourer. In 22 days Cast Lead killed more than 1,400 Gazans.

As Deeb pointed out, Israeli *hasbara* (propaganda) relies heavily on the sort of confusing misinformation that makes outsiders feel they can't really understand what's going on – so they lose interest . . . Example: Mahmoud Abbas, as an individual, was the Palestinians' lawfully elected President until 9 January 2009. But his *party*, Fatah, had no mandate to rule after January 2006. Therefore Hamas' pre-emptive strike against the CIA-backed Fatah militia, in June 2007, did *not* 'oust the rightful government from Gaza'. The CIA had intervened to destroy the National Unity Government set up in February 2007. Another example: in June 2006, five months after Hamas' election victory, the IDF reduced the new administration's talent pool by jailing dozens of Hamas ministers and elected representatives described by *hasbara* as 'terrorists'. *Very* confusing for the general public! Why were terrorists allowed to stand as candidates in an EU-funded and supervised election? *Hasbara* didn't explain that the 'terrorist' designation came after the election victory. Again – *hasbara* blamed Cast Lead's high death toll on Hamas' use of 'human shields'. The Strip is flat and bare, lacking hills, caves, woods or swamps. Where were 1.6 million Gazans supposed to take shelter?

Israel produced a new National Information Directorate to coordinate Cast Lead *hasbara* (lies that cancel each other out are blush-making). This was akin to the US-based Israel Project, responsible for a 100-page advisory document (stamped Not For Publication) which delighted Shimon Peres. He noted, 'This has given Israel new tools in the battle to win the hearts and minds of the world.' To complement such tools, all foreign journalists – embedded or freelance – were excluded from Gaza throughout Cast Lead. As an exercise in censorship this backfired badly; millions of viewers and listeners became dependent on al-Jazeera's show-it-all reporting and in many cases switched their loyalty to that station.

*   *   *

It was a relief to be able to move around unchallenged by the IDF, yet their mechanised nearness soon came to seem far more threatening than those personal encounters unavoidable on the West Bank. Gunboats patrol Gaza's coast, unmanned drones and F-16s patrol Gaza's sky, tanks, jeeps and APCs patrol Gaza's border fence. Nor is there anything 'symbolic' about all this weaponry. Gaza, as a 'hostile entity', may legitimately (in Israeli eyes) be attacked at any moment from sea, air or land. Attacks are frequent though rarely noted by the international media; each kills or injures no more than a few Gazans. Warplanes also regularly bombard open spaces likely to be used as training grounds by resistance groups. Those massive explosions greatly distress children not yet recovered from the traumas of Cast Lead. Discussing all this with Nita, a Khan Younis cousin of one of my Balata friends, she told me that her youngest sibling, a five-year-old boy, has been permanently deafened by a sonic boom – another IDF terrorist technique. Then Nita offered to be my advisor and, crucially, my interpreter if I wished to visit some of the families bereaved since 1 January 2011. More of that anon.

Israel's blockade uniquely handicaps Gaza, yet in one respect the Strip resembles other economically divided societies, its rich class seeming quite detached from the surrounding poverty. When Khalil introduced me to a nearby small supermarket I realised that Gaza's privileged minority can buy anything transportable through tunnels. The rest of the population depends to some extent on food aid – from UNRWA, or an Islamic charity, or one of the few international NGOs still present. These keep their institutional heads well below the parapet; most offices and vehicles go unmarked, apart from Médecins Sans Frontières whose minivan twice caught my eye. In a month, a four-person International Solidarity Movement (ISM) team were the only foreigners I met; no expat workers were visible.

It upsets Gazans to hear sympathetic foreigners bewailing their 'humanitarian crisis'. Everyone with whom I talked emphasised that they do not want to be regarded as people in need of 'aid', like earthquake or famine victims. Their crisis is *political,* not humanitarian. Given justice, they are perfectly capable of running as efficient an economy as anyone else. Their past proves them to be hard-working, ingenious people – and proud, hating their present dependence on hand-outs.

*   *   *

All those dire warnings about Bedouin robbers in the Sinai had prompted a change of routine; instead of cash in a money-belt I carried a Visa, my bank being confident that credit cards work in Gaza. However, Nabil, Khalil and Mehat were not so sure – they had long since exchanged banks for known and trusted money-changers. Gaza has a problem of which my 'ivory tower' bank knew nothing – a problem linked to what is politely known as 'the informalisation of the economy'. In September 2007, when the 'enemy entity' label was slapped on the Strip, Israel's banks ended all direct transactions with Gaza's banks: future dealings could be done only through the Gaza banks' head offices in Ramallah. But Israeli regulations prevented large currency transfers from the West Bank to the Strip without IDF permission – not easily obtained. Gazans therefore suffer from a shortage of hard cash. And money-changers, who employ their own subterranean methods of acquiring shekels and dollars, have become more powerful than the spancelled bankers.

By 2011 local observers – people well placed to judge – reckoned that more than two-thirds of Gaza's economic activity was tunnel-related, centred on goods 'smuggled' from Egypt – and points beyond. I object to the term smuggled; its criminal connotation seems unfair since the blockade has left Gazans with no alternative but to transport goods furtively. Predictably this nice distinction irritated my Fatah friends who argued that Hamas runs the tunnel trade to fill their own government coffers. This no doubt is true but how else are they to fill them, given the Israel/US-led blockage of funding?

Gallantly Mehat volunteered to escort me into Gaza City's 'financial centre' where one of the three banks might be able to cope with a Visa card. This took courage: I could see how tense he became as we entered those enormous, dreary, Mandate-era buildings now associated in his mind with Hamas' world. The first two were moribund: silent and deserted apart from a few clerks slumped in cubicles, looking bemused and mumbling incoherently when we paused to enquire about the Foreign Exchange department.

Then – action! A bank with a queue! Just one short queue in a wide vaulted concourse but proof that here transactions could happen. These men were, said Mehat, public sector workers collecting their meagre wages – wages they couldn't have, I reminded him, without a tunnel economy. We were directed to the fourth floor and saw no signs of life as we ascended an unswept marble stairway.

The top floor had been partitioned into a network of mini-offices and in the remotest of these two formally dressed gentlemen, with tidily trimmed beards, seemed taken aback by our arrival. There were only two camp chairs in this tiny space (a very hot space, under the roof) so the four of us stood while the bankers conferred at length with Mehat before committing themselves to looking into the matter when the power cut ended. Their generator had broken down two days ago and they didn't expect the spare part to arrive for a week or more – possibly even a month. But if I left my Visa details and returned next morning for a further consultation, we should be able to sort the matter out (electricity permitting) – though of course it might take some time . . . I could feel the tentacles of a bureaucratic octopus tightening around me. Yet when I saw an electronic credit card terminal on the little table that served as a desk I knew all would be well – eventually.

Three rather stressful days later I escaped from the tentacles clutching a fistful of dollars.

*   *   *

On the evening of 11 June I was visiting a Beit Lahia family when news came through of the death of their fifty-year-old friend, Mohammed Sha'ban Mohammed Eslemm, who had been wounded in his own home on 15 January 2009 as Cast Lead was drawing to an end. That 2,000 pound bomb killed twelve people, including six members of the Eslemm family; its target was the Hamas Minister of the Interior, then being sheltered by the Eslemms. I remembered sitting in my Balata room reading the *Ha'aretz* account of Said Siam's assassination. A former teacher and founder member of Hamas, he had topped the poll in Gaza in January 2006 and gone on to become an extremely effective Minister of the Interior, largely responsible for the rapid restoration of law and order in 2007. The IDF flaunted him as their second most important Cast Lead 'trophy'. The first was Sheikh Nizar Rayan, 'eliminated' on 1 January 2009, together with his four wives and nine of his children. Mohammed Eslemm had been transferred to an Egyptian hospital on 24 February 2009 – then on 29 May 2011 to an Israeli hospital, where he died.

My friends were relieved to hear of Mohammed's death. 'He had suffered too much,' Sari said quietly.

Amira and Sari shared a small top-floor flat with two married sons and their families; both homes (near the buffer zone) had been bombed in 2010. We were sitting on the child-free roof where Amira grew pots of herbs for sale in the street market.

Sari had been among the 415 Hamas activists deported by Israel to south Lebanon in December 1992. Throughout the OPT this was seen initially as a brutal blow to Palestinians in general and Islamists in particular. The expulsions followed a series of Hamas attacks on Israeli personnel, calculated to secure Sheikh Yassin's release; he had been jailed in 1991. Hamas' campaign backfired – but so did the Israeli expulsions. In Palestinian eyes, these came to look like a panic reaction – said Sari – and for the first time made Hamas seem a possible political alternative to Fatah. Also, the Lebanese year drew the exiles close to Hizbollah who gladly provided military training 'more advanced than anything we had before'. When the Islamists were allowed home, because of international pressure, 'we had a welcome back like we were a winning army!'

Meanwhile Amira had been coping with six children under twelve and she remembered the 1992–94 years as one long nightmare. Then, partly as a result of the Second Intifada in 2000, economic conditions rapidly worsened throughout the OPT and, as Israel continued to expand its settlements, Arafat's support dwindled. Factional violence on the Strip increased when the PLO failed to persuade Hamas to join its ranks and pick the fruits of the overt (Madrid) and covert (Oslo) peace processes.

During this period of internecine bloodiness informers proliferated and in 1994 Amira's brother Riham was executed by al-Majd, a special intelligence unit set up by Sheikh Yassin to detect and punish collaborators. The family was never given proof of Riham's guilt but Sari said there was no reason to doubt it. Sheikh Yassin, being a wise and just man, made sure that all al-Majd recruits were well-trained and responsible. A Palestinian informer's shame stains his whole clan but almost always his immediate family is helped by ISIs and on the very day of Riham's killing his widow and seven children were 'adopted' by three ISIs.

On the West Bank I twice heard informers being shot close to my pad and I listened to a few debates with Internationals about the ethics of such executions. Happily no one ever sought my opinion. Under Israeli military rule collaborators are responsible for incalculable suffering, property loss, injury and death. One can't condone these executions but neither could I bring myself to condemn them where the alternative of life imprisonment is impractical. Every society abhors informers. I vividly remember, in the 1940s, two grey-haired maiden ladies moving from a distant county to my home town in rural Ireland and being identified, in whispers, as the relatives of an informer recruited some twenty years earlier by the Black-and-Tans. An aura of horror surrounded these unfortunate sisters of a man who had betrayed his own – for *money*!

The news from Syria was unsettling many Gazans and my friends felt concerned about Khaled Meshaal, Yassin's successor and a long-time exile from the OPT, for years based in Damascus as head of Hamas' Political Bureau. Sari then told me about the extraordinary events of October 1997, when Mr Netanyahu, in his first term as Prime Minister, ordered Meshaal's assassination during his residency in Amman, Jordan. Meshaal was already seen as one of Hamas' most talented young leaders. It's not nice to bomb or shell the resident of a friendly state, so two Mossad agents, bearing stolen Canadian passports, chose to spray poison on their target. When caught in the act they were arrested and Meshaal was rushed to hospital. As he lay there, his recovery uncertain, an angry King Hussein did a deal with Netanyahu. In exchange for an effective antidote, and the release of Sheikh Yassin and several other prisoners, Mossad's dudes would be freed. Soon after, Sheikh Yassin visited his friend, Meshaal, in hospital and found both the King and Arafat there to greet him. Then he was helicoptered to a Strip vibrating with cheers and enveloped in banners. These celebrated 'the Sheikh of the Intifada' – pictured beside Yahya Ayyash, Hamas' most efficient bomb-maker, known as 'The Engineer', who had been assassinated in January 1996. Sari later showed me the spot where Ayyash switched on his mobile and died. He had been given it by a collaborator.

For Hamas the Israelis' inexorable assassination campaign had been far more damaging, politically, than Cast Lead – or so Sari reckoned. Between 2002 and 2004 the IDF 'took out' most of their senior leaders – and any of their family and friends who chanced to be with them when the missile struck. In July 2002 a one-ton bomb dropped on Salah Shehade's Gaza home killed the target and fourteen of his relatives. Nine months later Ibrahim al-Maqadmeh was eliminated and five months after that Ismail Abu Shanab. His successor, Mohammed Deif, survived a shelling but was permanently maimed. The following year, in March and April, Sheikh Yassin and his second-in-command, Dr Abdel Aziz al-Rantissi, were the targets. Ahmed Yassin was paraplegic, confined by a childhood accident to a wheelchair, and the missile struck early one morning as he was being pushed home from his neighbourhood mosque.

In January 1996, when the first post-Oslo elections happened, the imprisoned Sheikh Yassin wrote regularly to his followers, advising them to take part in the voting. For some years he had been considering a prolonged truce during which Hamas, converted into a non-violent political party, could work to dismantle Oslo from within. In 2000 he sought a ten- or fifteen-year truce in exchange for a genuinely independent Palestinian state in the OPT (as distinct from the crippled creature born of Oslo). Again, not long before his death he looked ahead to the IDF's 2005 'withdrawal' and suggested power-sharing with Fatah on the Strip. A leader so persistently focused on 'peace with justice' could only be a serious embarrassment to governments having a very different agenda. The Bush administration openly approved of the murder of Hamas' top layer.

Unlike the Popular Front for the Liberation of Palestine (PFLP) and Black September, whose deadly militancy kept the Palestinian cause in the world's headlines during the 1970s, Hamas has never advocated or defended attacks on third party countries or their nationals within Palestine. No such scruples inhibit Israel from assassinating Iranian nuclear scientists or any other third parties deemed undesirable. By now senior Mossad and IDF officers feel free to boast in media interviews that Israel has made assassination 'internationally acceptable'. Their reasoning seems to be that a crime committed often enough is somehow drained of criminality.

*   *   *

When I first met Gaza's International Solidarity Movement (ISM) team they were still in a state of shock and none mentioned their murdered comrade, Vittorio Arrigoni ('Vik'), of whom I had heard much over the past few years from mutual friends. Born in 1975 in a small town near Lake Como, he was a freelance journalist, an uncompromising pacifist, a fervent binationalist and defiantly brave – ever ready to take risks in defence of Gaza's farmers and fishermen. He had spent the 2005 Christmas season in Ben-Gurion airport's lock-up and been several times beaten and wounded by the IDF though they knew he was permanently on medication for a chronic heart condition. The *Jerusalem Post* repeatedly denounced him as 'an enemy of all Jews'.

Every week Vik rang his mother, then mayor of Bulciago, and on 12 April she rejoiced to hear that after an 18-month absence he was planning a holiday. At once rumour blamed his apparent kidnapping on a hitherto unknown Salafist gang calling themselves Tawhid-wa-Jihad (Monotheism and Holy War). They were said to be guaranteeing his release within thirty hours (by 5.00 pm on Friday) if Hamas freed the Salafist Sheikh Abu Walid al-Maqdas and his two sons (detained a month previously). A brief YouTube video showed Vik bruised, bloodied and blindfolded. Early on the Friday morning police searchers found his body hanging in a derelict house in northern Gaza.

Hamas then allowed the circulation of misleading information, to spare Vik's family. This fabrication was believed by many – including me, until an 'insider' friend reported the facts. Vik, ignoring sound advice, had gone to that house voluntarily and been murdered by a Jordanian who, as the police approached, killed himself to avoid arrest. This essentially unIslamic action (suicide bombers are *martyrs*) prompted much speculation about the real motive for Vik's murder and the identity of those behind it. Of course there were mutterings about Mossad. Could this well-publicised crime, coming only eleven days after the West Bank assassination of the film director Juliano Mer-Khamis, have been calculated to unnerve the foreign supporters of Freedom Flotilla II, due to sail to Gaza in July? A few of my Fatah friends insinuatingly recalled that Vik's blog had more than once openly criticised Hamas – e.g., 'Since winning the election they have deeply limited human rights by trying to impose hardline Islam.' Responding to those friends, I deplored this ill-considered judgment; one can't reasonably blame Hamas for Salafist influences percolating through on the Strip.

In August 2009, during the Rafah mosque siege, a Syrian imam proclaimed Gaza to be an Islamist caliphate. Hamas had long been patiently negotiating with this fanatic, seeking to lead or push him towards moderation. Therefore the five policemen who entered the mosque, hoping to end the siege peacefully, were unarmed. They died beside the imam when he blew himself up and in the chaos that followed Hamas killed twenty-four of the 'caliphate's' adherents. The subsequent discovery in the mosque of hundreds of suicide vests, packed with *Israeli* explosives, generated another swarm of speculations.

Vik had long since been granted honorary Palestinian citizenship and Gaza's Prime Minister, Ismail Haniyeh, telephoned condolences to Vik's mother. During mourning ceremonies in Gaza City Dr Mahmoud al-Zahar, Hamas' co-founder and elder statesman, condemned 'this awful crime against our friends' and during similar ceremonies on the West Bank Fatah's Mahmoud Abbas addressed the crowds. It would have pleased Vik to see this spontaneous surge of grief uniting so many Palestinians. Meanwhile a Salafist minority, tiny but shrill, continued to jeer at Italy as 'an infidel state' and to accuse Vik of having spread corruption by encouraging men and women to meet in public as independent individuals.

* * *

On 14 June the ISM team invited me to a commemorative five-a-side indoor soccer tournament at the Rafah community centre where Vik had spent so much time coaching boys who for lack of space could never play normal soccer. This centre, in a cleverly converted factory, is another example of Gazan energy, ingenuity and fortitude. It will take a very long time to blockade these people into demoralisation.

At sunset, in a vast first-floor chamber, we joined a dozen men around a banquet-long table overlooked by tall showcases crowded with trophies won during the past half-century: cups, bowls, urns and trays, all engraved and embellished. The only other woman present was a fiery young Anglo-Egyptian ISM-er, famous for subduing Israeli naval officers. Handshaking became incessant as sporting (and other) notables continued to arrive from all over Gaza. Many men eagerly enquired about my compatriot, Caoimhe Butterly, a great friend of Vik's, whose courage as a paramedic working throughout Cast Lead won't soon be forgotten. Everyone received a T-shirt depicting Vik above an Arabic inscription and below the crossed flags of Italy and Palestine. The notables spoke emotionally and at length – until suddenly a piercing whistle signalled the start of the tournament.

In a hangar-like hall, tiered seating for 1,000 rose on one side above a chalk-marked soccer pitch (also marked for netball and volleyball). I found myself in the front row beside Mohammed, born in Rafah camp in 1973. He had graduated in Italy but 'at the start of the Second Intifada I wanted to be with my family'. He was proud of his wife who, having tasted freedom in Italy, refused to wear the hijab or jilbab. 'She's maybe the only Gazan woman so brave in these times! Though not brave enough to wear a swimsuit.'

On my other side sat Khalil, with whom I had already talked several times at the Palestinian Centre for Human Rights (PCHR). A small, slight, middle-aged man, he was pale and fine-featured and abstractedly cold in manner – perhaps a cover-up for the sorrow and frustration felt by all such workers throughout the OPT unless they are simply 'in it for the money' (which can happen). The PCHR is a rare and precious source of reliable information about contentious events on the Strip. Unreliable information comes by the truckload.

This tournament consisted of four 30-minute matches and the hundreds of youthful spectators were loudly partisan in a cheerful way. The not-so-young players wore soft shoes and quite often had to pause when the chalk dust aggravated their smokers' coughs. Kicks now and then rebounded from the walls, one just missing my head, but in general there was something soothingly ritualistic about the slow pace and gracefully controlled movements.

Then I became aware that Mohammed was worriedly reading text messages. When I looked at him questioningly he explained. His fifty-eight-year-old mother was on dialysis and in dire need of a drug at present unavailable. That afternoon the doctor had warned, 'She may die within 48 hours.' Now a text had told him of a relevant drugs consignment being held in Ramallah because the donor (or some PA bureaucrats?) didn't want Hamas to benefit from it. There was nothing to be done, though a mother lay dying. Gaza truly is a prison, not metaphorically but in reality. Had some tragedy befallen my family, requiring my immediate departure, I could not have left the Strip before 2 July.

Mohammed showed me pictures of his son, now aged eight. During Cast Lead the child thought their shrapnel-victim neighbours had been killed by flying glass and decided to build himself a house without windows.

The muezzin's evening summons interrupted the second game.

All shoes came off and, though there could be no washing, both teams formed a line led in prayer by the referee. Mohammed commented, 'It's not that all are so religious, this is just the custom and the culture.' He glanced at Khalil who nodded his agreement. Yet again I heard the argument that 'the Middle East problem' does not have religion at its root though it so well suits the 'international community' (code for the US and its allies) to harp on about Islamic terrorism. Echoing many other Palestinians, Mohammed urged me always to use 'Zionist' rather than 'Jewish' in relation to Israel's multiple crimes. In Bologna he had shared a student flat with a Jew who became and remains a close friend. He recalled Palestine's pre-Zionist harmony and affirmed, 'We can live together again and we will! Some time in the future, in spite of everything!' Again he glanced at Khalil who nodded – then added, with quiet vehemence, 'Support BDS!' referring to the Palestinian call for boycott, divestment and sanctions against Israel until it complies with international law.

Between the second and third rounds all eight teams posed for photographs – with me as the reluctant centrepiece. Minutes into the fourth round the electricity went off, to no one's surprise. There were disappointed groans but no angry shouts. Matches flared here and there in the blackness and a few ISM torches enabled us to find our way out to the starlit car park. The tournament would be completed on the morrow. 'Gazans are adaptable,' observed Mohammed. 'It's how we have to be.'

As we drove out of the darkened town, candles were flitting like glow-worms through homes lucky enough to have them. Khalil remarked, in his precise, slightly squeaky voice, 'Isn't it sad to think how Gaza seemed in 1660. Travellers compared its cultural life and economic importance to Paris.'

I didn't feel it necessary to reply; he seemed to be talking almost to himself.

Three

Vik's closest Gazan friend was Mohammed al-Zaim, a tall, hand-some, elegant intellectual who for some weeks had been helping Tom, a volunteer from the United States. Tom was making a video about a Gazan family and Mohammed suggested I accompany what the Israelis describe as 'that propaganda network' – the ISM video-makers. (Once back home, ISM-ers try to educate their neighbours about what is really going on in Gaza.)

In 1948 Naser's newly married grandparents had fled from their home near Beersheva and squatted outside the village of Juhor al-Dik, close to what was to become the Erez border crossing. For many years the grandfather laboured in Jaffa, gradually saving enough to buy a patch of land and build a two-storey house measuring 100 square metres. After Israel's seizure of Gaza Naser's father had married, found work in a settlers' factory, lived frugally and by 2001 had acquired three cows, a small flock of sheep and goats and a shed full of hens. All were killed during the Second Intifada when the IDF dumped some of the carcasses in the family's two wells.

From the end of a motor track Mohammed, Tom and I followed Naser along a pathlet between unweeded fields of peppers, squash, some leafy green vegetable and a dunum of ominously dehydrated maize. Naser's house stands alone, only 400 metres from the border. When the IDF shelled it on 13 July 2010 Naser was living there with his widowed mother, his wife Ghada and their five children. Ghada, sitting outside the door with her two-year-old son, was killed instantly and two visiting relatives were badly injured.

Despite major structural damage, UNRWA couldn't help because the house had not been totally destroyed. While repairing it as best they could, the family moved into the village where Ghada was buried. Two nights later Naser woke to find only the two-year-old remaining in the children's bed. As he was rushing out of his one-room shack a neighbour arrived – the missing four had been found in the cemetery, crouching around their mother's grave shouting 'Wake up!' Next morning Naser took the children back to their damaged home, two miles away, where his younger brothers were camping while rebuilding.

In February 2011 Naser remarried – his perceived duty, to provide the children with a step-mother (and no doubt several half-siblings). The original fatal shell had been fired from a tank on a nearby hillock. At 9.15 pm on 28 April 2011, after dark, six more shells were fired from the same place, four finding their target and leaving it uninhabitable. Six adults and the children were then living there. Shrapnel severely wounded ten-year-old Alaa Adin's head and abdomen; he spent seven weeks in hospital. Shrapnel also penetrated the chest and abdomen of five-year-old Misa, who needed a month in hospital. Naser's brothers suffered face and leg injuries. An ambulance arrived within thirty minutes, after unusually rapid coordination between the International Red Cross (ICRC) and the IDF. Otherwise Alaa Adin might have died, as so many do when coordination is delayed. (Ambulances rushing to the rescue without coordination are often attacked by the IDF – the vehicle destroyed, the paramedics killed or wounded.)

Approaching the thrice-shelled house, we could see a donkey, a cow and a handsome pony tethered near a stack of hay bales (ersatz hay, more weeds than grass). On the only chair in the roofless hallway sat Naser's sixty-five-year-old mother – hunched forward, leaning on a stick, her face expressionless, seeming not to register our presence. Naser explained that she refused to leave her home again and slept under the remaining fragment of roof, at the back of the hallway.

Cautiously we ascended the semi-shattered cement stairway to two little bedrooms, one with an intact bauble-decorated dressing table against a half-demolished wall. The children's mattress on the floor was heavily blood-stained. Beyond the 'buffer zone' two army jeeps were visible, trailing dust along the ridge. From the closest watchtower a soldier – doubtless angered by Tom's filming – yelled through a megaphone before firing a shot in the air. In December 2010 the kitchen opposite had been hit by a solitary shell which just missed the cooking gas cylinder.

At the foot of the stairs we sat on stools of concrete blocks while the brothers boiled a tea kettle on their Primus stove; they were camping beside their mother. Three of her twelve children were dead, another three were being held without charge in Israeli detention camps. As we talked a helicopter gunship flew low enough to stop the conversation and the army jeeps reappeared. Then Tom asked Naser, 'How can you go on living here, never knowing when the next attack will come?' Quietly Naser replied that after all his family's efforts to buy land and build a home no one could intimidate them into moving. This is a Palestinian quality not understood by Zionists, comprised of courage, obstinacy and a calm sort of pride. The IDF have the weaponry, the Palestinians have *samoud*.

Naser was a tall, well-built man, clean-shaven and dressed in his best for the video but looking much older than his years. He began to limp slightly while escorting us back to the taxi; it was parked beside three rudimentary tents holding four single beds donated by an Islamic charity. Here lived most of the family and the two convalescent children sat together on a bed, playing with a string of beads, the scar still visible on Alaa Adin's scalp. Courtesy required us to wait for Naser's new wife to brew tiny cups of Turkish coffee with a kick like a mule. As a drone passed overhead, and three more jeeps patrolled the ridge, Naser drew our attention to newly planted olive saplings, replacing a grove bulldozed in

2008. An adjacent bushy patch half-hid the village's communal beehives. Gazan honey is superb and I was paying the equivalent of £11.50 per kilo in the Rimal grocery store. These villagers sold their harvest, in bulk, for little more than £3 per kilo.

In 2005 the 'withdrawing' IDF declared a 'free-fire' buffer zone, some 500 metres wide, on Gaza's side of the border. After Cast Lead this was extended to a kilometre or so, encompassing 30 per cent of the Strip's cultivable land. 'Free-fire' means Israeli soldiers can shoot, without warning, any who venture into the zone. Of necessity many Gazans take this risk and among farmers and rubble collectors the death toll has been high. ISM-ers regularly accompany such families and remain close to them all day, making random murder less likely. The international reaction to the deaths of Rachel Corrie and Tom Hurndall (ISM-ers killed by the IDF in Gaza in 2003) affords foreigners a degree of protection.

The Strip's ISM-ers, like their West Bank comrades, also support the weekly non-violent protests held at strategic points. In northern Gaza a talented group of activists organises Tuesday demos not far from Erez. 'Local Initiative Beit Hanoun' also run educational and cultural events; they attribute their high energy level to memories of a November night in 2006 when an artillery shell killed nineteen sleeping Beit Hanounians. On that occasion the IDF apologised – 'a faulty target device', the shell had been aimed at a nearby rocketeers' base.

One Tuesday morning I joined the ISM-ers. We were first at the meeting point on the northern edge of Beit Hanoun outside a bombed Agricultural Research College where a lone donkey wandered through the rubble finding a weed here and there. Within the next hour *serveeces* delivered a few score young men and a dozen young women, several carrying megaphones. Sitting in the limited shade of a crumbling wall I talked to a petite twenty-year-old wearing jeans and a carelessly tied hijab. At intervals she stood up to shout – 'I hate non-violence!' With relish she mentioned the previous week's casualty, a young man kneecapped by IDF forces from a watchtower.

Eventually the 'Local Initiative' minivan arrived, driven by an older man with an air of authority. He distributed yellow jackets and supervised everyone's possessions – apart from megaphones and flags – being stowed in the van. Then our noisy, flag-waving march, led by three brothers carrying a sheet-sized banner, straggled down a rough slope, past a noisome smouldering garbage dump, along a laneway between prickly pear hedges – now within sight and earshot of IDF watchtowers. Our chanting became more defiant as we crossed a field of thorny scrub brightened by a tall weed with golden flowers – land no longer cultivated, so many local farmers had been shot. As we stood in a line on a long ridge of earth, some 500 metres from the fence, there was no reaction: nothing and no one moved on the army road or in the watch-towers. My companions began to look a little foolish and turned up the volume on their taunting chant – apparently calculated to provoke a response which could later be rightly described as 'excessive'. Soon we retreated – more slowly, in small groups – and Tom teased me. This anti-climax was all my fault: seeing an ancient female International, the IDF chose to hold their fire.

On the West Bank I had felt uneasy about certain ISM-ers and other Internationals who seemed too eager for angry confrontations to 'enhance' their video albums. Sometimes I wondered – do these set-piece protests, often attended by small groups of sympathetic Israelis, achieve anything? The publicity generated has slightly benefited a few communities but such demos can't Stop the Wall – or halt house demolitions – or curb settler outrages. Since 2008 they have been organised by the Popular Struggle Coordination Committee (PSCC) which since October 2009 has been receiving from the PA a monthly subsidy of 50,000 shekels – adding up to US$125,000 annually. However, I felt no such reservations on the Strip, where the ISM-ers I met were protecting fishermen at sea and farmers in the buffer zone – an enterprise very different from 'professional' demonstrating.

As we passed the reeking garbage, tons were being loaded into three metal trucks (Second World War models) for transport to – where? Nobody knew. Perhaps to be dumped offshore because Beit Hanounians had complained about the fumes.

An al-Azhar student wearing a Freedom Flotilla T-shirt overtook me and introduced himself as Mehat. He talked of Vik, recalling that in 2009 a US right-wing website had issued death threats against the 'Jew-hater', giving details of how to find him. In exchange, I recalled Juliano Mer-Khamis's reference, when I spoke with him a few months before his assassination, to death threats from Salafists within Jenin camp – thugs who reviled him for running a 'mixed' theatre group. Mehat feared for all ISM-ers, given the resurgence of extremism in Israel, in the US and among Palestinians themselves. Unlike NGO employees, ISM-ers are not controlled by bosses attentive to advice from wimpish governments. They can take risks when compassion seems to demand courage rather than prudence – and so they have their own 'martyrs'. Mehat also spoke of his (and Vik's) close friend Sharyn Lock, who worked 20 hours a day as a paramedic throughout Cast Lead, sometimes riding in 'uncoordinated' ambulances. Her understated record of those 22 days (*Gaza Beneath the Bombs*, written with Sarah Irving) must surely become the classic account of Israel's shame.

Our rickety *serveece* paused in Beit Hanoun's centre to pick up three youths and a Canadian woman volunteer who sat on Mehat's lap in the front passenger seat. Now the taxi was comically overloaded – everybody sitting on somebody else – and soon our survival seemed to me rather unlikely. Rebel songs were played, all the Gazans loudly joining in, and the driver often took both hands off the wheel to conduct an imaginary band as we dodged through the Strip's erratic mix of horse and motor vehicles. Mohammed later remarked that such episodes of reckless jollity are part of the Palestinians' coping mechanism.

*　　*　　*

When Alexander conquered the Strip in 332 BC, Gaza's port had long served as one of Persia's most important harbours. Now it is a sad, stagnant place, the nearby luxury hotels seeming to mock its dereliction. Pairs of Hamas naval policemen sit outside a hut by the wide gateway, not needing to look vigilant. On the opposite walls graffiti artists have painted portraits of Vik, for years among the most daring escorts of Gazan fishermen. On various occasions he was arrested at sea, wounded, imprisoned, deported. When I wore my commemorative T-shirt the police cheered.

Strolling around the almost-deserted harbour, I noticed numerous small bullet-holed fishing vessels. One sun-blackened grandad wore a short ragged beard and a ravelling woollen cap on tousled grey curls. He spoke basic English and pointed to a dismantled engine belonging to his son – a father of nine, dependent on fishing. The engine had been badly damaged within the three-mile limit; repairs would cost 3,000 shekels – an unattainable sum, unless the hard-pressed al-Tawfiq Fishermen's Co-op could help. Yet grandad assured me that not all Israeli sailors are bad, some treat you fairly . . . I often marvelled at this willingness, on the part of older Palestinians, to give Israelis their due – if earned.

Gaza's 40,000 or so fishermen are not refugees, therefore don't qualify for UNRWA support. Yet the blockade has reduced them to destitution. Their average annual catch used to be around 3,000 tons, now it is less than 500. Families who were earning about £350 a month, before the Second Intifada, now earn less than £80. The traditional deep-sea fishing in international waters has been illegally forbidden by Israel. Boats must keep within a six-mile limit – often diminished, in practice, to three miles. Israel's navy is even more blatantly aggressive than its army if it even suspects the limits have been crossed. Nets are ripped to bits and explosives often used to disperse a shoal as crews make to draw in their catch. Boats are regularly rammed – or all lights may be shattered, causing the craft to drift off course. This can provide a pretext for arresting the crew, destroying their equipment and impounding their vessel. Water-cannon are a favourite weapon, their load of foul liquid (sewage or some chemical brew?) causing nausea, headaches and rashes. Naval trigger-happiness is so common that by now gunshot wounds are almost taken for granted as an occupational hazard.

Over the past decade, the ISM has assembled a solid body of evidence, visual and aural, proving that in the persecution of Gazan fishermen Israel violates the Fourth Geneva Convention every day and night. Volunteers often sail with the crews; less often, their own tiny boat (costly to run) joins a fishing fleet. Twice I hoped to sail but on the first morning a mini-gale confined everyone to harbour and on the second morning the ISM boat's engine resolutely refused to start and was pronounced by an expert to be in terminal decline. This was a big worry; to maintain its independence, the ISM is funded only by its volunteers.

*   *   *

Nabil and Nermeen were uneasy about my wandering alone around Gaza; having spent most of their adult lives in Saudi Arabia they couldn't adjust to my way of being. Granted, it soon became apparent that as an improperly dressed woman, walking alone, I was hated by Gaza's fanatics, men quite capable of killing a non-conforming relative. Extreme disapproval may be disguised but hatred is unmistakable and looks so loaded have the force of something physical. I thought about the al-Helous' warning, then decided it would be silly to allow a tiny minority to come between me and the welcoming majority. Perhaps because of their peculiar isolation, the Gazans seemed even friendlier than the West Bankers, even more eager, despite the prevailing poverty, to offer hospitality

57

– maybe no more than a mug of water but one sensed that the gesture of *giving* was an important assertion of their identity.

Casual heart-warming encounters were frequent. In the Ash Sharqi district, one too-hot forenoon, I rested in the shade of a fig tree, its roots thrusting through the concrete of steps leading down to a bomb site. Rebuilding was being attempted without the aid of machinery. A donkey-cart had drawn rubble from elsewhere to be recycled by four men, two of whom were wrestling with a 300-foot-long plastic pipe. It stretched from a domestic water main to an improvised concrete-mixer, an ingenious mating of tar-barrels with an old-fashioned bath tub. Quickly little boys gathered around me, then were joined by teenage brothers – all smiling, curious, polite, seeming astonished by my sweat-flow rate. One lad ran into the hosepipe house, then emerged to present me with a chipped mug of water. An impromptu English lesson followed, illustrated with photographs of my granddaughters and dogs.

In a little café near Shatti Camp, on the ground floor of a half-bombed apartment block, all the shelves and showcases were bare but a large circular tray of syrupy pastry stood inside the door. As I entered a small girl, raggedly dressed, was buying a takeaway triangle. I requested two triangles and a coffee, and was invited to sit at the one tiny table. The owner and his adult son repeatedly asserted 'Hamas good, Fatah bad!' At the mention of Ireland both exclaimed in unison – 'Bobby Sands!' They envied me because now 'no more fighting'. But they were not interested in Gerry Adams' visit to Gaza to talk about reconciliation. While the Occupation continued they didn't want to stop fighting. We talked for over an hour and my cup was twice refilled but no payment would be accepted.

At noon one day, as I walked slowly uphill from the port, an elderly man noticed my crossing the road to avail of a high wall's shadow. He was returning to his Rimal flat and spontaneously invited me in 'to drink coffee'. His widowed daughter lay on a divan watching al-Jazeera in a large comfortable living-room overlooking a garden ablaze with flame-of-the-forest. Majda's husband had been killed in the 2007 conflict, less than a year after their marriage. A yellow Fatah flag flew on the balcony. She was a jobless though highly qualified teacher. Gaza's overcrowded schools work in two or three daily shifts, some classes starting at 6.00 am, but no one had enough money to pay enough teachers . . . An older brother lived in Stockholm, was married with two sons and had invited his father to visit – even sent a return ticket. But so far it had proved impossible to get either a Swedish tourist visa or an exit permit from Hamas. A younger brother, Yousef, soon joined us and Father urged me to stay to lunch. He looked incredulous, then peeved, when I explained that I eat only at breakfast time but would be happy to drink more coffee while the family lunched. Yousef was a tense twenty-four-year-old chemistry graduate hoping to migrate to a Gulf state. But because Hamas likes to punish Fatah families he, too, might be refused an exit permit.

Mrs Halaweh's invitation was equally spontaneous. We met on the beach where this great-grandmother was supervising the aquatic gambols of five-year-old twin boys. They were bright-eyed and bouncy and already confident swimmers but impressively attentive to great-grandmaternal directives. Mrs Halaweh, another Rimal resident, went bareheaded – a loud statement. She invited me to drink coffee on the following Friday when the twins' UNRWA-employed parents would have the day off and we could enjoy a tête à tête.

A native Gazan, born into 'old money', Mrs Halaweh had no time for either Hamas or Fatah. When she was young, women didn't have to swim fully clothed and wine with a meal was taken for granted. Her photo albums held scores of Brownie black-and-white snaps, as sharp as the day they were printed, showing bathing-suited Gazans of both sexes posing beside picnic hampers and ballroom dancing on floodlit platforms laid across the sand below what is now the al-Deira Hotel. In those good old days, under Egyptian military rule, it seemed the Strip was becoming 'civilised'. The biggest album held all the studio portraits, from infancy to graduation, of Mrs Halaweh's children: six sons, three daughters. The twins' paternal grandfather, I noticed, was himself an identical twin.

Suddenly my hostess let her anger off the leash. Egypt's exit had allowed 'those Mujamma people' to infiltrate. She hadn't been able to counter their influence, had seen how their grip tightened, until now her grandsons wouldn't let their wives go bareheaded and her own granddaughters wouldn't be seen in public without a *thobe* and didn't *want* to be free. That was what most upset her. In the '70s and '80s her grown-up daughters had resented the Mujamma's bullying and scorned the Islamists' perverting of Koranic texts. Now their children, as young adults, believed in those perversions, felt it would be sinful to break the rules – sinful *and* unpatriotic. Only by being 'faithful to Islam' could the infidel be defeated and the Occupation ended. 'But *I'm* faithful to Islam!' declaimed Mrs Halaweh. 'Every Friday I go to the mosque, I keep the Ramadan fast – but I'll never wear the *hijab* and *thobe*.'

My hostess was of course exaggerating; not all young Gazans are as broken-spirited as she considered her grandchildren to be. Many students admitted to me, sotto voce, 'We'd like to live normal.' Also, The Strip has a hard-working though low-key branch of The Palestinian Working Woman Society for Development which valiantly runs a Gender Resources Centre. In December 2010 they produced a harrowing report, 'Testimonies from the Gaza Strip', which stated that 'The practice of violence against women in the Gaza Strip is based on man's belief that violence is the suitable tool to control women's behaviour. Practising violence is not only limited to housewives or uneducated women, but also extended to working and educated women'.

*   *   *

Not for many years have I visited a crowded place as tourist-free as Gaza beach, where I was seen as an object of interest, a stranger to be offered help and hospitality. When I paused to rest, people soon gathered around me, curious and welcoming, the small children enchanting – playful and affectionate, neither shy nor pushy, never begging.

At intervals high wooden platforms are manned by lifeguards who also serve – said my Fatah friends – as Morality Police, looking out for couples who behave improperly (e.g., hold hands or lean a head on a shoulder) and for men who bare their torsos or women who bare anything but face and hands. As I sat one forenoon on the bottom rung of a platform's ladder a large jolly family 'kidnapped' me, insisting on my lunching with them in Shatti camp. Hanaa was a wiry little septuagenarian great-grand-mother who long ago had worked for UNRWA and acquired a smattering of English. She introduced me to all her companions (three generations, both sexes) and my later efforts to remember and pronounce those ten names caused much merriment. As we strolled towards Shatti the usual interrogation brought the usual reactions; deep sympathy because I live alone, an inability to believe that I do so by choice, an insinuation that Allah may be punishing me for not marrying and having a quiverful.

Shatti is an asphyxiation of more than 80,000 very poor people confined within an area allotted to 23,000 in 1949 (and even then space was short). Because Cast Lead left so many homeless (again!), thousands must now endure the worst living conditions I have ever seen. People shelter below and behind jagged lengths of corrugated iron, shreds of carpet, ragged curtain fragments, sheets of cardboard nailed to half-burnt door panels, battered plastic trays inscribed 'Adam Hotel'. In most such shanty-towns, sections of motor vehicles are conspicuous but in blockaded Gaza every ounce of metal must be recycled. Spatially this camp forms an integral part of Gaza City but it has its own distinctive aura – and not only because of sewage problems. Incongruous CCTV cameras are mounted high on gable walls at several alleyway junctions, seeming to mock the destitution all around. Quite a few of the Israeli assassins' 'high-value targets' live in Shatti where the Strip's grim contest (Informers v. The Rest) is at its most stressful. Only in this camp was I asked (once) to show my passport, by a burly, black-uniformed, black-bearded security officer who scowled at me and told Hanaa she must do a détour – foreigners are forbidden to enter certain alleyways.

It was exactly four years since the 'Five Day War', Hamas' easy though bloody defeat of Fatah's uncoordinated forces – armed and funded but not well-trained by the CIA. During Shatti's brief bursts of fighting a rocket-propelled grenade penetrated Ismail Haniyeh's modest breeze-block house, injuring no one. The damage was soon repaired and Hanaa proudly pointed out that the Prime Minister's family home has not since been 'improved'. The message was: Hamas leaders don't get rich quick. Fatah of course say otherwise, in voices trembling with rage.

Within this maze of alleyways we had to concentrate on not dislodging people's laundry. The Palestinians are sticklers for personal cleanliness, however repellent their environs, and even in Shatti water is somehow found to wash garments and space is found to dry them. But they must be guarded; here village standards of honesty cannot be expected to survive.

As a solo foreigner, I was quite a novelty; the various international organisations who have been 'studying camp conditions' for the past half-century (rarely taking action to alter them) usually travel in groups with local handlers. Therefore cheerful excited children followed us in droves, rushing forward where there was space to stare up at me intently before – 'What is your name?' Throughout Gaza's camps the general level of juvenile high spirits and friendliness is remarkable. However, on the fringes of any such crowd one sees the others – some maimed, some crudely scarred, some physically sound with all the pain in their eyes.

Hanaa and her family of sixteen lived in three small stifling ground-floor rooms all clean and tidy. (Granted, tidiness in not a challenge when possessions are so few.) They cooked on a gas ring in a lean-to and shared a lavatory with three other families.

When we arrived Hanaa's first-born, aged fifty-eight, was trying to sooth a whimpering three-year-old with earache; this boy was his fifteenth child, the fifth by his second wife. Cast Lead had taken his two oldest sons and a daughter-in-law. He believed those three died because the IDF delayed negotiations with a Red Crescent ambulance. That morning the beach-going party had left him in charge of a vast pot of rice (Shatti's 'New Man') and now four pairs of hands quickly prepared an equally vast salad and luncheon was served in traditional style – the menfolk and the guest eating first.

Afterwards, while fruit shopping with the children, I noticed how much lower prices were here than in Rimal. Beside the greengrocer's stall, on a comparatively wide laneway, stood a very fine horse enjoying a nosebag. The care lavished on many Gazan horses delighted and surprised me. Obviously hours of regular grooming were lavished on this glossy scion of some noble Bedouin line. His cart was not quite empty of its vegetable load and one of my companions hastily collected wilted sprigs of parsley from crevices.

As we drank tea, Hanaa asked me to visit friends of hers who had been grievously affected by Cast Lead. In 1949 the Elmadhoun family didn't need to register with UNRWA; from Jaffa they had brought enough cash to start a small business and eventually to buy a ramshackle but roomy house in the Old City. A foreign visitor would cheer them up.

*   *   *

I like the Old City with its remnant of a fifteenth-century covered souk (mostly demolished by British bombs in 1917), and its potters who conserve ancient techniques, and its Hammam al-Sumara which was *renovated* (mark you!) by a Mamluk governor in 1320 and still uses wood-fired boilers. The sixteenth-century al-Omari mosque – closed to infidels – is said to be built on the site of a temple to the Philistine god Dagon. The church of St Porphyrius was always locked so I couldn't see the tomb of this fifth-century Bishop of Gaza – reputedly a valiant defender of Christianity in the Holy Land which probably means he was another Byzantine bad egg. In 1967 the IDF looted this church for the benefit of Jerusalem's museums and the Strip's tiny Greek Orthodox community can't afford to repair the damage done by repeated Israeli attacks. In 2006, in reaction to Pope Benedict XVI's anti-Islam remarks, the exterior was defaced by angry Muslims ignorant of Christendom's East/West split.

Whether in a vehicle or on foot one has to move slowly through the narrow streets around Palestine Square. Crosscurrents of shoppers, hawkers and porters flow this way and that between hundreds of small, tunnel-dependent stalls and bigger lock-up stores. Many Rimal residents distrust this noisy, smelly, multi-coloured scene; they feel safer on the quiet streets of 'developed' Gaza where it's hard to believe that the Strip is one of our planet's most densely populated areas.

Hanaa's Arabic scribble in my notebook helped me to locate the Elmadhoun home on a short squalid street of tall, early nineteenth-century houses, outwardly neglected. The ground floor, where Ya'qub had continued the business started by his father, was now let to two Jabalya camp families rendered homeless by Cast Lead. The blockade had killed the business. Upstairs, seventeen Elmadhouns (including grandparents) occupied two floors, the long high-ceilinged rooms shabby but comfortably furnished. The building's wide, flat roof was a bonus, a safe play area for the eleven children (five girls, six boys). Before the electricity, water and other crises, the Elmadhouns ran a normal middle-class household complete with a two-oven gas cooker and a giant fridge. Not any more: unlike my Rimal friends they could not afford a generator or complicated water-purifying technology – or gas cylinders, when long border closures inflated prices.

In January 2009 two daughters, then aged ten and twelve, were playing on the roof when the shell came. The ten-year-old died instantly; her two older brothers, having rushed up, momentarily mistook her twisted body for a big doll discarded by the parapet. Her sister, Rana, lost both legs from the groin and will always be confined to a wheelchair. Two shrapnel-torn young cousins have recovered – at least physically. One of them, now aged ten, dreads leaving her home, has to be forced to go to school and when in the classroom can't concentrate.

Soon after my arrival Rana's mother persuaded her to join us, then pushed her through a high double door from the adjacent bedroom. The mechanism in her electric wheelchair (a Swedish donation) had long since failed and might or might not be replaced. At once I realised that my visit wasn't helping: Hanaa had got it wrong. Rana greeted me sulkily, clearly seeing herself as some sort of grist for a predatory foreigner's mill. My not wanting a photograph of myself with Rana and myself with the family surprised everyone. I wondered then if Hamas had been using this tragedy in their legitimate campaign to publicise the criminality of Cast Lead.

Samira sat beside her legless daughter – a youthful-looking forty-year-old, despite everything, with a wide pale face, blunt features and the sort of eyebrows some women have to pay for, in time and money. She smiled a lot, Rana not at all. She had miscarried after the shelling but soon conceived again and as we talked Ya'qub dutifully dandled the baby who demanded constant attention. A three-year-old sprawled on the sofa beside them, helping to entertain her little brother, whose impulse to crawl was being frustrated: Ya'qub believed crawling delayed walking. He spoke more English than his eighteen- and nineteen-year-old UNRWA-schooled sons. A US-born Israeli business associate had given him impromptu lessons in the good old Oslo days when the construction industry flourished. He had, it emerged, worked briefly for Atef's father.

When Samira began to pour fruit juices other children appeared from various directions, each equipped with a mobile phone for use during conversational interstices. This incessant fiddling would grate on me, if I lived in such a household. Presumably most parents know nothing of the possible health risks – anyway Gazans are occupied by more immediate concerns.

According to her father, Rana was doing well at school, would probably get a degree (or two) from the Islamic University of Gaza (IUG) and wished to become a university lecturer. Her two older brothers lacked such ambitions and couldn't find jobs. They were available every day to carry her down and up the long, narrow, unlit stairway. Her twelve-year-old sister pushed her to and from school along war-roughened streets. Both those young men were cultivating beards and looked quite severely damaged, emotionally. They lounged on another sofa, beneath a much enlarged photograph of their 'martyr' sister, her chubby face framed in Koranic quotations. Unusually, a few words had been translated into English by the dead child's Swedish teacher – 'they wish for that which may cause you to perish'. During my short visit the youths referred repeatedly to Israel's advanced military technology ('they sell it to *America*') which proved that an attack on an open roof, where four children were playing, could only be deliberate . . . Who could blame them if they yearned to become militants? The beards were suggestive and I sensed their parents' fear of this contingency.

As Ya'qub escorted me to a taxi route near the Gold Market he spoke of Cast Lead's long-term consequences: children blind, deaf, burn-scarred – young men paralysed – mothers maimed – homeless families with no possibility of replacing bombed dwellings – enfeebled grandparents left to succour disturbed orphans – orchards bulldozed, wells maliciously poisoned. Statistics can blur all this. So many killed, so many injured, the deaths usually fewer than the injuries. Too often we tend to focus on the heartbreaking finality of death, the desolation of the bereaved, and not to think enough about the injured and those who love them, the lives thwarted and distorted because 'wars' are no longer fought by warriors. Modern weaponry, callously deployed, makes nonsense of the concept of 'professional armies' fighting 'just wars'.

Four

The Strip provided only one frisson of fear. I was on my way home from visiting a village family whose eldest son, Yousef, had recently been 'eliminated' while training with a Qassam unit, the armed wing of Hamas. The young man's father insisted on showing us (Nita and me) the orchard death-site, a hole five feet deep and ten feet in circumference, surrounded by charred lemon trees and overlooked by three-storey houses with shattered windows. Little bits of cordite were scattered far and wide; I was given one as a souvenir.

Nita, being in a hurry to get home, left me at a busy junction on the outskirts of Khan Younis, where communal taxis parked under an improvised tin roof. As I sat behind the driver's seat in an empty minibus, awaiting fellow passengers, I noticed the busy traffic dwindling to a trickle. Then two figures appeared on the far side of the wide road, walking some fifteen yards apart, carrying rockets over their shoulders. Two others followed, carrying tripods. Each wore black slacks, black long-sleeved shirts, black ski-masks with narrow eye-slits. My first reaction was to chuckle; they looked too like stereotypical 'terrorists' to be taken seriously on a sunny afternoon among ordinary people going about their ordinary business – women dragging bulging sacks, a youth driving a horse-cart loaded with jerrycans, small boys kicking a deflated football, two old men hauling a handcart of broken concrete blocks. As eight other *jihadis* appeared in the distance – carrying AK-47s, also walking yards apart – their leader slowly crossed the road to stand in the shade beside my minibus, so close that I could smell his vice (nicotine) and by reaching through the open window could have touched his rocket. He stood very still, staring straight ahead as his comrades walked towards Gaza City, keeping to the far verge. They moved with military precision but oddly – as though on their own, not in a public place. By then both the motor and pedestrian traffic had almost stopped. Was my neighbour aware of an International's presence? I didn't turn my head but swivelled my eyes and noted that the rocket looked very home-made, no more than six feet long with wobbly tail-fins. Then came my scary moment. I remembered that drones target rocket-launchers – quite often and sometimes accurately. Yousef had been carrying a launcher when 'eliminated' and now I was within cuddling distance of another. But that moment, though chilling, was brief. The statistics reassure: not many Internationals become collateral damage.

Ten minutes later my companion moved off to form the rear-guard. Normally, during that time, the taxi would have been filling up; now, as the *jihadi* crossed the road, passengers crowded in, having been waiting at a discreet distance. I wondered, are these young men deliberately provoking the enemy or is this the 'It can't happen to me' syndrome? Even if personally indifferent to death, it seemed callously irresponsible to risk exposing others to attack for the sake of proving they're still armed and ready for action – though action is no longer being officially encouraged.

We soon overtook the unit, still walking yards apart along the verge. A long-bearded young man in the front passenger seat spoke English and I decided to be tactless. 'Are they al-Qassam?' I asked in a bright curious-tourist voice. 'We don't know them,' came the curt reply. When I put the same question to Deeb he prevaricated – 'They were going to some training ground' – which didn't tell me who 'they' were.

Moh, one of my unconstrained student friends, was prepared to speculate. They might of course have been al-Qassam. Or they could've been an al-Quds unit from Islamic Jihad's armed wing. Or a Saladin Brigade unit from the Popular Resistance Committee's armed wing. Or maybe a unit from the al-Ahrar Brigade, an armed wing without a body.

Acidly I remarked that if Gaza grew fewer wings it might not fly into such sterile grief. Yousef's mother had told me of his boast on 19 March – around noon, warplanes had fired two missiles in an attempt to kill him and three of his comrades. The next attempt succeeded. His father said, 'He always wanted to be a martyr.'

Moh thought it inevitable that quite a few young men were keen to prove that Gazans could and would continue attacking Israel, even when Prime Minister Haniyeh was in conciliatory mood. Supposing Moh had it right, the long-term implications are disquieting. If a small armed group could do its own thing wherever and whenever it chose, who was governing Gaza? Was the relative calm of June 2011 more apparent than real?

Another friend, a middle-aged Cast-Lead victim who made light of being one-legged, said, 'Really, nobody is governing. Hamas tried but the whole world is against them. Remember they're terrorists! Part of trying to control is letting those groups show their strength.' As Nizar saw it, if Hamas were recognised as the legitimate government it would be different, many more Gazans would respect their authority. He continued, 'Those you saw, I can guess who they are. I know what they're like. They are not mad Salafist dogs, they're young Palestinians wanting respect. They don't feel they have it when everyone says their fairly elected government is terrorist, criminal – can't have any tax money or normal funding. For self-esteem they need to go marching around with guns saying "We're not terrorists or criminals! We're Palestinians fighting the Occupation, never giving up!" Yousef, whose family you visited, he was that sort. They don't care if they can't do much damage in Israel, if their rockets' real victims are their neighbours. For them it's the ritual that matters. Taking action, being daring, two fingers to the IDF and death's OK if it comes. Martyrs get more respect than anyone else around.'

* * *

A few days later, en route to Abassan village, Nita insisted on our visiting some of the Samouni family survivors. Their fate ranks as the most barbarous of Cast Lead's many atrocities and her plan made me vaguely uncomfortable; this crime scene has become a macabre parody of a tourist attraction, a 'must' for foreign politicians, human rights teams, NGO delegations and journalists. But then, as we sat with three survivors, I sensed that our visit was being appreciated. Perhaps it helped them to know that their sufferings have not been forgotten.

Zaytoun is a semi-rural district of Gaza City, quite close to the sea. From the main road we followed a sandy, tank-ravaged track past the shelled remains of mini-industries surrounded by bomb craters and hillocks of rubble sprouting that tall yellow weed. A substantial new villa – startling amidst the drab desolation, painted orange and brick-red with white trimming – was not yet lived in. It stood on the site of the mass-slaughter. Three short rows of olive saplings had been planted nearby: the *samoud* gesture, seen so often where IDF tanks or bulldozers have savaged ancient groves. Fifty yards further on, at the base of a high thorny hedge, four pale skinny little boys sat beside a tray of the cheapest possible sweets. Who were their customers? There was no one else in sight. An opening in the hedge gave access to the small yard of a three-storey house missing half its roof and one gable end. Nita called a greeting and Mohammed appeared, a tall man in his mid-thirties needing a crutch and with bags under his eyes. Ahmed followed, a very tall, painfully thin nineteen-year-old whose paralysed right arm could possibly be fixed elsewhere – but not in Gaza. Then came twelve-year-old Hassan who put a tea-kettle on the Primus stove before rolling up a trouser-leg to show me his shrapnel-scarred thigh. We sat on the ubiquitous white plastic garden chairs under a sturdy vine, gnarled but fertile, trained to provide ample shade between hedge and house. All around lay shattered gable-end stones, shards of roof-tiles and twisted sheets of corrugated iron.

On 3 January 2009 the IDF attacked several Zaytoun homes, rounded up 97 people (the Samounis and a few of their neighbours) and herded them into the main Samouni dwelling with orders not to come out. On 5 January, when four men emerged in search of firewood, a shell at once killed two and wounded the others. Minutes later a precision guided weapon hit the house, instantly killing 21 and wounding the rest. Within the next two days 27 of the wounded died because ambulances were not permitted to reach them. During those days four toddlers clung to their dead mothers. Hassan lost both parents but was 'lucky': they died quickly. Ahmed's parents survived in agony until the ambulances were allowed through; both soon died in hospital. The ICRC reported: 'The Israeli soldiers stationed nearby must have known of the people in the houses but the wounded died as they waited for medical care due to the slow negotiations for access.' After the survivors' removal on 7 January the IDF quickly bulldozed the house, preventing corpse retrievals or any medical examination of the remains. Soldiers then cordoned off the area until 18 January when the truce began and a Red Crescent team hurried to Zaytoun with body-bags and surgical masks to help the locals dig out their rotting neighbours.

A collage of photographs of the dead, mounted on a sheet of hardboard some five feet by three, included elegantly scripted quotations from the Koran. Names and ages were in Arabic and Roman and everyone had 'martyr' status. This consoled the survivors for reasons I have tried to understand – but can't. When the weapon was laid beside me I noted its details.

US Contract Serno

Guided Missile, Surface

Attack: AGM 114 OXYD8

Manufacturer 1410 01-425-4459 13415050

NAIL STOCK No. PART No.

LOT no MGP05 J529 – 014

As I wrote I remembered that in June 2009, as President Obama made his famous Islam-friendly Cairo speech, the US was replacing the many multi-ton bombs dropped on Gaza. And in 2010, US military aid to Israel was the single largest expenditure in the US Foreign Aid budget. Since 1972 the US has vetoed 41 Security Council resolutions condemning Israeli violations of international law. Until the US is willing to play the international law game the concept is meaningless.

While ambulances were being denied access to the Samouni home, IDF graffiti artists were having fun. Within yards of their dead and dying victims – within earshot of the latter's desperate cries – they spray-painted those houses still standing. ARABS NEED 2 DIE – DIE YOU ALL – 1 IS DOWN, 999,999 TO GO – ARABS 1948–2009 – that last on a sketch of a gravestone.

Nita said, 'Those soldiers are sick. They're worse damaged than us though we're more hurt. They act like people with no education.'

I said nothing but Professor Sofer came to mind. A demographer, Professor of Geostrategic Studies at the University of Haifa, advisor to Ariel Sharon – a man not lacking education. When 'disengagement' and the blockade of Gaza were being planned, the *Jerusalem Post* (20 May 2004) reported his vision of the future.

We will tell the Palestinians that if a single missile is fired over the fence, we will fire 10 in response. And women and children will be killed and houses will be destroyed . . . When 2.5 million people live in a closed-off Gaza it's going to be a human catastrophe. Those people will become even bigger animals than they are today, with the aid of an insane fundamentalist Islam. The pressure at the border will be awful. It's going to be a terrible war. So, if we want to remain alive, we will have to kill and kill and kill. All day, every day. Until collective imprisonment produces voluntary transfer. If a Palestinian cannot come into Tel Aviv for work, he will look in Iraq, or

Kuwait or London . . . I believe there will be movement out of the area.

The uniquely bizarre nature of the Palestine/Israel conflict is even more obvious on the Strip than on the West Bank. Here we have a wannabe Western-style democracy treating their neighbours' democratically elected leaders as suitable targets for assassination while mass-slaughter eliminates those who elected them. They are 'terrorists' because they oppose an illegal occupation and blockade calculated to get rid of them, to leave the way clear for more Zionist expansion – as both the IDF graffiti and Arnon Sofer's oft-repeated statements make plain. In 2003 Anthony Hurndall, a London lawyer, spent some time in Rafah investigating the IDF's murder of his son Tom, an ISM volunteer. His 50-page report concluded that 'The IDF chiefs of staff had given the clear signal to their soldiers and to the international community that in Israel soldiers can and do deliberately kill and maim innocent civilians, Palestinian and international, without cause and with impunity.'

Back on the road, awaiting a taxi under a fig tree, Nita and I were joined by two local women and a youth. One woman had recently lost a thirty-year-old son, a Saladin Brigade volunteer killed by a warplane at sunset on 8 April. His two companions were still in hospital in Gaza City. On the same day, at sunrise, another warplane had targeted a motorbike carrying two al-Qassam volunteers. The rider was killed, the passenger left permanently brain-damaged. A few hours later a tank on the border shelled a civilian gathering near al-Shuja'ia cemetery, killing two (one a child) and seriously injuring ten others including four children. I assumed these strikes were rocket-provoked but no one would confirm this. It intrigued me that Gazans were so open with one another (though not with the foreigner) about martyrs' affiliations, labelling them al-Qassam, al-Ahrar or whatever and always distinguishing between 'civilians' and 'volunteers'.

In all, between 3.00 pm on 7 April and 6.00 am on 9 April, shelling killed eighteen Gazans: nine civilians, nine volunteers. The thirty-eight severely wounded included two paramedics and fourteen adolescents. Dozens of houses and several training sites were damaged. A few quarrels broke out between the owners of shelled homes and volunteers who argued 'our training spaces are so limited we can't avoid all residential areas'.

During our taxi ride I asked Nita, 'Did Cast Lead not convince most Gazans – apart from the chronically belligerent – that fighting Israel physically is futile for all and suicidal for many? Wouldn't it be comparatively easy, now, to bring the volunteers, of all brands, under control?'

Nita smiled, seemed genuinely amused. 'For normal people, yes you're right. But sixty-three years of Zionism have made us not normal.' She was halfway through her thesis on the Muslim Brotherhood in Gaza and eager to explain. The men who brought the Mujamma ideology to the Strip were good Palestinians from the camps, born into stark poverty, knowing how much the majority who didn't have their educational opportunities needed help. They associated Westernisation with the Zionism that had made them refugees and used the Muslim Brotherhood sort of Islam to heal their wounded pride. Nita emphasised the refugees' humiliation – deprived not only of their material security but left with feelings of guilt and inadequacy because they hadn't put up a fight – couldn't, against Zionist wealth, but they'd lost sight of that valid excuse. For many, the past made it hard to be rational about how to confront Israel *now* . . . As is the case for many of Palestine's friends in the west.

Abassan is east of Khan Younis, not far from the border, a village where high, unlovely concrete walls conceal women from unrelated male eyes. Often a small child opens a wooden door just enough to see who's there. In response to our knock a scared-looking nine-year-old peered through the crack but Ibrahim was expecting us and called reassuringly to his son. Then a neatly bearded fifty-two-year-old, wearing a grubby *galabiya*, came to greet us – not shaking hands, he and Nita exchanging the ritual Arabic murmurs.

Olive trees half-filled the large yard and around them hens scratched and pecked and clucked. The one-storey breeze-block dwelling had tiny unglazed windows and a solitary, aged walnut tree grew by the narrow hall door. There our chairs were placed on a square of shattered concrete – shattered by the drone-delivered missile that a few weeks previously had instantly killed Ibrahim's forty-one-year-old wife and nineteen-year-old daughter as they sat chopping vegetables at 12.20 pm. At 1.30 pm Israel Radio announced, 'We are sorry a missile went astray in the Khan Younis area.' Two other daughters, aged eighteen and fifteen, were badly shrapnel-torn but had escaped maiming and would soon be home from hospital. The three youngest of the motherless eleven (all boys) did not appear; they were indoors with a twelve-year-old sister. As we talked, the nine-year-old and his seven-year-old sister sat on the ground beside their father's chair, each with a hand on a paternal knee. At intervals Ibrahim stroked their heads. Both looked tense and bewildered, had not yet been able to bounce back as many children quickly do (or so we're told).

Ibrahim himself was still in shock, his handsome face expressionless, his voice low and calm. 'It was Allah's will. We must be patient, trust in Allah. The Holy Koran tells us truth. Allah will bring all that is bad to an end. Then will be no more Israel.'

The buffer zone excludes this family from most of its land. Together the parents used to venture out – sometimes with ISM 'protection' – to grow parsley (an exceptionally profitable crop) but the children had begged their father never again to take that risk. On 19 March the minaret of Abassan's village mosque took many hits during three hours of artillery firing from the border across Ibrahim's land. And everyone knew about Sha'ban Qarmout, aged sixty-four and unconnected to any 'volunteers'. He had been killed recently by several bullets to the heart as he drove his donkey-plough one afternoon, 550 metres from the border.

Out on the road, Nita rang Jameel the taxi driver; he was roving around the village, hoping to buy apricots. Then she said, 'This family, they make me want to cry many tears. You see Ibrahim's *galabiya* is not clean and here is the one time no one gives us to drink. I know those girls, it's a family full of love. Already I hear the old women planning the next wife and soon they'll put pressure on. That's cruel! Ibrahim is too sad, you can see the broken heart in his eyes . . . '

Jameel drove us to the market area of Nussairat camp, picking up four more passengers on the main road. The Strip's tortured landscape offers few visual rewards yet had it not been mid-summer I would have chosen to walk between villages. When I said as much to Nita she startled Jameel by loudly shouting 'No!' I must never be so silly – there were crazies around who might try to please Allah by killing an uncovered infidel woman brazenly walking alone. When I protested, 'There can't be that many crazies!' Nita swiftly retorted, 'And how many Salafists does it take to kill a granny?'

The 16,000 refugees who in 1949 squatted in then-rural central Gaza have since become 70,000. Nussairat 'camp' is in fact a cramped, overcrowded, grimly impoverished city – but with a notably spirited and imaginative Popular Camp Committee, on whom a rising percentage, unregistered with UNRWA, are becoming dependent.

Nita planned to spend the evening here with a favourite uncle, another recent drone victim though in a less drastic way; there had been many injuries but no deaths. Kemal owned a three-storey building on the edge of the market, divided into twelve flatlets and four mini-offices, all seriously damaged when a drone fired two missiles into an adjacent car-park in the middle of the night. Even worse, Kemal's engineering workshop on the ground floor was wrecked, all the expensive machinery beyond repair. And it had provided jobs for four young fathers while helping to sustain Kemal's own extended family (nine children, twenty-eight grand-children and many more to come).

We found Uncle helping a shopkeeper neighbour to contrive a substitute for a metal security shutter warped by the blast. Up and down the street were shrapnel-pocked doors; most of the broken glass had been swept up but the loose chunks of cracked pavement were treacherous.

Kemal was short and stout with features dominated by worry lines. He invited us into his temporary office, a dusty, twilit cubby-hole opening onto the street. Despite Nita's protests he was determined to brew tea on an alarmingly defective gas ring that seemed more likely to explode than to boil water. While coaxing it along he told us about his narrow escape when he drove past the nearby Palestine Naval Police compound five minutes before a mighty bomb destroyed two empty police vehicles. Rumour suggested the IDF had been misinformed, and expected to eliminate a group of senior Hamas officers who should by then have boarded those vehicles. 'That's how it is,' said Kemal. 'Allah decides do we live or die.' In his view, no human agency was going to improve the Palestinians' lot. But the Holy Koran tells that all things end and so Israel will end and the Palestinians will regain their land. 'We must be patient,' said Kemal echoing Ibrahim. 'We must believe and have trust in Allah. All is his will.'

Suddenly I felt another Islamophobic surge. I rarely swear but now I wanted to while pointing out, 'What's happening to the Palestinians is the *Zionists'* will!'

Looking at Nita, I suggested, 'Why not stop waiting patiently? Why not have a bold rethink and some sensible action? Like petitioning Hamas to rewrite their Charter. It embarrasses most Palestinians I know.'

Nita promptly looked embarrassed, Kemal admitted he'd never read the Charter but often heard it quoted in the mosque. He hadn't liked my bluntness which perhaps was too blunt. (It's a common defect of the old, who assume they're entitled to say what they think and know there's not much time left for saying it.) Later, a shrewd observer of Gaza's mosque scene told me that certain imams advocate patiently waiting for Allah to sort it out as the only prudent course at present – given the ferocity of Israeli retaliations.

When Nita and I had arranged our next 'misery tour' (her phrase) I took a taxi to the shore and in the cool of the evening paddled home along the beach brooding on the 1988 Hamas Charter. I first read it in 2008 and then many passages sounded hideously familiar, an echo of the Vatican-inspired anti-Semitism prevalent in Ireland from the 1890s to the 1950s. Rabid Christianity in Ireland, rabid Islam in Gaza, rabid Judaism in the Holy Land – tolerance and compassion being overridden wherever religious fanaticism is hitched to nationalist bandwagons. And yet – on rereading that pernicious document, and discussing it with Muslim friends who knew something about its genesis, I saw that it could be melted down, purged of its dross and recast as something valuable. To Deeb I said, 'There's the most crucial and dangerous task for the next generation of Hamas leaders.' He didn't disagree.

Other Hamas friends were nonplussed when I asked what they thought could be done about both the Charter and the obstinate rocketeers. With Salafists beckoning the thousands of male adolescents who have nothing to do all day, Hamas reformers must proceed cautiously. To revise the Charter too abruptly, boldly, aligning it with the more constructive strands in current Hamas thinking, could destabilise not only Gaza but regions far beyond where Salafists have their spiritual home. As for the rocketeers, even though non-violence had become the official flavour of the new decade, not much could be done to restrain them. Said one young man, 'They might start more internecine stuff if held down too hard.'

In the Department of Foreign Affairs, my unlikely home-from-home, I did occasionally get glimpses of a better future. Many conversations were predictably confused and confusing but now and then – as when mountain trekking through shifting clouds – there was a clear space, a bright expanse of beauty, all the details plain to be seen. Beyond a doubt, those comparatively youthful Hamas members saw Palestinian unity as a first step without which nobody could get anywhere. They took heart from Khaled Meshaal's quiet assertion and reassertion that 'There is no political horizon if Hamas is not included as a legitimate element of the Palestinian people.' (An interesting turn of phrase, not presaging a takeover by Islamists – until recently the goal of some of the first generation of Hamas leaders.) But then there were bleak moments as the clouds closed in again. It had been too easy, deploying a ruthless army, to punish all Gazans for the majority's election of a Hamas government. How to achieve unity when the saboteurs were so implacably against it, knowing 'Divide and Conquer' to be essential for the maturing of their 'Eretz Yisrael' project?

One morning Deeb beckoned me to his computer. He had found an *Ha'aretz* item (18 April 2009) with an 'if only' headline that stabs the heart: 'ISRAEL COULD HAVE MADE PEACE WITH HAMAS UNDER YASSIN'. Kobi Ben-Simhon, interviewing a retired Israel Prison Service chief intelligence officer, Zvi Sela, recorded that in the mid-'90s Sheikh Yassin recognised the State of Israel and, said Sela, 'He was smart and brave. Cruel but credible. He gave his life in the war for the freedom of his people. I tend to think that if we tried for an agreement with him, we would have succeeded.'

Several years before Zvi Sela talked with Sheikh Yassin in his prison cell, a close friend of the Sheikh, Dr Mahmoud al-Zahar, had visited Shimon Peres, then Israeli Foreign Minister. Although not formally representing Hamas, the doctor was known to be a founder member. That was in March 1988, a few months into the first Intifada, when Israel was still treating Islamist officials as social reformers rather than militants. To Mr Peres, Dr al-Zahar presented a suggested long-term solution to the Problem. This potential discussion document revealed a softening of the Mujamma/Hamas determination to view all of Palestine as a *waqf* (Islamic endowment) – a position equalling in dottiness Gush Emunim's view of Palestine as Abraham's legally and morally binding bequest to his descendants. Had Peres not declined to discuss that proposed solution, would the catastrophic Charter, proclaimed five months later, have been so rabid?

Soon everything changed for the worse. In February and May 1989 two Israeli soldiers were kidnapped and killed. Hundreds of Hamas activists were imprisoned, among them Sheikh Yassin and Dr al-Zahar. In December 1989, two years after its founding, Israel outlawed Hamas.

Yet at intervals, over the years, other tentative attempts were made to bring about reconciliation, both between Hamas and Fatah and Hamas and Israel. The multilateral 1991 Madrid conference was followed by eleven rounds of futile 'peace negotiations' which were of course no such thing. In August 1991 Hamas was invited to sit on the powerful Palestine National Council but only under unacceptable conditions. Then the offer made four years previously to Shimon Peres was withdrawn and Hamas formed its armed wing, the Qassam Brigades. Little more than a year later, at the January 1993 Fatah/Hamas talks in Khartoum, Hamas was loudly preaching 'Jihad until Liberation!' while Fatah was ready to cede 'land for peace' in pursuit of the two-state solution. Those talks collapsed when Arafat refused to quit negotiations destined to lead to Fatah's collaboration with Israel.

Hamas leaders often criticised Fatah on religious as well as political grounds, referring disdainfully to their representatives 'debauching themselves, drinking, singing, carrying on here as they did in Jordan, Lebanon and Tunis'. Yet immediately after the

Oslo signing those same leaders appealed publicly for an avoidance of civil conflict with the PA and sought, throughout the OPT, to form conciliation committees which could cooperate on welfare work. But alas! the Accords allowed Arafat to bring in 7,000 armed Fedayeen, veterans of the PLO, and these forces, by drastically upsetting the power balance, rendered the committees obsolete. At this point Ariel Sharon (patron saint of the settlers and then Israel's Foreign Minister) asked with a smirk, 'Why should we chase Hamas when the PLO can do it for us?' Sure enough, on both the West Bank and the Strip PA security forces were soon fighting side by side with the IDF against Hamas. This prompted a series of vicious suicide bombings in Israel and on 17 November 1994 Arafat arrested some 400 Hamas leaders and followers. When 20,000 protesters gathered outside Gaza's Palestine Mosque, the PA police opened fire on them, killing fourteen and wounding 270.

In February 1996, less than two months after the assassination of Ayyash, their most skilled bomb-maker, Hamas despatched a retaliatory team of suicide bombers to Israel, killing 58 civilians and wounding hundreds. In response, thousands of Hamas activists were jailed, tortured and (if family money was available) held to ransom by Mohammed Dahlan's US-trained Fatah forces. Dr al-Zahar and his senior colleagues were among those arrested and Dahlan ordered them to be forcibly debearded before their interrogations. Afterwards Dr al-Zahar commented, 'Israel hoped Hamas would be isolated and weakened by Oslo but in fact it has allowed for the rise of a more vigorous, militant leadership. It also gained us much popular support even where we were not liked before.'

Eight bloody years later, on 24 May 2004 – not long after the assassinations of Sheikh Yassin and Dr Abdel Aziz al-Rantissi – a 'Document on the Approach to the Anticipated Withdrawal from the Gaza Strip' was considered by the Gazan Hamas leadership. It showed the influence of another paper, written in jail by Marwan Barghouti, leader of Fatah's al-Aqsa Martyrs' Brigade, who had suggested a role for Islamists in running the post-withdrawal Strip and who communicated regularly and amiably with his Hamas fellow-prisoners. The Hamas document's authors were Dr al-Zahar and Ismail Haniyeh. Assuming the PA would not continue to side with the IDF after its withdrawal, it advocated a power-sharing 'joint legitimate leadership', using all Gaza's 'nationalistic and Islamic factions'. Even were the PA to stick with Israel, making it impossible for the Hamas leadership to share power, this remarkable document recommended that in many areas Hamas members should

> dialogue with other factions, managing daily affairs in regions where withdrawal has taken place by actively participating in PA ministries and various institutions: local elections for towns and villages; participation in some of the security services of a police nature on movement affairs, criminal investigations and fire-fighting.

A lot of thought had gone into this document which was scarcely noticed by the outside world. It showed Hamas keen to move on from suicide bombing, with its misleading al-Qaeda resonances (Hamas and al-Qaeda had always been antipathetic). Now the leadership craved international recognition as a *legitimate* resistance movement and power-sharing on the post-withdrawal Strip would be a significant advance in that direction.

When Deeb announced that Dr al-Zahar would like to meet me I was slightly taken aback, remembering his justification for the Hamas ban on dancing – 'A man holds a woman by the hand and dances with her in front of everyone. Does that serve the national interest? If so, why have the phenomena of corruption and prostitution become pervasive in recent years?' And in an interview with Stephen Farrell in *The Times* (7 October 2005) he had ranted against gay marriage – 'Are these the laws for which the Palestinian street is waiting? For us to give rights to homosexuals and lesbians, a minority of perverts and the mentally and morally sick?' However, this would certainly be something to write home about, meeting the Hamas government's first Foreign Minister and the only founder member of Hamas to have (so far) survived the assassin state. Thrice Israel has tried to eliminate him, on one occasion breaking his wife's spine, leaving her invalided, on another killing two of his sons and a son-in-law while flattening his home (now rebuilt).

Hamas government departments don't run fleets of limos nor can their officials afford family cars. Everyone uses *serveeces* – or, for special occasions like calling on Dr al-Zahar, ordinary private taxis. Deeb escorted me and was puzzled by my lack of journalistic equipment: no camera, no tape-recorder, not even a notebook and pencil. I explained that I don't like interviewing people, I just like talking with them.

Perhaps the al-Zahars' new home is well protected but it doesn't seem so. From a rough laneway we turned into a wide vine-draped patio: there wasn't even a low gate, never mind any of those hi-tech systems used by rich gated communities fearful of the mob. Instead, two young men ushered us in, so courteous and discreetly armed they seemed like butlers rather than security guards. Afterwards, when I commented on this, Deeb pointed out that a gated community's defences are irrelevant if a drone is coming to get you.

Dr al-Zahar, wearing a white *galabiya*, sat in a corner at the far end of a long, sunny salon, the ceiling arched, the floor tiles blue and green, the décor white and gold, the furnishings austere. He didn't rise to greet me but shook hands – a firm, warm handshake that made me feel not only welcome but relaxed. As he gestured me towards an easy chair close to his own one of the 'butlers' appeared – jinn-like, through an invisible door – providing water and fruit juice. My host asked, 'Tea or coffee?' and Deeb, sitting on a sofa across the room, thoughtfully explained that I don't take sugar.

Above Dr al-Zahar's chair hung A4-sized photographs of his murdered sons and son-in-law, simply framed, not given the usual 'martyrs'' embellishments. As he didn't mention them, or the attempted assassinations, neither did I.

I began by saying, 'Politically I'm on your side but as a European woman Hamas is not where I belong.'

Dr al-Zahar nodded and chuckled and we never looked back. A handsome man in late middle age, he has the attractive demeanour of an elder statesman unaware of his own importance. He also has a humorous tilt to his mouth and kind eyes which contradict his reputation. For more than twenty years he has been vilified as a brutal, bigoted, irrational, anti-Semitic, homophobic psychopath. And yes, he had indeed backed the suicide bombing campaign, until it was unofficially abandoned before the withdrawal. Personally he had never ordered or organised an operation, but that was beside the point: he agreed with his paediatrician friend Dr al-Rantissi (Hamas's second-in-command until his assassination), who often reminded critics, 'We wouldn't use suicide bombers if we had F-16s, then we could kill without being killed.'

However you juggle them, two wrongs don't make a right. But you can better understand one wrong (suicide bombers occasionally indiscriminately murdering Israeli civilians) if you never lose sight of the other (Israelis daily terrorising and often murdering Palestinian civilians all over the OPT).

On some issues my host and I were in perfect harmony. I could detect no taint of anti-Semitism in him and our levels of loathing for political Zionism were about equal. Dr al-Zahar enjoys history and we spent an hour or so mulling over happier times – when, for instance, Muslims and Jews flourished together on the Iberian peninsula before Christians intervened. And likewise in Baghdad, for millennia, until political Zionism's poisonous fumes came wafting across the desert from Palestine. Dr al-Zahar could remember the exact dates when Jews were expelled from various countries or subjected to major pogroms. 'It's natural,' he said, 'they've been twisted by those experiences, going so far back before the Holocaust, making them always fearful and suspicious.' He wondered why Christians seemed unable to forgive the alleged deicide until Pope John Paul XXII made friendly noises. As a frivolous aside he added that if the Jews – like the Muslims – had accepted Jesus as a prophet there would have been no Zionists, political or otherwise. And then he remarked on a very sad fact: in Palestine anti-Semitism was virtually unknown before Zionism's advent. 'We're all sons of Shem,' he said, meaning Arabs and Semitic Jews. Sardonically he referred to the thousands of gentile Russians whose 'right to return' went almost unchallenged – and to the hitherto unheard of tribes recently arrived from Andean valleys and Burmese borderlands, 'Jews' desperately recruited for deployment on the demographic battlefield.

Dr al-Zahar obviously wanted me to believe that Hamas had driven the Israelis out of Gaza in 2005. Since 1992 he had been advocating violence because 'it is justified when all else fails and Israel will never voluntarily leave our territories'. I didn't doubt his estimate of Israel's mindset but there were, I ventured to suggest, complicated demographic considerations behind the unilateral pull-out which involved no talks or deals with President Abbas. Ariel Sharon would have been happy to see Gaza and its 1.5 million Palestinians being absorbed into Mubarak's Egypt. From a Zionist perspective, the Strip's land value is more than cancelled out by its dense and fast-growing 'enemy' population. Also, Sharon wanted more shekels to expand West Bank settlements and protecting 8,000 settlers on the Strip was judged not cost-effective.

'Yes!' said Dr al-Zahar. 'And why not cost-effective? Because of our resistance! That made Israeli voters restive about the disproportionate money spent on so few settlers – so politicians decided to "redeploy" which is the word they like!'

When Sheikh Yassin established Mujamma in 1973 its main

district leaders were Mahmoud al-Zahar, Ibrahim al-Yazuri and Abdel Aziz al-Rantissi. They and the other founder members were all of refugee stock but had qualified abroad as doctors, dentists, teachers, engineers, pharmacists, geologists, surveyors. At first Mujamma concentrated on providing healthcare, welfare assistance, sports clubs and an Islamic education to Gaza's poorest communities. The Islamic Revival was not yet of primary importance. Then, as the '70s ended, Dr al-Zahar observed Gaza's youth becoming more mosque-centred, possibly in reaction to the IDF's increasing obtrusiveness.

Extreme Islamists often speak of being at war, meaning the cosmic war between good and evil. In 2003 a book by one of Osama bin Laden's advisers came out, presenting all human history as 'a perpetual war between believers and unbelievers'. It sold well on the Strip. However, during the 1990s, when Osama bin Laden tried to recruit Palestinians, both Hamas and Islamic Jihad repeatedly rebuffed him, being convinced that any tinge of Wahhabism would fatally pollute their ideology. A half-dozen Hamas militants spent time in Sudan's training camps while bin Laden was based in that country (c.1991–95) but they never met him.

By March 2006, when Hamas named its first cabinet, assassins had eliminated most of the Mujamma/Hamas founders. Therefore Ismail Haniyeh was chosen as Prime Minister, Dr Mahmoud al-Zahar as Foreign Minister, Said Siam as Interior Minister and Dr Omar Abdel-Razeq, a high-powered, US-educated economist, as Finance Minister. The last-named, having closely considered the PA's account books, calculated that Fatah's spectacular corruption had bred a $1.2 billion debt – money owed to banks and suppliers. He also foretold that the collective punishment of Gaza would exacerbate Israel's security problem by immensely strengthening Qassam.

Meanwhile the Foreign Minister, having equally closely considered the PA's morale, foresaw a split; it seemed likely the US-sponsored Dahlan faction would oppose cooperation between Palestinians. He was also infuriated by US/Israel manoeuvrings to give the PA's President Abbas more significance than the Hamas-controlled legislature. 'This should not have surprised me,' said Dr al-Zahar. 'Democracy doesn't work even in democracies. Leaders go to war against voters' wishes.' The Palestinians' free and fair election was contemptuously dismissed by a UN-led 'international community'. ('Another humiliation,' noted Dr al-Zahar.) At once, all funding was cut off from a government that would have used it comparatively honestly. US legislation already in place ensured that very severe sanctions would be applied to any person or institution caught dealing with 'terrorists'. Before long Omar Suleiman, then director of Egypt's anti-Palestinian intelligence services, was warning the West: 'If you go on isolating Hamas, Iran will give them millions.' He was right. In the autumn of 2006 ministers of Gaza's new Hamas administration returned home via Rafah carrying large suitcases packed with dollar notes. These, they informed EUBAM, had been fetched from friends to pay public servants unpaid since Hamas' election victory led to the withholding of Western funds. Dr al-Zahar also denounced the PA's previous agreements with Israel, especially the 1994 Paris Economic Agreement (on trade and taxation) which had undermined what little there was of a Palestinian industrial sector by tightly tying it to Israel's – so tightly that Palestinians can deal only with Israeli suppliers. And Israelis can punish Palestinians by (illegally) withholding taxes collected on their behalf – as was done, for example, after the PA's ill-judged bid for statehood at the UN in September 2011.

Because of his attitudes on such matters, Dr al-Zahar's ministerial career was brief. On 8 February 2007 in Mecca, Saudi Arabia encouraged the establishment of a Palestinian government of national unity. A month or so later, al-Qaeda's voice was heard again from outside, accusing the Hamas leadership of 'surrendering most of Palestine to the Jews'. Some within Hamas smelled a plot to gain a Gazan toehold by making more trouble between Hamas' Salafi-tinted 'sons of Qassam' and the unity-supporting political leadership. The latter found this hypothetical threat (which never came to anything) quite useful in negotiations with Fatah cabinet colleagues.

Meanwhile the Foreign Minister had learned of the Bush administration's resolve to wreck the power-sharing government by donating $64 million (for starters) and many guns to the PA security forces. Without delay, Hamas significantly increased its import of weapons from 'friendly sources' (left anonymous by Dr al-Zahar) and set about training its armed wings 'to professional standards'.

The new cabinet allowed Fatah six seats to Hamas' nine and it soon became clear that none of the funding desperately needed for non-military purposes would be resumed until Dr al-Zahar and Said Siam, seen as the most inflexible hardliners, were replaced. This seems not to have embittered my host. He was indeed too inflexible to compromise his principles yet he recognised that the Unity Government's survival would alleviate the extreme hardships inflicted on all Gazans by Israel's closures. Despite his personal history, I found him remarkably free of bitterness on every level and sensed unusual reserves of calmness and strength – all derived from his faith in Allah, he himself would certainly say. We irreligious humanists have to acknowledge that religion, if it works for people, can work very well.

Dr al-Zahar spoke then of his ideal Palestinian state in which rulers would remember that Allah created everything to benefit all human beings of both sexes equally. People could choose for themselves whether or not to live by the Koran. There would be no discrimination against any faith – or lack of faith. With difficulty I resisted the temptation to ask why, if Hamas opposed discrimination, I could not buy a drink anywhere on the Strip –

not even in the UN Beach Club, for UN employees only, which was fire-bombed in 2005 to remind its owners that the sale or consumption of alcohol is a sin. I didn't doubt my host's sincerity when he spoke of his 'ideal state' but I did wonder who – if anyone – now has Gaza's diverse groups of fanatics under control.

When Dr al-Zahar complained about 'relentless Israeli anti-Hamas rhetoric' I could have pointed out (but didn't) that its own Charter defines Hamas as 'the spearhead of the circle of struggle with world Zionism' and is generally suffused with a shameful anti-Semitic hysteria. This would have been the moment to ask who (or what) coterie had compiled that Charter. Given its ignorant acceptance of the 'Protocols of the Elders of Zion' and a general crudeness of tone it doesn't read like the sort of document Dr al-Zahar himself (author of twenty-two scholarly books) would have been involved with either as author or adviser. Hence my shying away from the subject; it would be hard to mention something so abhorrent without sounding confrontational and accusing – to what purpose?

Dr al-Zahar wondered if US support for Partition had been strengthened by reluctance to accept into the States those thousands of destitute Jews who settled in Palestine only because the US wouldn't admit them. Not admitting them was much easier when they had a 'homeland' to go to – never mind that it was in fact someone else's homeland. We agreed that one of the Palestinians' major handicaps is public ignorance of the conflict's historical background, starting in the 1880s. And we felt angry together about the widespread misrepresentation of the Occupation as a Problem that could have been solved decades ago but for unreasonable obstinacy on both sides.

Some simple facts seem so trite, banal, almost puerile their repetition is best avoided. Dr al-Zahar helped me to see that in the Palestinians' case we err by not stating the obvious again and again, continuing to repeat simple facts in simple words instead of trying to operate on a higher plane where the accretion of complexities around the Problem requires language more sophisticated and subtle. Suddenly I remembered a walk with my Nazareth friends across the site of a demolished village, long since hidden by tangled bushes, grasses, ground creepers. From a little distance this place looked like a tranquil corner of the Galilee; its dynamited foundation stones became visible only as one pushed through the overgrowth. In the same way, I now thought, a tangle of arguments, assertions, accusations, denials, definitions, analyses, theories, claims and counter-claims has been allowed to obscure the foundations of the Palestinian tragedy.

I liked Dr al-Zahar's steady focus on the essentials. After the Ottoman defeat Zionists colonised Palestine with British assistance. The Palestinians were not consulted at any point before the UN vote. Israel exists only because Europeans drove some 800,000 Palestinians off land their ancestors had been cultivating for centuries. In 1967 Israel seized more land. Its military occupation of those territories is designed to complete the Zionist project. There has never been a 'peace process'. The Zionists always wanted all of Palestine and they continue to play happily with negotiators while building settlements. Israel has a security problem not because the neighbours are nasty but because Zionists forcibly dispossessed a defenceless people. By using IDF terrorism on the West Bank and blockading Gaza, Zionists hope to make life so intolerable for most Palestinians that they will migrate. 'But we won't!' said Dr al-Zahar.

Nowadays all those facts, so obvious and accessible and crucially important, are too often fudged in the mainstream media – even by some of the Palestinians' friends.

As Dr al-Zahar walked me out to the laneway I thanked him for raising my spirits. He had achieved that not by saying anything extraordinary but by being what he is, a man of such integrity I felt the better for those hours in his company. An elusive quality, integrity – but you know it when you meet it. And, mysteriously, it breaks down the barriers put up by such issues as homophobia and women's rights. That evening, having described our meeting in my journal, I ended:

> Despite his qualified support for suicide bombers, Mahmoud al-Zahar is not a hawk in dove's plumage. More like a crow (but better-looking) – intelligent, practical, adaptable, tenacious, loyal to his own.

I'm reminded of my 2009 conversation with a Gush Emunim linchpin, in the notoriously hardline settlement of Kiryat Arba near Hebron. In that case, too, all the barriers went down – undermined by integrity. A memorable encounter, but it belongs in another book.

Five

Access to the Faraj Allah home in al-Nussairat camp is through a passageway so narrow it entraps the granny – a diabetic, immobilised by obesity at the age of sixty-three. (She was born under a lemon tree during the Nakba, as her family fled from Ashkelon.) Nita called a warning greeting as we approached a ragged blanket hanging in a doorless doorway. The two-roomed, earthen-floored concrete shack was windowless and furnished only with bed-rolls, serving as divans by day. Granny sat just inside the doorway, fondling a toddler. Her daughter Tahany, mother of nine, was the most beautiful woman I saw in Gaza, with a sweetness of expression to match perfect features. The room's only decoration was a 'martyr's' photograph of nineteen-year-old Ibrahim – Tahany's second son, shot dead three weeks previously.

In fact this young man was not a 'martyr' (i.e., volunteer/ militant). He had never been in the armed – or any other – wing of any organisation. But all Israel's victims are given this status, however civilian their lives may have been. Most families accept the convention though a few resent it. Several times Tahany repeated that Ibrahim was not a fighter, had never been in any sort of trouble, only wanted to work. His colourful 2′ x 5′ memorial poster was misleading; crossed rifles formed a fringe motif but the beaming youth wore a T-shirt and carried a football.

For weeks Ibrahim had been telling his friends that he couldn't settle to a life of permanent idleness. (Were Gaza an EU government jail, occupations would have to be provided for the prisoners.) But he told no one of his plan to enter Israel illegally, in search of a job. On 20 May, when he was not home by midnight, his parents became anxious; al-Nussairat is not known for its nightlife. At

93

1.30 his father tried unsuccessfully to ring him. At 1.50 his brother Adel got through and Ibrahim admitted to being near the border. Everyone begged him to come home. Further calls brought no reply and around 3.00 am neighbours reported hearing two artillery shells and ten minutes later many gunshots. Then the police were contacted.

The IDF cruelly postponed their convoluted negotiations with the ICRC and the Red Crescent Society. Not until 1.00 pm was a medical crew allowed to search for the body. The IDF of course knew exactly where it lay – one metre from the border – but they refused to cooperate and Ibrahim wasn't found until 4.00 pm. By then, according to Awni Khattab, a paramedic who led the search, dogs had eaten most of the abdomen and thighs, inflicting on his stricken family a refinement of emotional torture. Then, inevitably, there were self-torturings – had nobody rung Ibrahim's mobile, perhaps he'd have got safely over the border . . . ? Nita and I emphatically dismissed that notion. Poor Ibrahim, his only equipment a mobile phone, had no chance of defeating the technology that keeps 1.6 million Gazans imprisoned.

Tahany said, 'And he only wanted to *work*, he didn't want to harm anybody.' She took an envelope from under a divan and showed me four photographs: Ibrahim aged from two to eighteen. She stroked them with a forefinger and said, 'I've nine children, each different, special. People with one or two think if you've nine losing one isn't so bad. They're wrong.'

Translating this, Nita had tears in her eyes.

Adel, a handsome twenty-year-old, spoke a little English and with Nita's help voiced strong views on the IDF's use of psychological torture (considered by some to be clinically sadistic). At noon one day, in nearby Khoza'a village, sixty-year-old Mahmoud was ordered by phone, 'Evacuate your house now!' His was one of three small houses built some fifty yards apart; married sons occupied the others. He and his wife gathered their few cherished possessions and took refuge next door with Hussein, whose wife and three children were absent, queuing at an ISI vaccination clinic. At about 2.00 pm a drone shelled Hussein's house, penetrating the roof but causing only minor injuries because no one was upstairs. The three 'lucky' ones retreated, badly shaken, to Mahmoud's house. An hour later the IDF phoned again, this time ordering Mahmoud to leave his home *within five minutes*. Everyone hastened away from the three houses – but none was attacked. And that sort of thing, said Adel, happens frequently up and down the Strip, playing on nerves already stretched taut.

A seventeen-year-old girl sat close to Tahany, never speaking. Her wedding, planned for that week, had been postponed. Children of varying sizes romped cheerfully; there were no toys in sight. The toddler had left granny and was staring hard at Ibrahim's poster, taken from the inner room and placed opposite the doorway for my benefit. But the centre of attention was a sturdy nine-month-old speed-crawler of infinite charm and energy who paused just occasionally to refuel at the breast. His ambition was to escape into the Great Outdoors, a tiny space between concrete shacks. Whenever retrieved from the doorway he chuckled gleefully instead of yelling frustratedly, then rolled his gleaming eye at everyone before zooming off on his next circuit of the floor, dribbling as he went. Adel, especially, was quite besotted by his hyper-active brother and lamented my being cameraless.

Not all Gazans can afford gas cylinders and this family cooked in a lean-to on a mud-stove built by Father and fuelled by whatever flammiferous substances the children could scavenge. Given so few shekels, and these cramped living conditions, how did Tahany manage to rear such a happy, healthy family? All were neatly dressed, well groomed, well-disciplined and affectionate with one another – while she herself remained unfussed and quiet-spoken, amidst all the to-ing and fro-ing and frequent demands on her maternal inventiveness. To me she seemed a superwoman, one of many I've met among Palestinians. Some experts describe what they observe in the camps as 'a great waste of human resources'.

Tahany and Adel urged us to stay for lunch: soon Father would be back from his camp co-op job (a fruit-growing co-op; Gaza is famous for its strawberries). I would have liked to spend much longer with this enchanting family but Nita's time was limited. On realising this, Tahany sent a couple of children to a shop (I later discovered) to buy two plastic boxes in which to pack delicious rice and vegetable lunches for Nita and me. A variant of Mohammed and the mountain: if guests won't stay for a meal they must take it with them. Before we left, I arranged to visit again on the following Friday afternoon when Father would be back from the mosque.

As our taxi bumped through Bureij camp we heard bouts of sustained shooting. According to the other passengers, trouble had started at sunrise when the IDF moved 200 metres into the buffer zone. There they levelled wide areas under crop, a brutal loss for the farmers concerned who had already risked their lives to plant those seeds and were being kept off the scene by irregular random shelling. Next day, we heard the IDF withdrew at sunset and no casualties were reported (apart from the crops).

The al-Tarabin home in Rafah camp – two-storeyed with a patch of back garden – was minimally furnished and unwired for electricity. We were received in an empty living-room by seventeen-year-old Yazan, handsome and charming and head of the household since 7 April, when his thirty-eight-year-old father, Saleh, was killed with two friends, twenty-five-year-old Mohammed and seventeen-year-old Khaled (Yazan's classmate). The three (all civilians) had been stunt-riding on Saleh's vintage motorbike at the former Gaza International Airport, one of the Strip's few open spaces. At about 4.00 pm, ten artillery shells came from the nearby border and moments later two helicopter gunships opened fire. Mohammed and Khaled were killed instantly, Saleh lay bleeding on the ground for two hours while the ICRC and a Red Crescent ambulance tried frantically to start negotiations. At 6.00 pm a brave group of despairing neighbours (all civilians) risked approaching the bodies without IDF authorisation. At once a shell killed twenty-year-old 'Obaid al-Soufi. Fourteen others, including five teenagers and a paramedic, were seriously wounded. By then Saleh had bled to death and 'Obaid's family couldn't reconcile themselves to the idea that their son was 'wasted for nothing'.

Haia appeared then, carrying a baby and followed by her six other children who sat in a silent row against one wall, staring at the stranger. She was a tall, heavily built thirty-six-year-old with a chronic eye infection – caused by too much weeping, said the doctor. Her hands trembled as she filled little tea glasses and she hadn't slept normally for two months. The most tormenting thing, Yazan explained, was the image of Saleh slowly bleeding to death because no help was allowed. The paramedics said he would certainly have lived but for 'negotiations'.

Haia came from the West Bank and had no family on the Strip; her mother lived in Tulkarm and now longed to be in Rafah. Since the day after Saleh's murder she had been trying doggedly to get an 'emergency permit' to visit, with little hope of success. The phrase 'on compassionate grounds' has no meaning for Israeli officialdom. Mother and daughter spoke daily on their mobiles – a costly routine, subsidised by a rich man in Tulkarm as part of his *zakat*, his charitable duty as a Muslim.

The children reflected their mother's distress. During the summer holidays Saleh often took them all to Gaza's most beautiful beach, near Khan Younis and previously reserved for settlers. Now they didn't want to go, they missed him even more when remembering the games they used to play together. Apart from that, the three girls – aged thirteen, fourteen and sixteen – couldn't go to the beach (or anywhere else) without an adult male relative; and Yazan had inherited his father's truck-driver job. Nita caught my eye and made a soothing gesture. She could guess what I was thinking –

'How outrageous that a girl old enough to be married can't take her younger siblings to the beach!'

Haia beckoned us into the larger room where big cardboard cartons, with childishly written name labels, were stacked in corners; improvised chests-of-drawers. High on one wall, facing the window, hung a triple 'martyrs' memorial', photographs of the murdered men wreathed in Koranic quotations with no hint of militarism. Then we were led out to the yard and a shed door was unlocked to show us the shelled motorbike – a sinister contortion of metal, scarcely identifiable for what it was. Saleh had been very proud of it, said Yazan. Trying out new stunts was his hobby. As we were leaving, Haia embraced me, began to sob and said I reminded her of her grandmother who had white hair and didn't wear the hijab.

A private taxi took us to our next destination; it was off the *serveece* routes and involved culture shock on a seismic scale.

The driver speculated about the airport killings – perhaps yet another case of 'collaboration gone wrong'? Someone with a grudge against one of the dead men's clans fingering them as terrorists? Or the IDF misinterpreting information? Or simply an informer so frantically in need of IDF cash – maybe for a good purpose, like buying medical care abroad for a dangerously ill child – that nothing else mattered and lies were invented. Gaza's blockade creates unique exigencies. And Israel's 'war on terror', with its heavy dependence on buying information from within a grievously impoverished population, has inevitably led to some degree of moral degeneracy. As she translated, Nita emphasised that all this was no more than speculation, though sufficiently grounded in past events to be noted. She was meticulous about my 'getting the facts straight'.

Outside a metal double gate, set in a long, fifteen-foot-high brick wall topped with razor-wire, Nita startled the driver by saying 'Stop!' This was an unexpected vision on the outskirts of a Gazan village and he waited, looking curious, while Nita dealt with an electronic device. When nothing happened he laughed and made some teasing remark which provoked her to bang on the metal. Moments later we were admitted by a young manservant who eyed me suspiciously. Ahead rose the Oslo-era home of a notable family which had prospered during that brief boom. It was very large, incorporating pinkish stone, brownish marble and garish stained glass. The architect had come under the influence of many styles, discordant when combined. We were led across a wide palm-fringed courtyard, its centrepiece an elaborate fountain unlikely ever to spout again. An abundance of crimson and yellow shrubs flowered in tall, bulbous pottery jars. Many balustraded steps led to a wide, tiled verandah furnished with well-crafted wooden benches – uncushioned. When the bereaved mother joined us, wearing a wondrously embroidered Palestinian traditional gown, she called for the standard plastic garden chairs. Then she welcomed me in English – kissing me on both cheeks, as is not the custom – and I guessed she was used to meeting foreigners.

Our hostess's composed cheerfulness surprised me, less than two months after the shelling of her twenty-five-year-old first-born and his comrade – members of a Qassam unit which had just fired a home-made rocket into Israel. The family hadn't known of his activism, had treated as a morbid hobby his lifelong obsession with weaponry and the resistance movement. (Masks are multi-purpose.) He worked in his father's thriving business; not all martyrs are seeking to escape from misery to Paradise.

Looking through three family albums we saw the toddler with his water-pistol and the primary schoolboy always wearing realistic military gear, surrounded by an extensive collection of weaponry and brandishing a wooden AK-47. One chilling picture showed him, aged nine, standing threateningly over a small brother, pressing a pistol to his temple. 'This is how he wanted to be with Israel,' explained his mother. But one had to suspect that without a resistance movement this young man would have been elsewhere, seeking 'action'. His mother may have been better able to conceal emotion than the camps' bereaved, but her cool detachment disconcerted me. And I didn't feel it was contradicted by the shrine in the basement.

Dainty slippers were provided before our hostess led us into a vast circular space, almost mosque-like, with multi-coloured light pouring down from a stained-glass dome fifty feet above. Slender marble pillars rose on either side and low carved archways led to who knows what other splendours. Scattered about were divans and coffee-tables and inconsequential solid sideboards that surely came from nineteenth-century Germany – all looking like doll's-house furniture in this unhomely space. Ahead, beyond a high archway, we glimpsed a sweeping double staircase – then were led along short vaulted corridors and down several flights of steps to the basement, cool and well ventilated and big enough to house half-a-dozen camp families. Yet it seemed to be unused, apart from the shrine at one end – virtually a chapel. A triptych 'altar-piece' stood on a long table supporting four large vases of irises and a display of the martyr's possessions – toy weapons, a massive Lego tank and other military vehicles, football boots, boxing gloves, surf board, laptop, cell phone, an al-Aqsa University briefcase, watch, worry beads and framed school certificates showing how well he had done in all his exams. The 10′ x 6′ triptych should have been spotlit but the electricity had gone off (hence the hiatus at the gate). The central panel depicted a lightly bearded, heavily armed Qassam officer in full uniform with a white dove (butterfly-sized) perched on his right forefinger and another on the tip of his rocket while a third (full-sized) flew above his left ear. These, explained our hostess, symbolised the resistance fighters' longing for a just peace. The side panels showed masked volunteers setting up and firing imported (rather than home-made) rockets. At both ends of the table/altar stood flags bearing the insignia and mottos of the Qassam Brigades. Before going on our way we each received a large glossy poster from the pile kept under the table for presentation to worshippers.

Outside, Nita asked, 'What's the English word for a place like that?'

I thought hard. Villa, mansion, fort, palace, manor, castle – nothing fitted. Then the word came. 'It's a folly,' I said. 'Much bigger than average but undoubtedly of that genre.' One doesn't expect such excesses in Gaza but I'm told similar follies shelter Fatah nabobs on the hills around Ramallah.

Nita joked that she was training herself to be a tourist guide in the unimaginable post-blockade future. She had planned a relaxed end to our day, on a Central Strip poultry farm where all the F-16's victims had been feathered.

Another private taxi took us past al-Zawaida village through an unpeopled landscape close to a section of the buffer zone where many have been killed or wounded. Then stands of palms and fruit trees marked a scattering of small houses, all to some extent damaged when an F-16 bombed the al-Hayeks' poultry farm. That was at 11.30 pm on 5 March and our driver, as usual, speculated. Had the IDF wanted to avoid human casualties while destroying an important enterprise? It was important for the sustenance of the surrounding population and everyone knew economic warfare was an integral part of the Zionist campaign. Or had they meant to kill people in their beds and got the poultry by mistake?

This was one of those moments when suddenly the sheer improbability of the whole tragedy overwhelmed me. We were talking about the airforce of a government armed and supported by the US, the UK and all their allies. Yet had Israelis chosen to kill the al-Hayek family no one outside Gaza (or no one who is listened to) would have heard of their deaths. Or, if they did hear, they would have made no more than a token protest. Improbable, yes – yet a reality not only accepted by 'the international community' but *made possible by those governments.*

There is little traffic hereabouts and our taxi's sound brought Hani to welcome us: a genial fifty-year-old, tall and elegant – the sort of elegance that has to do with bearing rather than clothing. He showed us the bomb crater, twenty metres from the house; 120 pairs of birds had been killed, including precious representatives of three rare breeds (his wife's hobby). 'Morning after' photographs proved how hard the seven al-Hayeks had worked to clear up the devastation. There were five children, aged twenty-one to eight, the youngest girls.

Hani remarked, 'Having three strong boys helped.' Then we joined his wife and daughters – all stoning apricots – in a palm-thatched summerhouse amidst a fabulous cacti collection, some blooming exotically. They varied from thimble-size to an unlovely giant recently officially recognised as a record breaker (I forget by whom). Hani gazed down at this prodigy the way mothers gaze down at their first-born, reminding me that beauty lies in the eye of the beholder. All around distinguished-looking hens wandered and pecked (the vanguard of the replacement stock) and a few turkeys gobbled in the adjacent olive grove. This orderly oasis of silence and comparative greenness felt deceptively tranquil and remote – absurd adjectives in the Gazan context.

Here was another refugee family unregistered with UNRWA. Hani's citrus-farming parents had left Jaffa with enough cash to start a business and eventually buy a house in Jabalya town. By the mid-'80s Gazan resistance to the Occupation was simmering towards the First Intifada and making urban life increasingly unpleasant. Hani and his bride decided to buy these few dunums and, assisted by three brothers, they built a six-roomed, two-storey house with an outside staircase and a flat roof. Gradually they established a modestly successful free-range poultry farm and an olive and cacti nursery – partly obliterated by the bomb but already Hani had replanted. All the children were born in Gaza City and ISI-educated, not because the family inclined towards

Islamism but because such schools were the best available and, if carefully chosen, did not proselytise (as they are all alleged to do, by people and institutions who should know better).

While the 11-year-old daughter brewed coffee, her plump blue-eyed mother plied us with stoned apricots and sadly explained that she cultivated rare plants as well as rare breeds and now all were gone and not as easily replaced as Hani's olives and cacti. But she spoke resignedly, not cursing the IDF as I would have done. According to Hani, her shrewdness and competence had made possible the success of the family enterprise. And immediately after the bombing her sense of humour had held the children together. Those girls were attractive to look at and fun to be with but not yet back to normal. As we were drinking our coffee both went wide-eyed with fear on hearing a short burst of artillery fire from the nearby border. Before the attack on their own home they had ignored such IDF intrusions.

By then two of the sons had joined us, also attractive personalities, and intelligent, but with poor job prospects. However, because they were prepared to live frugally and work hard Hani believed the farm could support them all – unless the IDF struck again. This was a family united by the challenges of Gazan life and sufficiently aware of its own relative good fortune to be content.

Before we left, the boys showed us their home's interior damage. It had been solidly constructed, using good quality materials, but now dangerous cracks gaped in several walls and ceilings. The minimum repairs estimate, using family labour, came to US$6,000 – for Gazans a formidable sum.

I promised to visit again, when unconstrained by Nita's time-table, and our farewell gifts were bags of apricots and glorious bouquets of irises. Then Mrs al-Hayek urged us to call on Izbat, a bereaved friend who needed support, and Hani drove us to the main road, in a minivan redolent of poultry, and waited to see us safely aboard the *serveece* that would take us to Izbat's village.

From the junction we walked between a long line of blank grey 'purdah' walls and a cultivated space where several men, tending a guava crop, paused to stare at us. Around a corner, youths kicking a football also paused to stare and shouted something hostile. Nita looked uneasy. 'It's because you're uncovered,' she muttered. 'This area has gone a bit Salafist – know what I mean? I shouldn't have brought you here without a hijab.'

I laughed. 'So much for your plan to end our day on a relaxed note!'

'Don't laugh!' said Nita. 'Maybe they think you mock them!' She called a greeting then, cleverly asking for Izbat's house. His son was one of four Islamic Jihad volunteers recently killed on their training ground by an F-16 missile. The youths, still scowling but no longer jeering, indicated a nearby door. They moved closer to watch as Izbat, after some delay, admitted us to a large yard with the now familiar combination of hens scratching under olive trees. He waved us towards chairs and a little table, without shaking hands or looking at us directly. His dazzling white *galabiya* seemed to add to his height and gravity.

This twenty-eight-year-old martyr had been an only son, the eldest of seven children. Five of his sisters were married, leaving the youngest to comfort her mother who had, said Izbat, under-gone a personality change, didn't want to meet even close friends, stayed in the bedroom and had lost her appetite. Later Nita told me the full story. This was a Fatah family, loyal in a necessarily subdued way to President Abbas. The son's open membership of Islamic Jihad caused his parents and sisters much distress and anxiety. A year ago his mother had begged his father to scheme, to contrive to have him jailed by Hamas – then he couldn't be active on training grounds and go marching around in broad daylight carrying rocket launchers. But Izbat knew nobody in Hamas who might have arranged such a thing.

The 'martyr's memorial' was missing. Izbat said his wife would have found it offensive. He spoke always in a low voice, looking down at his worry-beads, not letting his expression show any emotion. Then abruptly he made a dismissive gesture and began to talk of times past. He had been born in 1956, of parents terrorised out of their village near Beersheva, and he could remember pleasant features of the Egyptian occupation. His joiner father was never out of work and the children enjoyed listening to dance bands playing on the beach. Even under the Israelis, until the Second Intifada, Gazans were much better off than now. The blockade was inflicting the worst suffering on Palestinians since the Crusades. It was meant to 'cleanse' the Strip, leaving it empty for settlers and a new Israeli naval port. For the first time Izbat smiled as he said (I could see it coming) – 'But we won't go!'

As though to celebrate this declaration the sunset flared – an immense expanse of redness spread to the zenith, momentarily the whole world glowed and Izbat's *galabiya* was tinted pink. 'It's a good omen!' I exclaimed. Nita however had a more prosaic reaction. 'It's late! We can't walk past those heroes outside – I'll ring a taxi.'

Izbat intervened: we mustn't be so extravagant. His neighbour's two adult sons would gladly escort us to the main road. A good plan, I thought, but Nita insisted on a taxi: until then, I hadn't realised how much she feared the Salafist influence.

Reviewing our day, I was again puzzled by the Palestinians' apparent lack of anger and bitterness and impressed by their resilience – the quiet determination to start again, not to be daunted or demoralised. Nita commented, 'It all goes together. People *are* angry and bitter but won't let outsiders see it. That would be not dignified. The anger makes the resilience. The resilience tells the Zionists "You can't win". In the end it will be stronger than suicide bombers and rockets.'

* * *

Nita did not accompany me to Tunnelopolis, an area of topo-graphical turmoil where foreigners are not popular and a Foreign Affairs escort was deemed appropriate.

'Why,' people ask, 'does Israel allow all the tunnelling?' Of course some tunnels are bombed, killing quite a few Gazans, but the network is never attacked on a scale seriously affecting the flow of goods. One theory is that without such a well-organised 'informal economy' the extremity of Gazan suffering, as recorded by UNRWA and other agencies, would compel Israel's allies to take action against the blockade. Therefore tunnels suit Israel. But this theory doesn't fit with a rumour that took off in 2010. Allegedly, the Egyptian authorities and US government engineers had begun to construct a solid steel barrier, ten kilometres long and 25 metres deep; beneath that, not even the most daring Gazan could tunnel. But if the tunnels suit Israel, why would the US invest so much on a counter-tunnel measure? A suggested answer: profits from the informal economy, run by Hamas and its associates, have become one of the government's major sources of income and anything that 'sustains terrorism' must go, regardless of the Israeli viewpoint.

Many people reminded me that June 2011 marked the fifth anniversary of the full blockade of Gaza, a process begun after the 2005 withdrawal. Until June 2006, 4,000 'approved products' were allowed into the Strip. Then the nineteen-year-old corporal, Gilad Schalit, was captured, and two of his mates were killed, in a raid – through a 600-metre tunnel – on Kerem Shalom military base. In retaliation, Israel reduced the number of 'approved products' to 73. And the IDF, driven berserk by their inability to rescue Schalit, bombed several bridges and Hamas government offices and, at Gaza's only power station, destroyed transformers for which no replacements could be imported. This was/is sustained, com-prehensive collective punishment on an unprecedented scale. Imagine the global reaction if the RAF, in retaliation for the killing of two British soldiers and the capture of a third, had bombed Sinn Fein offices in West Belfast and Derry and the bridges and power supply of South Armagh.

Given a 'mixed' community, the British government, even if so inclined, was not free to behave thus. Gaza is singularly unmixed. During the Oslo era, Israel severed the Strip from the West Bank and East Jerusalem. As Amira Hass wrote in the *London Review of Books* (26 February 2009), this isolated Gaza 'from its population, its education and health services, from jobs in Israel and from family members and friends'. Then came the withdrawal of the settlers, leaving the Strip open to uncontrolled collective punishment, and giving the *coup de grâce* to the two-state solution, already undermined by ever-expanding West Bank settlements. Yet in 2012, the two-state solution is still being earnestly promoted in the Highest Places: the US State Department, the British Foreign Office, the EU Commission, the duplicitous Tony Blair-led Quartet – promoted by people who are either culpably ignorant of 'the facts on the ground' or too lily-livered to face them. Facing them would mean challenging Israel's right to exist in its present phoney incarnation as a 'democratic Jewish state' – doubly phoney because the 20 per cent of its citizens who are Palestinian do not enjoy those equal rights granted to citizens of genuine democracies. Meanwhile a contemptible fiction is being maintained – that Israel's 'security' requires the relentless repression of Palestinians until the 'peace process' hatches a peace agreement. In reality there is no peace process and never has been. (I am deliberately repeating myself.) The Zionists have always wanted all of Palestine; a 'just peace' doesn't interest them. The elaborate 'peace process' pantomimes, staged over the decades by Israelis and their allies, masquerading as peace seekers, perfectly suited the Zionist purpose. Off-stage, government-sponsored settlers are being allowed ample time to seize more and more Palestinian land unhindered by the 'international community'.

When Hamas took over the Strip in June 2007 the blockade was tightened again and eighteen months later Cast Lead brought about the almost total collapse of the private sector. In the 2006–2010 period Gaza lost at least 95 per cent of its industrial enterprises (3,759) through border closures or bombing. Between 100,000 and 120,000 workers were left without work. On 19 July 2007 John Ging (then Director of UNRWA in Gaza and a compatriot of whom I can be proud) was quoted in *The New York Times*: 'If present closures continue, we anticipate that Gaza will become nearly a totally aid-dependent society, a society robbed of the possibility of self-sufficiency and the dignity of work.' Given 65 per cent (approximately) unemployment, it is unsurprising that dependency on food aid has gone up from 30 per cent in 2001 to at least 75 per cent (and increasing daily) in 2011. A UN report stated in November 2009: 'The evidence shows that the population is being sustained at the most basic or minimum humanitarian standard.'

Farming, too, has collapsed. One doesn't need to look up the statistics; travelling from village to village the evidence is heart-breakingly visible. Some 35 per cent of the Strip's most fertile land has been put out of bounds by the IDF; 305 wells and 5,000 acres of farmland were destroyed by Cast Lead; widespread soil and water contamination is frustrating most of the gallant replanting efforts. The tree losses, on those 5,000 acres and around bombed homes, are linked to a recent perceptible decline in children's health and have been precisely recorded by Gaza's Union of Agricultural Work Committees: 140,965 olive trees, 136,217 citrus trees, 22,745 fruit trees, 10,365 date palms and 8,922 other trees (figures obtained by Sara Roy in January 2010).

Tunnelopolis is not conducive to the collection of reliable statistics . . . Some say there are a thousand tunnels which, given the area involved, seems very unlikely. Others refer vaguely to 'hundreds'. I was told, 'We've dug 400 but we're using only about 200.' The rest, apparently, were bombed or – more usually – collapsed of natural causes. It's obviously absurd to label them 'illegal' – an adjective more properly applied to the open-air imprisonment of 1.6 million Gazans for whose survival those tunnels are essential. Yet some commentators have given them gangland connotations. Beverly Milton-Edwards and Stephen Farrell, in *Hamas*, write of the withdrawal:

> This made it simpler for Palestinian factions to smuggle in weapons from Egypt, using tunnels bored through the loose sandy soil underneath the border by criminal clans with decades of experience transporting weapons, drugs, cigarettes, alcohol and people. By 2010 Hamas enjoyed control over hundreds of these tunnels, using them to bypass Israel's policy of sealing off Gaza.

Naturally arms come through, plus raw materials for home-made rockets. But on the West Bank and the Strip and in East Jerusalem (let's repeat this) Palestinians are every day being repressed with weaponry supplied by the US and other members of the UN Security Council. All who have witnessed the IDF in action know that the indigenous population is being held down by force – with help, since Oslo, from foreign-funded Palestinian collaborators. No wonder militant 'factions' consider themselves entitled to acquire weapons, through tunnels or by sea or anyhow else, from Iran or anyone else, for use against an occupying army. It is tragic, for all concerned, that they lack a responsible leadership able to restrain them from attacking Israeli civilians within Israel.

Pro-Palestinians often argue that international law allows the people of the Occupied Territories to take up arms against the IDF but by now I'm weary of the 'international law' concept. It has been consistently flouted by Israel since that state's creation. Laws lacking any means of enforcement are '*Humbug!*' (This is being written on Christmas Day and I've just been rereading *A*

Christmas Carol.) I prefer to argue that natural justice is on the side of any people whose land has been stolen by armed robbers, or invaded by powerful alliances using specious excuses ('spreading democracy') to install puppet governments in strategically interesting regions.

In December 2010, on my last evening in Jerusalem, I talked with my Israeli friend Ben. Sagely he observed, 'By now the Zionists have convention on their side. People see the IDF as a regular army, weaponised by the world's leading democracy. They don't doubt its credentials. They forget regular armies can't make up the rules as they go along. I enjoy reminding them that everyone has a moral right to use force to get back their land. Afghans are entitled to kill NATO troops and Iraqis to kill Americans or whoever. People's shocked confusion can be funny. Even if they hate the Occupation, a national army is fixed in their mind as something somehow *respectable*. Peasants who pop out of caves to kill them must be bad. It's the "Peace Now" syndrome – liberals with their guts drawn, dodging the full Israeli reality. In our Holy Land human rights groups try to make non-violent resistance the flavour of the decade – OK, very nice, except the IDF stay with violence.'

Serveece taxis don't casually enter Tunnelopolis and from Yibna camp Shujaeya, my FO minder, led me across a grim wasteland levelled by Cast Lead. We paused to climb a hillock of rubble giving a view of the Sinai's edge; a long stone's throw away, just beyond the border wall, stood a neat little whitewashed mosque. Ahead we could see, amidst high mounds of excavated sand and rock, a colony of large ragged tents and crude corrugated iron shelters, marking the tunnels' entrances/exits. Several horse-and donkey-carts awaited loads, the unharnessed animals nosing though the detritus, finding occasional weeds or blades of grass. Every hundred yards or so huts like portable loos served as offices for long-bearded, black-uniformed customs inspectors and tax collectors. (If criminal gangs once smuggled drugs, alcohol and

cigarettes into Gaza, they don't any more. Allah is watching . . .)
These toughies, all tall and lean, glowered at the foreigner but were
reassured by Shu.

In the first tent we visited, crates and cartons of tinned foods
were piled high and a wiry little man with a grizzled beard and a
poverty-worn face was about to descend, sitting on a plank like a
playground swing seat. He was lowered quite quickly into a wood-
lined shaft, 30 metres deep with a two-square-metre entrance.
Peering down, we could see him using one foot as a buffer. His
grandson assistant, a gaunt poorly clad youth, was hoping to move
to the other side of Tunnelopolis – if the new people in Cairo
stopped supporting Israel. Ten minutes later the plank was being
winched up, laden with crates of fruit juice.

In the three-sided iron shed next door, two men handled each
gas cylinder as it appeared from the tunnel and a pair of weedy
adolescents were loading a donkey-cart. There had been an acute
cooking gas shortage since November 2010 – a crisis that began,
Shu said, in January 2010. Then Israel closed the Nahal Oz
crossing, where all fuel and cooking gas supplies used to enter, and
decreed that in future they must come through Kerem Shalom
where, for security/technological reasons, only a fraction of Gaza's
daily needs could be handled. Said Shu, 'We know some special
Israelis are paid to sit at a desk looking for new ways to make us
more stressed.' A ridiculous notion – until you stop to consider the
multiple constraints of daily life on the Strip.

The shaft in the next tent was wider, to accommodate big sacks
of a building material resembling fine gravel. Two muscular dust-
coated men together heaved these sacks over the parapet, then
lugged them outside to empty onto a pile; such sacks were precious
and had to be returned to Egypt for refilling. All these workers, I
sensed, found my presence discombobulating. The Tunnelopolis
vibes are an odd mix of the eerie, the mundane, the excited and
the watchful.

In a tattered tent of big-top dimensions, four men, including a customs officer, had gathered anxiously around a shaft and from its depths came the pathetic sound of a motherless, terrified calf being trussed and loaded upside down on the plank. When I saw how young it was I wondered who could afford to feed it and one of the men explained – it was a replacement, his cow had lost her calf. Then I wondered why it hadn't come through a pedestrian tunnel and Shu hinted that Tunnelopolis was a very complicated place: certain tunnels were controlled by certain people . . .

The customs officer looked rather amiable so I sought a personal 'tunnel experience'. Shu tried to dissuade me but permission was readily given. 'Then you go alone!' said my minder – being unduly influenced by the 59 tunnel deaths and 115 injuries since January 2010. At that the amiable officer – by name Latif – offered to escort me. We left Shu looking agitated, not realising that no Hamas official would lead an International into a dangerous tunnel.

Beyond the cave-like entrance came a brief gradual slope, then level going for 1,400 metres. Two people could have walked abreast but Latif led by ten yards, carrying a torch not needed; at regular intervals wall bulbs glowed brightly. Underfoot was a little uneven and occasionally damp; throughout, the air felt fresh. To one side ran thin metal rails for the easy transport of goods in what resembled a 25-foot currach made of hide. This tunnel's central stretch goes through solid rock, before and after through soft sand – contained by wood panelling, the roof beautifully barrel-vaulted. I had to walk only slightly more stooped than I am anyway (by virtue of the passing years). A very tall person might find this distance tiresome but only claustrophobics would regard it as an endurance test.

Where the ground began to slope up, Latif turned and made a 'Stop!' sign. Then, obviously pleased by my unfeigned admiration for the tunnellers' skills, he allowed me to go all the way – so that I could boast childishly of having dropped in on Egypt for thirty seconds. I glimpsed a big indoor space, quite crowded. After a thirty-second visit, I can say no more.

On the way back we met two women and three small boys, all carrying large shopping-bags stuffed with clothes. The women's mother, resident in Egyptian Rafah, was dying of cancer and when told they couldn't get an exit permit before 23 August they chose to go underground. Their husbands dared not accompany them; if detected by the Egyptians they might be jailed for years. This cruelty cannot be put on Israel's charge sheet. Some Gazan Interior Ministry clerk would have refused to move these women up the queue, possibly because their families were Fatah supporters. That's the dark side of the Hamas moon. As we Irish well know, a civil war's residual bitterness is peculiarly corrosive.

That evening, my friend Adnan had a very different suspicion: those unfortunate sisters might have been casualties of the next civil war. He said, 'Without an end to the blockade, we'll have bloodshed again. This time between Fathi Hamad (the Interior Minister) and the Qassam Brigades. An informal economy gives no one legal control and Hamas will split over who gets what and who decides what. The Brigades resent Hamad's officials swaggering around like the tunnels are all theirs when Qassam units organised most of the construction.'

Shu, a resident of Yibna camp, estimated that so far some 70,000 Gazans had got tunnel-related jobs and hundreds had been killed, including two of her uncles. On my praising the diggers' bravery she smiled wryly and said, 'They're not brave, they're hungry. They risk their lives for 50 shekels [10 euros] a day – a 12-hour day.' I wondered about her estimate but had no way of checking it. Without a doubt, maintaining and replacing tunnels, and operating Tunnelopolis's bureaucracy, is south Gaza's main source of employment. Shu believed that this informal economy generates fat private fortunes, especially for Egyptians.

On our way back to Yibna we passed three new cars (unregistered) being checked by a customs officer. They had come through a tunnel I was not allowed to see; exotic gifts from Iran may also use it. (Cattle certainly do, though not often; they tend to panic.) A car costing US$10,000 in Egypt is worth US$30,000 after its tunnel experience. In August 2010 the IDF publicised an end to their three-year ban on motor imports; 60 cars a week were to be allowed through. Ten months later, complained Shu, not one vehicle had been admitted – nor any urgently needed spare parts. Simple parts could be made locally – that's how her father earned half a living – but modern cars often need micro-surgery and stood idle all over the Strip for lack of it.

That misleading IDF statement had been part of a wider scheme. In May 2010, when a 'Free Gaza' flotilla tried to break the blockade, the IDF provoked global outrage by killing nine campaigners in international waters. On 20 June Israel's Security Cabinet met to recalibrate its Gaza policy. In future, we were told, only items *not* allowed into Gaza would be listed – 'weapons and war materials, including problematic dual-use items'. A year later, the Palestinian Centre for Human Rights reported:

> Israel's declaration of allowing new goods to enter the Gaza Strip constitutes an attempt to delude the international community, as such goods do not meet the minimal needs of the Strip. Measures declared to ease the blockade are vague, purely cosmetic and fail to deal with the root causes of the crisis, which can only be addressed by an immediate and complete lifting of the closure, including lifting the travel ban into and out of the strip. PCHR is concerned that the new policy is simply shifting Gaza to another form of illegal blockade, one that may become internationally accepted and institutionalised. Gazans may no longer suffer the same shortage of goods, but they will remain economically dependent and unable to care for themselves, and socially, culturally and academically isolated from the rest of

the world. The IDF have continued to ban the entry of raw construction materials and have continued to ban all exports.

No wonder Gazans resent Tunnelopolis workers being described as 'black market operators'. There is no other market to operate.

Six

Mrs Halaweh had introduced me by mobile to her nephew, Anwar, a retired professor of Political Science who, having spent most of his working life abroad, was now back in the Khan Younis family home. Prompted by his aunt, he invited me to breakfast.

On the Strip, places tend to merge into one another and it can be hard to see where a town or camp begins or ends. But Khan Younis's city centre is unmistakable, distinguished by the noble remains of a khan wall – 60 metres long and ten metres high, including a tower and gateway – built in 1387 by the Emir Younis Ibn Ala'en-Nawruzi to shelter merchants and their goods in the heavy two-way flow of Cairo–Damascus trade.

Anwar's ancestral home, within sight of the khan, took a battering in 1956 when Israel occupied the southern Strip during the Suez crisis. No family member was seriously hurt but Anwar, aged ten, permanently lost his hearing in one ear. The shooting of hundreds of civilians in the nearby al-Amal camp enraged him. The Israeli government told a subsequent UN inquiry that those killed were resistance fighters, misinformation eventually corrected by the publication of General Moshe Dayan's diary. Two generations later, at the start of the Second Intifada, further structural damage was done to a gable end as giant bulldozers rumbled past to raze scores of homes on the edge of the camp and destroy all crops in fields separating it from a settlement.

Anwar was tubby and short-bearded and almost bald with a soft slow voice, grey-green eyes and the sort of nose that used to be described as 'Jewish'. His English had a pronounced Indian lilt, a souvenir of eight years lecturing in New Delhi – his first venture out of Palestine. We sat in the restored wing, in a sparsely furnished room with a wide window overlooking a barren garden where two massive palm stumps made Anwar sad. 'I feel they knocked those deliberately,' he said. 'They enjoy knocking Palestinians' trees.'

Most of Anwar's very extended family (he was one of twelve) still lived in Gaza; several others were also returnees. It surprised me to meet so many Gazans who had voluntarily incarcerated themselves in this open-air prison. The Palestinians' attachment to their birth-places sharpens the Nakba's poignancy. However, as a widower with four married children settled in the US and Europe, Anwar would not have returned in 2004 had he foreseen how total the blockade would soon become.

Having spent most of his adult life abroad, this returnee viewed the Gazan scene with some detachment and an unexpected optimism. He intrigued me by defining, as one of Hamas' main strengths, an essential incompatibility with 'fundamentalism'.

'You look surprised,' he said, 'but our tradition is not fanatical, we don't have that temperament. So Hamas fanatics are easily diluted! For that much we can give thanks to Allah. Sure, the Mujamma seed took root when sown – but why? Because Zionism had changed the dynamics, distorted our social and political frame-work. The seed only flourished after the Occupation introduced "Judaism versus Islam". Our conflict is about land and justice. The Zionists didn't get rid of us because they were bigoted Jews who hated Muslims. They were secular Jews who had to drive us off land they wanted to settle.'

For a time Anwar had worked behind the political scenes, as an advisor to major decision-makers. 'I warned them against out-lawing Hamas, then imprisoning Gazans on the Strip. A territory sealed off from outside influences is a hot-house for extremism. Now more and more of Gaza's resentful young jobless go regularly to the mosque. They've nothing else to do. A world of packed homes and empty pockets offers no hope and the most popular preachers describe the martyrs' other-worldly rewards.'

Anwar's cautious optimism sprang from a conviction that Hamas' present heterogeneous support has the potential to cohere into something stable and constructive. He pointed out that it encompassed the impoverished masses in the camps and elsewhere who feel a certain loyalty because for generations they have been helped, free of charge, by Hamas-supported ISIs staffed by professionals. Then there are the disillusioned former Fatah followers (no longer deceived by posturing peace-seekers), many of whom are among the embittered victims of Fatah/PA corruption, a scandal unconcealed for years in the certainty that as long as officials toed the Israel/US line the donors of abused funds would choose not to notice. Very important, too, are the devout moderate Muslims, longing for peace and normality, by temperament apolitical yet valuing Hamas' refusal to compromise on justice. And around the edges, menacing the rest, are those incurably belligerent rocketeers who despise the Hamas leadership's conciliatory tendencies and shrug off the deaths and injuries suffered by their own communities when Israel retaliates. I said nothing to dim Anwar's optimism but as he listed those disparate elements I did wonder – *how* to cohere them all?

Anwar brought up a subject rarely discussed, the ambiguity enveloping UNRWA's role. On the West Bank a few mavericks had spoken to me, *sotto voce*, about that agency as Zionism's partner in crime. What if there had been no post-Nakba humanitarian intervention? If Gaza's Egyptian rulers, and the West Bank's Jordanian rulers, had been left to cope with hundreds of thousands of Displaced Persons – starving, homeless, ill and in rags . . .

Benny Morris has written:

Economically the war (1948–49) had done a limited amount of harm to Israel . . . This was largely offset by the massive financial contributions sent in by world Jewry and by the grants and loans that soon began to arrive from various Western countries . . .

The Arab states had notched up only losses . . . and all, to one degree or another . . . were forced to cope with the burden of the Palestinian refugees . . . However, this by and large did not harm them economically, as the 1950 advent of the UN Relief and Works Agency for Palestine Refugees in the Near East (UNRWA) . . . and a steady flow of Western relief capital more than compensated for any losses they may initially have incurred. The major economic harm was to the Palestinians, who lost much of their property to the victors.

I told Anwar about Noha, my octogenarian but keen-witted Balata friend, who remembered her unusually prescient father objecting to the camps' establishment. Looking beyond the immediate alleviation of misery, he saw the dispossessed Palestinians becoming institutionalised, being regarded as an acceptable though regrettable entity, their minimum basic needs regularly fulfilled. Minimum, yet enabling the world to forget about them. Noha wondered – without aid from the UN and Zionism's international allies, wouldn't the Nakba have been seen in perspective? Wouldn't Israel have been held responsible for the alleviation of the uprooted population's misery? Surely so many suffering so much would have made it impossible for the world to ignore the Nakba injustice?

To Noha I had replied, 'But the UN, having put a match to the Nakba by voting for 181, had to become the fire brigade. Otherwise the vote might have been condemned as a criminal error.'

Anwar concurred with this and added, 'At the time most refugees trusted they'd be rescued eventually by Arab armies taking back their land. Camp life seemed temporary – until 1967, when they realised their children and grandchildren and great-grandchildren were doomed to a landless, stateless eternity.'

On 7 June '67, as thousands fled across the Jordan from the Tulkarm region, Moshe Dayan, then defence minister, ordered his troops to leave the roads open. 'In this way,' records Brigadier-General Braun, 'the population of the West Bank would be reduced and Israel freed of severe problems.'

In September '67 Dayan urged senior IDF staff to promote emigration 'because after all, we want to create a new map'. Two months later, General Narkiss didn't disguise the Zionist project. 'We are talking about emigration of the Arabs. Everything must be done – even paying them money – to get them to leave.' On 14 July 1968, addressing a meeting in his ministerial office, Dayan said, 'Anyone who has practical ideas or proposals to encourage emigration, let him speak up. No idea or proposal is to be dismissed out of hand.'

A mild version of the two-state solution was mooted in 1967 immediately after the Six Day War, when certain West Bank notables suggested autonomy for the newly Occupied Territories. Predictably, as Benny Morris explains, 'Dayan rejected the idea, fearing it would evolve into Palestinian statehood. He, like the rest of the Labour Party leadership, firmly opposed such statehood, deeming it a mortal threat to Israel's existence.'

Anwar said, 'When you see the IDF graffiti, and the shocking results of their retaliations, remember there's a 45-year build-up of frustration! Always the Zionists have desperately wanted us out – but we're not going!'

Throughout those 45 years a reprehensible pattern has been repeated: Israel destroys, her foreign friends restore – usually with their taxpayers' money. Anwar mentioned an example of which Shu had spoken: in May 2004 she witnessed some of the demolitions when Operation Rainbow was launched in retaliation for the killing of two Israeli soldiers. Within 24 days, bulldozers flattened 277 Rafah camp homes, leaving 3,451 Gazans without shelter or possessions. Anwar had just returned to Khan Younis and was among the many notables who appealed to the Quartet to intervene; clearly the IDF's murders of dozens of civilians and their destruction of civilian property were war crimes. Yet the Quartet did and said nothing, the killings and demolitions continued. Then, on 25 June, at a press conference at UN Headquarters in New York, Kofi Annan was pinned down and had to make a statement which Anwar showed me – sellotaped into his old-fashioned newspaper cuttings album. The UN Secretary-General, speaking as the UN Quarter of the Quartet, said:

> You would want to see immediate action by the Quartet . . . to stop the demolition of the houses, and that is going to take the kind of action and will and resources and confrontation that quite frankly, today, I don't see anybody in the international community willing to take.

Anwar said, 'That tells us pandering to Israeli killers is more important than protecting Palestinian civilians. Soon after came the usual "compensation" – guilty governments donating millions to rebuild homes. But you can't resurrect the dead with donations.'

Anwar's blood pressure rose perceptibly as I recalled my private view, in November 2008, of Tony Blair's three armoured vehicles in their cordoned-off corner behind Jerusalem's American Colony hotel. To the man and woman in the street such monster machines symbolise aggression and mistrust while ensuring that the Quartet's leader can have no real contact with those he is being overpaid to help. Their cost (more than US$400,000) came in 2007 from the UN Development Programme's 'Programme of Assistance to the Palestinian People'. They are little used; Blair has many fish to fry and the Palestinian People are mere minnows – for whom $400,000 could do a lot if invested in a refugee camp.

The Quartet's headquarters, where Blair appears now and then for a few days, occupies a whole floor of one of Jerusalem's most expensive hotels and Britain's taxpayers foot most of this seriously astronomical bill. 'But doesn't Britain have austerity now?' said Anwar. 'Do the taxpayers know . . . ?'

I guesstimated. 'Perhaps 0.5 per cent know and even they may not care. In democracies people who work hard and pay taxes are conditioned not to fret about *how* their money is wasted. Unless some media person goes on the trail of *who* is wasting it. Then citizens become indignant – in a passive way, and not for long.'*

During my residency in Balata refugee camp Blair briefly visited the neighbouring city of Nablus, allowing me to glimpse the Quartet's methodology. For security reasons, only the staffs of the city's various UN agencies were aware of his presence among us. Not until he was safely back in his American Colony nook did the word get around – 'Blair's been here!' Balata's 26,000 refugees (four generations of them by now) were not on his agenda. In recent years, while the unemployment statistics become ever more harrowing, most UNRWA camps have suffered a reduction in funding. How come another UN agency can afford to spend $400,000 on three vehicles *to assist the Palestinian People*?

My breakfast visit had extended into the afternoon. 'Come again!' said Anwar. 'I want to talk about the future.' We fixed a day, then I left him with a cheering observation. In Israel and on the West Bank, I had found at least one sentiment uniting Israelis and Palestinians – scorn for Tony Blair.

* * *

On the Quartet's first appearance in 2002 I pounced on the name as a fudge probably presaging new rounds of fake 'peace talks'. (The reality is worse.) Russia, the US, the EU, the UN (always represented by its Secretary-General) – how to unravel that knot? Russia, the US, the EU's member states – all are among the UN's 191 member states. So what's going on here? Ten years later, we know.

This international sponsor for the fictional 'Peace Process' is

---

* In September 2011 UK's Channel 4 produced a Dispatches documentary investigating Tony Blair's financial frolics in the Middle East.

another tool with which the US shapes the Palestinians' destiny for Israel's benefit. An ad hoc committee, with no mandate from anyone, it has been led since his retirement from No. 10 by Tony Blair who uses it to collect an astounding selection of valuable feathers for nesting purposes.

In April 2003 President George W. Bush unrolled his Quartet-endorsed 'Road Map to Peace' which aroused tremendous international enthusiasm amongst those Middle East commentators who know not of what they speak or write. Apparently everyone was heading towards 'a final and comprehensive settlement of the Israel–Palestine conflict by 2005'.

Within a year Bush Jnr had in effect torn up his lovely new map by writing to Ariel Sharon (then prime minister) assuring him the US would never expect Israel to quit the West Bank's city-sized settlements. This merely echoed President Clinton's 2001 letter to Palestinian and Israeli leaders, approving 'the incorporation into Israel of settlement blocks'. Yet to some eyes it brought tears of disillusionment.

In 2005 Quartet statements misinterpreted the withdrawal from Gaza and more than 5,000 journalists arrived in Gaza City to report on this momentous event and write up 'Ariel Sharon, Man of Peace'. The Quartet had made no mention of the blockade and a few months later were embarrassed when James Wolfensohn, former World Bank president, complained after visiting Gaza, 'Israel is almost acting as though there has been no withdrawal.'

Meanwhile the Quartet's leader had a few other things on his mind. A private firm, Tony Blair Associates (remember Kissinger Associates?) feeds on very private consulting contracts linked to the sort of Arabs you get to meet if Israel favours you. The Emir of Kuwait paid $40 million for advice on 'reforms'. More millions came from UAE coffers. Tony Blair Associates enjoyed an annual $2 million retainer from JP Morgan for 'strategic' advice. In 2007 JP Morgan arranged a $2 billion loan for Qatari telecoms company

Q-Tel to buy the mobile company Wataniya. Wataniya wanted to operate on the West Bank and in November 2009 Blair successfully persuaded Israel to release the necessary frequencies – in exchange for the PA's promise to forget the *Goldstone Report* on Cast Lead war crimes.

The Strip's territorial waters hold an estimated $6 billion worth of natural gas fields and for their exploitation Blair tried to fix a deal between British Gas and Israel. This would be 'good for Gaza', he proclaimed. Yet all negotiations were with Netanyahu, not a prime minister known for giving Gazans their fair share.

The Quartet spends vast sums of public money but because of its peculiar genesis Blair can forget all about the normal 'conflicts of interest' and 'disclosure' regulations that bind British government officials and UN employees.

This committee's main task seems to be to make it easier for Israel to breach the Geneva Conventions with impunity – a function so obvious that one of President Abbas's senior aides, Nabil Shaath, has gone public to denounce Blair for acting as Israel's 'defence attorney'. A French diplomat agrees with this. Anis Nacrour, once a senior advisor to Blair in the Quartet's Jerusalem office, now talks of ' . . . a smokescreen for the actions of the Americans and the tandem between Americans and Israelis. At the end of the day, all this was for buying time for allowing the Israeli government to do whatever they wanted to do.'

This explains why Ban Ki-moon accepts directives from the Quartet rather than from an authorised UN agency. The UN Human Rights Council in September 2010 agreed with the finding of the ICRC – Israel's siege and blockade of Gaza is illegal. Ignoring that, a UN Secretary-General, who has taken an oath to uphold international law, wrote in May 2011 to the relevant Mediterranean governments urging them to 'use their influence' to stymie the 2011 Freedom Flotilla II (in which I had invested quite a lot of energy and some money, hoping to arrive in Gaza by boat). Ban Ki-moon referred to the Flotilla as 'not helpful' because 'assistance and goods destined to Gaza should be channelled through legitimate crossings and established channels'. This semi-literate wording is taken from a Quartet statement put out as part of the US/Israel manoeuvre to avoid another confrontation on the high seas.

As Ali Abunimah has noted, nobody knows who hired Blair or who can fire him. Anwar had told me his Ramallah contacts were reporting rumours of a move to sack him – politely, of course, by sending formal requests to the United Nations Development Programme and the British government. Anwar sighed and shook his head. 'I told my PA friends that won't work, the Quartet is too valuable, he'll never let go.' I remembered this prediction on 6 October 2011 when *The Financial Times* reported:

> Mohammed Ishtayeh, a top member of Fatah and confidant of Mahmoud Abbas, said in an interview: 'I call on Tony Blair to resign. There is a consensus among the Palestinian leadership that people are dissatisfied with his performance' . . . Nabil Shaath, another aide to Mr Abbas, said, 'He simply does not want to do anything that angers the Israelis, which sometimes makes him sound like them.'
>
> A spokesman for Mr Blair denied the envoy had a pro-Israel bias. A Western diplomat said the Quartet was unlikely to dismiss him. 'At the highest levels, Blair retains the confidence of the political leadership of the Quartet, except maybe Russia, which I can't see wanting a massive fight over him.'

Take heed – how the political leadership of the Palestinians views this envoy counts for nothing.

*   *   *

The British glanced at a one-state solution, binationalism, before Partition in 1947. Finding themselves unable any longer to contain the guerrilla war in Mandatory Palestine, they proposed a temporary international trusteeship with local autonomy for both Arabs and Jews and a generously subsidised binational state as the eventual reward for living happily together. Enthusiastic backing for this plan came from the Jewish philosopher Martin Buber and the then president of the Hebrew University, Judah Magnes; most Zionists and Palestinians didn't even stop to consider it.

In 1967, a few weeks after the Six Day War, a distinguished French Jew, Maxime Rodinson, felt worried and wrote:

> How is Israel to keep the conquered territories under her dominion? Either the system becomes democratic, or even remains simply liberal and parliamentary – in which case the Arabs will very soon be in the majority, and that will be the end of the dream of a Jewish State for which so many sacrifices have been made. Or else the Arabs will be treated as second-class citizens, discrimination will become institutional, a kind of South African policy will be introduced. This, together with the necessarily increasingly savage repression of increasingly bold acts of sabotage and guerrilla warfare, will lose Israel the support of world public opinion.

This Sorbonne professor of Old South Arabian languages may have been the first outsider to discern the underlying affinity between South Africa's white Nationalists and political Zionism's Ashkenazi leaders. In 2012 his foresight seems quite uncanny.

In the late 1960s Fatah toyed with the notion of binationalism but were soon cowed by the height of the hurdles. Then Yasser Arafat took it off everyone's agenda by clumsily presenting it, in his 1974 address to the UN General Assembly, as a secular ploy for undermining the *Jewishness* of the State of Israel. In 1988 the PLO reluctantly recognised Israel's 'right to exist' and formally adopted the 'two-state solution'.

Digging deep in my Palestine/Israel file, I came upon a long essay

('Where is Israel Going?', *New York Review of Books*, 7 October 1982) by Nahum Goldmann, for many years president of the World Jewish Congress. Written shortly before his death, at the age of 87, it is a sad and angry reaction to Israel's 'presumptuous invasion of Lebanon and the siege of Beirut'. Thirty years on, it remains relevant.

> Undoubtedly, Israel will gain a military victory. However, up to now every military victory has only resulted in new political difficulties . . . Despite their arrogance and stubbornness the Israelis are smart enough to understand that without the support of the US they have no chance to succeed with their politics of aggression . . . Many members of the Jewish elite in America have protested to Begin against his policies . . . An Israel whose main achievements are military ones – an Israel that concentrates all its energies on military superiority – would deeply distort the image of the Jewish people in the eyes of non-Jews . . . If Israel's martial characteristics continue to prevail for a long time, the Jewish people will lose their unique character. In the long run this would endanger no less than the very foundations of its existence.

Seven years later, in the *International Herald Tribune* (14 March 1989), Steven Pearlstein, one of 'the Jewish elite in America' deplored Israel's treatment of the Palestinians.

> American Jews once could be counted on to give Israel everything it wanted . . . most of all, help in gaining the unwavering support of the greatest military and economic power on earth. These attitudes have begun to change . . . and I wonder whether it isn't time to think about giving Israel one last thing – its independence. Not an easy gift to deliver . . . Like any step-parents, American Jewry finds it difficult to cut the cord but Israel seems to need such a new relationship . . . US support has

enabled the country to make itself into the overwhelming military power in the Middle East, creating for its leaders a false set of choices as they attempt to make peace with enemies outside their border and within.

Fast forward to 6 December 1997 when *The Economist* reported that Benjamin Netanyahu's government had agreed to withdraw its troops from the West Bank. However, this decision

prompted gratified winks and nods as the 'greater Israel' loyalists in the cabinet and the Knesset assured each other that nothing would happen as a result of the peace initiative announced on November 30th and designed only to head off mounting American pressure on the Prime Minister.

Sure enough, nothing did happen.

Ten months later Ahmad Samih al-Khalidi (a Palestinian writer and negotiator) flew a kite in *Prospect* (October 1998). Following the Oslo debacle, he noted:

A small but increasingly influential circle of Palestinians is posing binationalism as a practical alternative . . . This solution may emerge *faute de mieux*. Most Israelis see it as a threat . . . but a credible and peacefully articulated Palestinian campaign for binationalism and 'one man, one vote' will demand a better response than the mere reiteration of faith in exclusivist 'blood and soil' nationalism . . . A concept of citizenship whereby every individual has the same rights, based not on race or religion, but on equal justice for each person guaranteed by a constitution, must replace all our outmoded notions of how Palestine will be cleansed of the other's enemies.

Since that powerful intervention the debate had become vigorous though chiefly confined to the *New York Review of Books*, the *Boston Review*, the *Arab World Geographer* and *Al-Ahram Weekly*.

In the last-named, Sharif S. Elmusa, professor of political science at Cairo's American University, has argued persuasively (27 April–3 May 2006) for a binational state in Greater Palestine: Israel, the West Bank, Gaza, and Jordan. For complicated reasons, lucidly explained by Professor Elmusa, the inclusion of Jordan (which has a majority Palestinian population) could solve more problems than it creates by catering for the needs of very many refugees. It's easy to forget those millions in al-Shatat – in exile, not allowed to return to any part of Mandatory Palestine. They have been shamefully neglected since Oslo spawned the PA, which concerns itself only with the West Bank and Gaza.

The ancillary argument, about an end to the US annual subsidy of $4 billion (from government and private donors), is heard wherever people gather to discuss this conflict. In a review of Jacqueline Rose's *The Question of Zion* (*London Review of Books*, 23 June 2005), James Wood put it thus:

> . . . one might wonder whether a key to it all would be the cessation of indiscriminate economic and political support of Israel by the United States. If the task is to persuade Israel to get in touch with its own demons, this might speed up the process . . .

Those demons have been unflinchingly diagnosed by David Shulman in the *New York Review of Books* (24 February 2011):

> There is a studied blindness to the cumulative trauma that we Israelis have inflicted upon the Palestinians in the course of realising our own national goals . . . This is no ordinary blindness; it is a sickness of the soul that takes many forms, from the silence and passivity of ordinary decent people to the malignant forms of racism and proto-fascist nationalism that are becoming more and more evident and powerful in today's Israel, including segments of the present government.

In *What Does a Jew Want?* (2011, ed. Udi Aloni), Judith Butler,

Professor of Comparative Literature at Berkeley, promotes the use of 'binational' rather than 'one-state':

> People have reasonable fears that a 'one-state' solution would ratify the existing marginalisation and impoverishment of the Palestinian people. That Palestine would be forced to accept a kind of Bantustan existence . . . 'Binationalism' raises the question of who is the 'we' who decides what kind of polity is best for this land. The 'we' has to be heterogeneous . . . Everyone who is there and has a claim – and the claims are various.

Another sort of warning came in 2002 from one of Israel's most eminent historians, Ilan Pappé, who in 2007 was forced out of Haifa University because he had referred to Zionism's 'ideology of exclusion, racism and expulsion'. He cautioned:

> We should be very careful now in adopting the American, the Israeli 'Peace Now!', and I'm sorry to say, the PA discourse about a two-state solution which nowadays would be not the end of the Occupation but continuing it in a different way with no solution to the refugee problem and the complete abandonment of the Palestinian minority *in* Israel.

Yet in January 2009 we find Olivier Roy writing in the *International Herald Tribune* that the two-state solution, though 'dead on the ground, remains on the diplomatic agenda'. Sadly, it still remains there, though the bleatings coming from its putative supporters sound increasingly feeble. The binational alternative is never discussed in polite diplomatic circles where collective inertia Rules OK. Its advocacy would involve taking action, being daring, telling the Zionists, 'You can't have your pretend "democratic" Jewish state, breaking international law every day of the week. But you could have a shared Land of Canaan, a real democracy in which all have equal rights and responsibilities.'

President George W. Bush's infamous letter (14 April 2004) to

Ariel Sharon, affirming US support for the settlements, apparently contradicted the Road Map and provoked much disappointment, fury, grief and frustration. It's interesting to reread it now, with binationalism in mind. The Bush administration is indirectly acknowledging that 'two-states' is dead and signalling their approval of a Bantuesque alternative. The letter said:

> In light of new realities on the ground, including already existing major Israeli populations [*sic*] centres, it is unrealistic to expect that the outcome of final status negotiations will be a full and complete return to the armistice lines of 1949, and all previous agreements to negotiate a two-state solution have reached the same conclusion. It is realistic to expect that any final status agreement will only be achieved on the basis of mutually agreed changes that reflect these realities.

Professor Rashid Khalidi of Columbia University has recently put it another way:

> We already have a one-state solution . . . I'm talking about how you could uproot what I call 'the settlement-industrial complex', which is not 500,000 or 600,000 in the OPT, it's the hundreds of thousands in government and in the private sector whose livelihoods and bureaucratic interests are linked to the maintenance of control over the Palestinians . . . Most of them live prosperous lives near the Mediterranean and wouldn't go near the occupied territories . . . But their livelihoods are utterly bound up with the people who live on the West Bank and, to the extent possible, with those who live in Gaza . . . You have to spend a lot of time in the OPT to understand what Amira Hass described as 'the matrix of control'.

*   *   *

Not since staying with Mazin Qumsiyeh in Beit Sahour had

I met such a dedicated and confident binationalist as Anwar. Listening to him, I remembered Mazin's conviction that a 'well-organised, united grass-roots movement could bring about a win-win situation for all the people of the Land of Canaan'. The key word is 'united'. Hence the unremitting US/Israel efforts to stoke disunity.

'After all,' said Anwar, 'binationalists are only seeking justice. We're ready to share, to become equal citizens in a one-man-one-vote multicultural state.' He paused, laughed, corrected himself. 'Forgive – I meant one-*person*! We're way ahead of our political leaders – even those knowing it's the only solution fear to say so. Or else have a vested interest in the status quo – though they'd be a minority. But an influential and unscrupulous minority! To the fearful it looks like defeat, after years of claiming total independence. But when that can't happen, why not march on to claim what could happen? We never were an independent nation-state the way Europeans think of it. We've been robbed of our lands, our water, our homes, our rights to trade and study and travel – not of our sovereignty because we never had it! If we must think of "victory" and "defeat", binationalism also defeats the Israelis. It really inflicts a worse defeat on them, losing their artificial "Jewish" state – which never really existed with its one-fifth Palestinian population. Naturally Zionism's political leaders can't bring themselves even to think about one state. But some Israeli intellectual heavyweights know the score, have spelt it out in their 2004 Olga Accord. What's needed now is open discussion all over the place – everyone having to think about the unthinkable, as Ali Abunimah might say.'

I mentioned the difficulty of 'selling' binationalism to Palestinian support groups in Ireland and Britain – and no doubt elsewhere. People whose favourite cause is a 'Free Palestine', and who haven't experienced 'the matrix of control', tend to reject the need for a new campaign. Especially one that may not bear fruit until the old among them are dead and the young themselves old.

Anwar thought my timescale too pessimistic. 'Barriers looking insuperable now could quickly come down if we unite to use clever weapons. Our foreign friends must learn two states were never on the Zionist agenda but served them well as a Trojan horse. They must stop calling for a free Palestine – that's backing the Trojan horse and blocking the only road to peace. They must invite more binationalists to address their rallies, explaining the twenty-first-century realities.'

One such meeting, I told Anwar, was held in Dublin in February 2010, addressed by Ghada Karmi, Ilan Pappé and John Rose. I couldn't go but a friend kept detailed notes and remarked, 'There was no real attempt made to engage with the horrendous difficulties of working towards a one-state solution.'

'That's OK,' said Anwar. 'What counts is those three being heard – all thinkers, much respected by our foreign friends. As discussions widen and deepen, attitudes will change.' I nodded, remembering how well Anwar's friend, Ali Abunimah, has put it in *One Country*:

> By talking of a common future and imagining it, we engage in the act of creating it; we introduce a different prospect to endless war. It is only through shattering taboos and articulating a vision that we can move the idea . . . from the far margins to the centre of discussion. Simply by admitting the notion to the range of possibilities, we change the landscape.

I quoted Ghada Karmi's plea for a mass-binationalist movement working with kindred Israeli groups and advanced through Boycott, Divestment and Sanctions (BDS). At that, Anwar grimaced and shrugged. 'For me, as a professional scholar and amateur diplomat – well, BDS has to be problematic, intellectually and emotionally. But we don't have a wide choice of weapons – I can't oppose it. Ghada is right. Run a global BDS campaign, demand one-person-one-vote and a constitution like South Africa's. When we're not demanding independence we can't be demonised as terrorists threatening security. All perspectives change!'

We set about stoking each other's optimism. I said, 'Now is the time for a big push, given so much more support for Palestinians since Cast Lead and the Flotilla murders. No more haggling about borders, simply asking for justice, asking Israelis to share the land the same as South Africa's whites do.'

'And the world is watching,' said Anwar. 'Watching like never before! Imagine our Tahrir Square – truly non-violent, no stone-throwing kids, no jeering slogans, no flag-burning – but all those Palestinians calling for citizenship, the vote, equality before the law . . . The IDF daren't attack, within micro-seconds they'd be seen by millions! They'd have to leave at home their rubber bullets, tear-gas canisters, sewage-cannons, prison vans!'

Here a big dark cloud of realpolitik overshadowed my optimism. 'How are the US reacting to all this? How long before their foreign policy shifts?'

'Maybe only years, given a certain convergence of pressures. We're sensing so many tremors, like aftershocks – Egypt the earthquake. I know you've talked with Mahmoud al-Zahar – don't look so surprised! The Strip is small and you're conspicuous. He probably knows you're sitting here now! From him and your younger Hamas friends you'll have picked up atmospheric changes – right?'

I nodded. 'They told me their manic Charter didn't feature in the '06 electioneering – and we went on from there.'

'On Fatah's side,' said Anwar, 'Abbas's stupid "Statehood" game with the UN signals more change – some West Bank PA factions falling out of step with the US-funded Dayton Brigade. In the short term it's a bad game, confusing and deluding people like Oslo did. It's meant to be anti-binationalism but it's so crazy it's having unintended consequences. I've many grand-nephews and -nieces here on the Strip and they and their friends on the West Bank have registered the end of an era. To them Abbas, Netanyahu, Obama – all look irrelevant, so moulded by the past. And so focused on personal concerns – like winning the next election – sensible kids can't take them seriously. The young are in the majority. And they want new leaders, nearer their own age, creatively concerned about their future. They're much more willing than their grandparents and parents to consider binationalism. The recent input from young Mizrahi Jews is part of the same pattern. Some of them want to jump barriers, be with their Palestinian peers, have people admit all Israelis are not Europeans settled in the Middle East. There's change too across the Atlantic. Even AIPAC, the ADL and the rest of the constellation – my US friends tell me they can't recruit enough replacements as the grandads die off.' (A few months later I had an email from Anwar saying, 'Net's 29 standing ovations in the US helped us a lot by giving such publicity to AIPAC's control over US politicians. We laughed over the choreography with the background music of dollars streaming into bank accounts!')

Even among Israelis, BDS has been gaining momentum since Cast Lead. The 'Boycott, Divestment, Sanctions' movement acquired a coherent strategy in 2005, following a Palestinian Civil Society call for a global support group that would steadily concentrate on the essential coloniser-colonised relationship at the root of Palestine's tragedy. In the words of Lisa Taraki, a co-founder, 'The basic logic of BDS is the logic of *pressure* – not diplomacy, persuasion or dialogue.' Understandably, activists like Anwar find this strategy testing. Can it be right to punish ordinary decent Israelis who need to export their produce? Is it wise to boycott cultural and academic exchanges when communication is so often prescribed as the cure for conflicts? (Don't shoot! Talk to the IRA! To FARC! To the Taliban! To Hamas! To everyone . . .) In fact all my Israeli BDS friends are exceptionally dedicated communicators – but time has proved that their government, and all its institutions and international backers, are allergic to talking honestly about justice as the basis for peace. Although BDS never targets individuals, its successful operations will inevitably penalise some academics, artists and writers who are amiably disposed, in a vague way, towards the Palestinians. However, as one of my Haifa friends observed, 'If you're vague you're supporting the Occupation. Not liking it but going along with it. As BDS bites, those *Ha'aretz*-reading liberals will have to see themselves as others see them.' And when it comes to ordinary decent citizens – given the 'silence and passivity' of Israel's majority, it seems nothing less stringent than BDS will prompt them to overcome their 'studied blindness'.

Anwar was among several Palestinian friends who registered disappointment – rather than surprise – when the Irish Palestinian Solidarity Campaign failed to organise a boycott of a four-day, state-funded Israeli film festival in Dublin. As the *Irish Times* reported on 24 November 2011, the Israeli ambassador to Ireland, Boaz Modai, claimed that:

> This festival aims to prove that there is more to Israel than the Palestinian conflict. It is not political; we are trying to show the different faces of Israel. But we have found it quite a challenge to present this festival . . . It became a problem for the Government of Ireland, one about freedom of speech. We have protests outside the embassy every week, but not to allow Israel to stage a non-political event takes things to another stage. It became more than just an Israeli problem. It was important to show this phenomenon is not to be accepted.

'Freedom of speech' is a tricky one and sure enough the pressing of that button gained Tánaiste Eamon Gilmore's official attendance at the festival's opening night.

Perhaps the Government of Ireland is uninformed about 'Brand Israel'. This global campaign, launched (coincidentally?) in 2005, is funded by various Israeli government agencies and major pro-

Zionist international (mainly US) groups. Its primary purpose is to promote Israel as a 'normal' country involved in tourism, sports, innovative science, cultivation of the fine arts, a vibrant youth culture – and so on. 'Brand Israel' can afford to employ high-powered PR firms and all Israel's consulates and embassies are kept busy on its behalf.

In 2008 the Israeli writer Yitzhak Laor revealed the 'price tag' attached to government sponsorship of 'Brand Israel' operations. Any Israeli accepting funding from the Foreign Ministry for taking his or her cultural or artistic work abroad is obliged to sign a contract undertaking 'to act faithfully, responsibly and tirelessly to provide the Ministry with the highest professional services. The service provider is aware that the purpose of ordering services from him is to promote the policy interests of the State of Israel via culture and art, including contributing to creating a positive image for Israel'.

So much for freedom of speech.

Mr Modai's claim that the Dublin film festival was non-political is scuppered by Judith Butler's reflections on BDS and 'normalization':

> Israelis have the power to oppose the Occupation through BDS, the most powerful nonviolent means available. Things change the minute you say 'we cannot continue to act as normal'. To work to the side of the Occupation is to participate in its normalization. And the way that normalization works is to efface or distort that reality within public discourse. As a result, neutrality is not an option.

Many of Judith Butler's family were Holocaust victims. She grew up in the US in a household sympathetic to the new State of Israel and is now Maxine Eliot Professor in the Department of Rhetoric and Comparative Literature at Berkeley. One of her closest friends, Udi Aloni (Israeli-American writer and film maker), has referred to:

The local strain of apartheid policy nurtured by Israel which is precisely the reason why so many Jews all over the world have joined the BDS campaign, a key issue for those of us who are trying to prevent violence against Israel while simultaneously countering its arrogant and aggressive policies . . . Thus BDS actions do not amount to negative, counterproductive moves, as many propagandists try to portray them . . . They are actions of solidarity, partnership and joint progress serving to pre-empt, in a non-violent manner, justified violent resistance aimed at attaining the same goals of justice, peace and equality.

During Dublin's film festival fracas Ireland was accused, in the Israeli press, of being 'the most anti-Israel country in Europe'. This brought a frightened squawk from our addle-pated Department of Foreign Affairs: 'We are not hostile to Israel. We are critical of certain policies, particularly in the Occupied Palestinian Territories. These are not the same things.' Here is a vivid illustration of Judith Butler's point: 'To work to the side of the Occupation is to participate in its normalization.' For whatever reasons, the Irish government (and most others) want to 'continue to act as normal', to maintain friendly relations as though Israel's repression of the Palestinians were some isolated error of judgement, the choice of a wrong policy in a specific case, when in truth it is central to the State's existence and has been since 1948. 'Neutrality is not an option'; we all have a moral duty (usually occluded by realpolitik) to be hostile to a government that deliberately and relentlessly inflicts so much suffering on successive generations of a people who did nothing to deserve the Nakba and its consequences. To make our hostility effective, BDS is 'the most powerful non-violent means available'. If millions were saying, 'We cannot continue to act as normal' while the repression continues, then things would change – and everyone would be that much closer to binationalism.

Tony Judt was one of the many Jewish supporters of BDS. Not

long before his death, in an interview with Kristina Božic in the *London Review of Books* (25 March 2010), he repeated his call for the EU to use its 'enormous leverage' and say to Israel, 'So long as you break international laws, you can't be part of the EU market.' Why don't we do this? Because of 'ridiculous self-blackmail'. Tony Judt's Dutch and German friends said to him:

> 'We couldn't do that. Think of what we did to the Jews. We can't use economic leverage against Israel. We can't be a critic of Israel, we can't use our strength as a huge economic actor to pressure the Jewish state. Why? Because of Auschwitz' . . . I understand that; many of my family were killed in Auschwitz. However, Europe can't live indefinitely on the credit of someone else's crimes to justify a state that creates and commits its own crimes . . . Israel should not be special because it is Jewish. If Jews are to have a state just like everyone else, it should have no more rights than Slovenia and no fewer. Therefore, it also has to behave like a state . . . Furthermore, other countries have to behave towards it the way they would towards any other state that broke international law . . . The European bad conscience is part of the problem.

I had occasion to quote Tony Judt in Jabalya as I talked with angry members of a football club which had just signed a letter to UEFA's president, Michel Platini, condemning the suggestion that Israel might host the 2012 Under-21 tournament. Gaza has 42 football clubs and though their kicking spaces are so limited their enthusiasm is boundless. Each had signed this letter, denying Israel's 'right to be treated as a member of the community of nations'. One young man, Uthman, an English Literature graduate of al-Aqsa University, asked with tears of despair in his eyes, '*Why* does Europe treat Israel so kindly? In Europe there's no AIPAC!' Yet again I tried to elucidate the European bad conscience but those young men were impatient of Holocaust talk. Although not Holocaust deniers (of whom I did meet a few among the younger Palestinians) they might be described as Holocaust sceptics – doubting the numbers and gruesome details. For this, Israeli *hasbara* and some fanatical imams share the blame. Zionists have consistently inflated the role of the Holocaust in the creation of the State of Israel. *Hasbara* presents their State-building as an understandable/forgivable consequence of the Holocaust. Who, after that attempted genocide, could blame the Jews for seeking to establish a 'safe homeland'? The reality, as recognised by the historian and former Israeli Foreign Minister, Shlomo Ben-Ami, is that Zionism, since the 1890s, has been partly 'a movement of conquest, colonisation and settlement . . . forced to use the tools of colonial penetration'. Moreover, the dominant Zionist attitude to Hitler's Jewish victims was revealed by Ben-Gurion's chilling calculation, made a few weeks after the *Kristallnacht* pogrom (9 November 1938). Israel's future Prime Minster explained: 'If I knew it was possible to save all the [Jewish] children of Germany by their transfer to England and only half of them by transferring to Eretz-Yisreal, I would choose the latter – because we are faced not only with the accounting of these children but also with the historical accounting of the Jewish People.' Exactly four years later, in December 1942, when Jews were being murdered by the million, Ben-Gurion reminded his followers, 'The catastrophe of European Jewry is not, in a direct manner, my business.' No doubt this sentiment partly explains why the Holocaust was little spoken of between 1948 and the 1961 Eichmann trial in Jerusalem. After that came the founding of 'the Holocaust industry' and since then, as Norman Finkelstein puts it, 'The Nazi holocaust has been fashioned into an ideological weapon to immunize Israel from legitimate criticism . . . Whenever Israel comes under renewed international pressure to withdraw from occupied territories, its apologists mount yet another meticulously orchestrated media extravaganza alleging that the world is awash in anti-Semitism.' No wonder some young Palestinians are Holocaust sceptics.

A classic Zionist fabrication was provided by Ruth Zakh, Israel's deputy-ambassador to Ireland, in an *Irish Times* 'Opinion' (1 June 2011). It was headed 'Political Stunts not the way to end Gaza Conflict'.

> The new flotilla to Gaza is all about delivering provocation rather than aid, just like last year's . . . In 2005, Israel implemented its 'disengagement plan', completely withdrawing both its military and civilian presence from the Gaza Strip. While Israel hoped disengagement would serve as a springboard for improving relations with its neighbours, the opposite occurred: Hamas . . . took control of Gaza and stepped up rocket attacks, firing more than 10,000 rockets and mortars at civilian targets . . . within Israel proper – targets that have included kindergartens, school buses and marketplaces. The heavy armament used in these attacks is smuggled into Gaza via land and sea.

From this we gather that Gazan weapons inflict widespread damage on Israel's population, a message regularly reinforced by the international media. What percentage of the general public is aware that in ten years (2001–2011) Gazan rockets and mortars killed 23 people (22 Israelis and one Thai farm labourer)? Admittedly, 23 too many. But in 22 days Cast Lead killed more than 1,400 Gazans and since the end of that operation the IDF have killed another 200 plus – despite Ruth Zakh's misleading statement about Israel having 'withdrawn both its military and civilian presence from the Gaza Strip'.

The Gazans respect for John Ging led many to expect more support from the Irish government. Uthman asked me, 'Why does your country not talk strong for us? Your Foreign Minister came visiting for a few hours but afterwards said nothing strong. Did you burn too many Jews?'

'No,' I said, 'we didn't burn any Jews but for economic and sentimental reasons Ireland has always been subservient to the US.' Then I confessed that Shannon airport is permanently at the disposal of the US armed forces, however illegal their missions, and of the CIA as it flies its captives in unmarked planes to unnamed countries for courses of 'enhanced interrogation'.

It took time to explain all this in simple English. Five of us were sitting in the shade of a half-collapsed wall, looking across this club's pitch – a cleared bomb site, strewn with fragments of metal and splinters of glass. Soon it would be lost to the club; new shacks were planned.

On the far side rose a towering monument to Cast Lead's savagery, the bisected remains of a ten-storey, Oslo-era block, designed to US corporate specifications and constructed of reinforced concrete. Its ground floor had been let to many stores, a car showroom, bakers, barbers, a restaurant, a few cafés, a dentist's clinic, a gas cylinder store. On the next two floors were offices, above them, flats. Scores of women and children were among the 210 killed here, Uthman told me. Then immediately after the ceasefire many others died while trying to salvage something from within the unstable ruin. The bomb had left one half upright, in an extremely perilous condition. Tons of jagged slabs still hung by lengths of steel 100 feet or more above four children whose donkey-cart was being loaded with scraps of unidentifiable substances – for use in Gaza's 'building trade', where a wealth of ingenuity makes up for a dearth of materials.

We crossed the 'football field' and within this macabre edifice Uthman insisted on leading me by the hand across a narrow causeway of rubble – shifting beneath the feet – to a point from where I cold look far down into the depths of the basement. There lay the bomb's massive case, by far the biggest of the many 'souvenirs' displayed to me on the Strip. Two visiting ISMs had longed to auction it on eBay, to raise money for its maimed victims. A kind impulse, but no one could think how to haul it up – and anyway, unless the top bidder lived in Gaza, there would be an insoluble transport problem. One wonders, why the Goldstone Enquiry? To drop such a bomb on a shopping centre-cum-residential block is in itself a war crime for which there could be no possible excuse or explanation.

*   *   *

On a very windy morning I walked the length of Gaza Port's breakwater with Fahd and Yaser, two of Anwar's bilingual grand-nephews. They were first cousins, jobless graduates of Gaza's al-Azhar University, politically on the same wavelength but in appearance almost comically dissimilar. Tubby Fahd took after his great-uncle, Yaser was unusually tall for a Palestinian with conspicuously long features: long nose, long chin, even long ear lobes. They felt none of Anwar's reservations about BDS and worked hard on their computers as organisers for its National Committee. It cheered them that Dexia, a persistently targeted French-Belgian bank, was about to sell its Israeli subsidiary. And two French companies, Alstom and Derail Veolia, were loosening their ties with Israeli partners while numerous other companies had begun to register the effects of negative publicity. The University of Johannesburg was boycotting Ben-Gurion University. In Britain the University and College Union (the UK's largest academic labour union) and the University of London Union (Europe's largest student union) had voted to cut all links with Israeli institutions. Also, David Cameron had resigned, with minimum publicity, from his position as Honorary Chairman of the Jewish National Fund, a powerful Zionist agency. And Marc Almond and Andy McKee had cancelled visits to Israel. When I asked 'Who are they?' my companions looked worried and sympathetic; no doubt to them this lacuna suggested the onset of Alzheimer's.

At the end of the long breakwater we perched on smooth boulders, the Mediterranean being boisterous on three sides, cooling us with showers of spray. The only people visible were a few fishermen in the far distance, repairing their boats' bullet holes, and Fahd noted that here we were beyond range of eavesdroppers – unless Israel's latest pride and joy, a mini-drone known as 'the Ghost', incorporates some lip-reading device.

It heartened these keen campaigners to know that Israel was about to legislate against BDS, thus proving its effectiveness and gaining it much valuable global attention. The Law for Prevention of Damage to the State of Israel was passed a few weeks later, on 10 July (by 47 votes to 38), and a government spokesperson described BDS as 'an existential threat'. Already this legislation had ignited controversy; thirty-six distinguished law professors considered it unconstitutional and leading civil rights groups were preparing to challenge it in the courts. On the West Bank, settler businessmen were also preparing lawsuits – against BDS organisations and individuals, who would be compelled to pay reparations at a fixed rate (30,000 shekels: US$8,700) without the injured party having to provide any evidence of actual injury. Companies complying with boycotts will be barred forever from doing business with any government office or agency.

Said Fahd, 'All this helps towards what Zionists most dread – the delegitimising of Israel! Which prepares the way for bi-nationalism . . . '

Yaser added, 'The joke is, people backing the law say it's to block delegitimisation efforts! On Facebook I saw "Peace Now!" car stickers saying "Sue me, I'm boycotting settlement products". But only brave people will use those.'

'Another new law bans Nakba Day,' said Fahd. 'Schools and institutions commemorating it will lose all funding – it denies the Jewish and democratic character of the State! An amendment to the Penalty Code protects that character – people denying its existence can be jailed. Even though with a normal IQ you can see it's not possible to be Jewish and democratic with one-fifth Muslim citizens.

Tied in are the "acceptance committees" – naked apartheid! Every village and community built on public land can have a committee to reject Muslim newcomers. The bill calls them "candidates who fail to meet the fundamental views of the community". So how can they get mad when we publicise their apartheid system?'

'The positive bit,' said Yaser, 'is how all this unites some of us, Israelis and Palestinians protesting together. Next month Jerusalem will see a big joint demo. It's being organised by Daniel Argo from the Sheikh Jarrah Solidarity group and Murad Shafea from Silwan. We've had a video conference with them. Dan says we must have a unified state called Israeli-Palestine and all of us as equal citizens. He's brave!'

Fahd was suddenly looking gloomy. 'This government plans about twenty new laws, all meant to criminalise new ways of thinking, like binationalism. They feel they're being pushed to the exit. When I first heard them saying BDS is an existentialist threat, I cheered. Now I've nightmares about another Cast Lead because they feel pushed. Or an all-out attack on Iran instead of just assassinating nuclear scientists. I wish they could see Israeli-Palestine as a model for the whole region – we're demanding rights people don't have in most Arab states. They could get a lot of respect if they shared with us what your friend Mazin calls the Land of Canaan.'

I asked, 'At present, how do you see one-state support on both sides?'

Fahd shrugged. 'What would you expect? Very little on the other side until BDS bites harder – far harder! But Desmond Tutu says for us it's picking up speed faster than it did for the ANC – in reaction to Cast Lead.'

'Among us,' said Yaser, 'attitudes changed, specially in our age-group, when al-Jazeera published the Palestine Papers. Then we saw the dung-heap in the PA's backyard. And we realised honest people were trying to persuade them to go one-state as a credible alternative. Hearing Erekat boasting about PA forces killing "terrorists" to "help" Israel – that was shock-therapy! We knew it went on, but boasting about it is different . . . '

Fahd was emphatic. 'For certain we'd accept if Israel made the offer. If you asked people now most might say "No!" because they can't imagine such a thing. That's why it needs to be talked about loudly, in public. If the offer was genuine we'd say "Yes!" We're tired – very tired – of conflict. We want justice before peace but we do want peace – badly.'

Yaser lit his last cigarette and tossed the empty package into the sea. I said nothing with difficulty. He made an obvious point too often overlooked. 'While outsiders go on and on about two states we *know* we can't have an independent Palestine. We live here, with the reality. The Zionists have won, they've taken so much land there's not enough left to fight over, even if we could fight.'

'Which we can't,' said Fahd. 'No one gives us F-16s, helicopter gunships, Merkavas, gunboats and drones.'

Strolling back to the beach, our thoughts turned to Freedom Flotilla II. We had heard news that morning; the Irish MV *Saoirse* (of which I am the proud part-owner to the extent of perhaps half an ounce) was in dry dock in Turkey having its propeller mended after sabotage by Israeli frogmen (or their proxies). The US ship – *Audacity of Hope*, ironically named after President Obama's second book – was languishing in a military marina near Athens while her skipper, John Klusmire, languished in Greek police custody. He' was soon to appear in court, charged with ignoring an order to remain in port and with risking the lives of passengers who could be harmed by the IDF en route to Gaza. The obedient Greek government had confined the other eight boats to various ports – an illegal move, according to Nikos Chountis, a Greek Flotilla activist. The Free Gaza movement, organiser of these international flotillas, had been told of a compromise Greek–Israeli deal favoured by the ever-compliant Mahmoud Abbas and that celebrated US stooge (aka the UN Secretary General) Ban Ki-moon. The Greeks had offered to transport to Israel, for delivery to Gaza, the boats' cargoes (goods and mail). Rejecting this offer, a Flotilla spokesperson reminded everyone that in 2009 and 2010 the cargoes of captured boats were allowed to spoil in Ashdod warehouses; humidity destroyed cement, heat destroyed medications. And the delivery of some 3,000 private letters, many containing cash gifts, had overtaxed the Strip's UN agencies.

My companions had reservations about the Flotilla project. Both appreciated the hard work and courage of the participants – especially such dogged activists as the eighty-seven-year-old Holocaust survivor, Hedy Epstein. But they felt it would be wise to abandon the pretence that badly needed humanitarian aid was being shipped to Gaza. Those few ships could carry only token amounts. The Israelis can prove their cargoes are unimportant and accuse the organisers of staging political stunts.

'Better to focus on *freedom*,' said Fahd. 'The freedom to arrive and depart, keeping all attention on that central problem, our *imprisonment*.'

Yaser agreed. 'We're not starving Africans dying in a drought-stricken desert. Our tragedy is not a food shortage but a *freedom* shortage.'

'D'you remember '08?' Fahd asked. 'The Israelis allowed several boats through the blockade. Later they sailed away with passengers who urgently needed out but couldn't get permits. All publicity should concentrate on that lack of freedom to lead normal lives – as students, businessmen, builders, musicians, friends, patients, pilgrims, holiday-makers.'

Yaser nodded. 'The next Flotilla should say it doesn't want to take anything *in*, only take people *out*. Patients to get to specialist hospital units, students to get to foreign universities while scholarships are valid, relatives and friends to visit bereaved people. The Israelis couldn't sneer then about political stunts.'

'But they'd go on about the *Victoria*,' said Fahd. For my benefit he explained, 'The Israelis captured this commercial ship a few months ago, carrying fifty tons of weapons from Iran for Gaza – the IDF said.'

Yaser laughed. 'Iran's too smart to try getting past the blockade! Those weapons were for someone else – maybe Assad, via the Lebanon. Iranians love him and he's in big trouble. But the story made good propaganda. Media people repeat what the IDF tells them – "See the danger! We must keep Gaza cut off from all these heavy armaments!" Like there were no tunnels! The Flotilla should get friends of Zionism to check cargoes on the way – then what could Israel say? What excuse for stopping Gazans going to hospital or college or visiting relatives? The Flotilla is there to help them, they're not asking to go through Israel where they might stop off to blow someone up. Why won't Israel let them out of prison? It could be a dual-purpose campaign, "Free Gaza!" and big publicity for BDS!'

Already there is a strong link between BDS and the Flotilla. Zionism and its faithful followers may ridicule the latter as an alliance of archaic Lefties, shrill eccentrics, thwarted minor politicians, faded Flower People, professional publicity-seekers, covert Communists, and cheerleaders for terrorism. In fact, as Mark LeVine, history professor at the University of California, often points out, 'The political and strategic implications of the Flotilla are quite real. It symbolises that the Palestinians and their international supporters are refusing to play by Israel's rules . . . ' BDS also carries this message.

Back at Anwar's house, we heard that a Scandinavian boat had also been sabotaged. And that a US State Department spokesperson had praised the 'established and efficient' methods of supplying Gaza's needs through Israel.

*   *   *

A few days later I had a different sort of conversation in a dismal café, reeking of over-used cooking oil, near al-Azhar University. Jamal and Salim were English Language and sociology students (the language barrier limited my range of student acquaintances) from Jabalya camp. Unlike Anwar's atypical grand-nephews, with their sights fixed on binationalism and BDS, these young men – both close to graduation – seemed confused and on edge.

The recent 'Unity Agreement' between Fatah, Hamas and a few minor splinter groups and individuals bothered them. Salim thought it a bad omen that the signing took place in Cairo's Mukhabarat, the Egyptian government's intelligence headquarters of ill repute, where so many Palestinians have been tortured on Zionism's behalf. He couldn't believe in that 'unity'; past experiences made it seem chimerical; he imagined betrayal of the overall Palestinian cause being plotted behind its façade. Jamal condemned Hamas for compromising their principles, going after the mess of pottage that would reward their working within the PA structure – in other words, collaborating with Israel.

Salim said, 'Hamas leaders are getting afraid, losing support. After the war [Operation Cast Lead] they got very popular again. Now with no jobs and always people being killed – women and children – most see these rulers can't help us. Even worse, while they keep power, Israel won't let others help us, all must suffer because they won't let go. I'd like a real Unity Agreement, leaders united, power-sharing, like in Northern Ireland. But that's not what got signed in Cairo. Hamas have no unity inside themselves, must talk two ways at once. Last year, to make calm their own mad dogs, Haniyeh said Fatah "wages war against Islam". But he has waged war on Islamic Jihad.'

Salim was referring to August 2009 when Islamic Jihad raged against Hamas' participation in 'secular' elections and attacked Qassam units – the first armed opposition to the ruling party since 2007. Not many Gazans objected when an unspecified number of

149

captured jihadists were promptly shot in defiance of every international law and convention. Your average Palestinian is sensibly afraid of Salafist-types who seek to please Allah by slaughtering all brands of infidels and throwing acid in the faces of 'naked' (i.e., bare-headed) women.

When I asked how much regional changes might affect the Palestinians Salim replied that, as Mubarak was being removed, exhilarated crowds gathered on city streets throughout the OPT, suddenly feeling empowered. But on the Strip they were roughly dispersed by unlabelled 'security forces'. 'Those men wore no uniform,' said Salim. 'They looked like Salafists getting that job to let them be violent. They like acting military but Hamas wants them only political. We were out in Palestine Square, calling for unity against the Zionists, when the Salafists made us run home. Is it a crime to ask for something good, like unity? For that we got beaten by men who don't want Muslims working with other Muslims who read the Holy Koran differently!'

Jamal cited the Nakba Day (15 May 2011) protest march from Gaza, Syria and Lebanon towards Israeli borders. 'That couldn't have happened before Tahrir. We got courage from seeing how big governments, even with American friends, can go weak!' On the Lebanese border the IDF killed ten Palestinians and afterwards explained, 'They tried to damage the fence.' Four were killed on the Syrian border and one in Gaza. Israel predictably accused Iran of having organised these border breaches to promote terrorism and deflect attention from the current woes of the aptly named Bashar al-Assad. Jamal assured me the 'event' was pure Palestinian, Facebook-organised by exiled activists. I said I hoped there would be many more and much bigger marches – without deaths.

'There was a big plan,' said Salim, 'for millions to march on Israel, all arriving at borders around the same time. It got everyone excited – thousands to march from Egypt, Syria, the Maghreb, the Gulf, Jordan, Lebanon, even Europe and America, the whole al-Shatat!

The IDF heard and got panicked. They said to a newspaper they'd got no way to stop a mass non-violent march on the West Bank, even 4,000 couldn't be stopped if the PA police wouldn't help. Then they saw they'd no problem – we had no leaders to organise us and no money to move so many Palestinians around the world.'

'Wrong!' said Jamal. 'Fatah and Hamas can find millions. Hamas maybe from Iran or some Saudi prince. Fatah from Abbas's billion-dollar hidden slush fund!' (This is money much spoken of and allegedly accumulated by the CIA-funded operatives.) 'We know the problem is bad leadership, not needing money.'

'We don't *know* anything!' retorted Salim. 'How could we? All is lies and secrets. Hamas puts around that slush fund story – is it true, not true? Keeping people not knowing is one control method.'

'Whatever way, Americans won't let Palestinians be like Egyptians.' Jamal was looking angry. 'Obama's people yelled against that Unity Agreement – no government including Hamas can have aid!'

Salim smiled slightly. 'From here on, maybe what America says isn't so much important?'

I made no comment but, taking the short term view, found it impossible to share in Salim's optimism. On the very day of Mubarak's departure, the *New York Times* reported, 'The White House and the State Department are already discussing setting aside new funds to bolster the rise of secular political parties.' I wondered then – how many millions will it take to secure political power for secular parties in a Muslim country? The answer soon came from Hillary R Clinton:

I'm pleased to announce today (17 February 2011) that we will be reprogramming $150 million for Egypt to put ourselves in a position to support our transition there and assist with their economic recovery. These funds will give us flexibility to respond to Egyptian needs moving forward.

A month later Mrs Clinton again gave tongue:

151

The US government also thinks there are economic reforms that are necessary to help the Egyptian people have good jobs, to find employment, to realise their own dreams. And so on both of those tracks – the political reform and the economic reform – we want to be helpful.

Two months after that President Obama made a chilling announcement (19 May):

First, we've asked the World Bank and the International Monetary Fund to present a plan at next week's G8 summit for what needs to be done to stabilise and modernise the economies of Tunisia and Egypt. Together, we must help them recover from the disruptions of their democratic upheaval, and support the governments that will be elected later this year.

So it was definite; whatever seeds of hope had been sown in Tahrir Square were not to be allowed to germinate. Genuine self-determination would be thwarted.

By the end of 2011 the Obama administration had decided to talk to the hitherto condemned Muslim Brotherhood. Early in 2012 William Burns, Deputy Secretary of State, travelled to Cairo for a meeting with Khairat al-Shater, one of the Brotherhood's most powerful leaders. The main US concern, at that date, was Egypt's peace treaty with Israel. Mr Burns conveyed that the US could obtain for Egypt, through the IMF and the Gulf States, an extra $20 billion aid money – if the treaty continued to be honoured. During that and later meetings, US representatives brought the Muslim Brotherhood to heel. The movement showed willing to favour a free-market economic model (with a few minor concessions to Egypt's impoverished millions) and always to take US security needs into account.

In June 2012 Dr Mohammed Morsi of the Muslim Brotherhood was elected President of Egypt. Almost immediately, according to DEBKA, President Obama was able to reassure a White House gathering of Jewish-American leaders that 'President Morsi would be required to devote a section of his earliest speech on foreign affairs to the specific affirmation of his profound commitment to the peace pact with Israel'. (DEBKA is a website linked to Israel's intelligence agencies.) Sure enough, within hours Morsi was announcing that the new Egypt would honour all its old treaty obligations. An invitation to visit the White House in September 2012 promptly followed. Then came his first state visit as President – to Saudi Arabia, on 11 July. On his return he made several public statements guaranteeing that Egypt would never interfere in the Gulf States' domestic politics, would 'respect the regional balance of power' on Iranian issues and would not allow its relationship with Erdogan's Turkey to grow too close. In Riyadh he had announced that 'Egypt would keep the same distance to the Palestinian factions' – meaning his regime would be even-handed in its dealings with the collaborationist secular West Bank regime and the defiant non-secular Gaza regime. Yet during his election campaign he had promised to end the blockade of Gaza. When Hillary Clinton visited Cairo and Jerusalem in mid-July, Israel reported that she had compelled President Morsi to agree to maintain the blockade. On Israel Radio, Danny Ayalon, the Deputy Foreign Minister, explained: 'She is bringing a very calming message. President Morsi's agenda will be a domestic agenda. There is no change and I surmise there will not be for the foreseeable future.'

US strategists describe this sort of skulduggery as 'a managed transition of power'. The *New York Times* noted that Mrs Clinton had to abandon her plan to give a 'significant' speech in Alexandria lest it might further enrage those many supporters of the military who believed the US had gone over to the Muslim Brotherhood. An odd illusion: General Tantawi and the Military Council knew that Egypt would continue to receive an annual military subsidy of $1.3 billion, plus an extra $1 billion aid package to get them through 'the transition'.

Seven

The Islamic University of Gaza (IUG) is disconcerting. Behind high walls oil money has created another world, seemingly not part of the Strip – yet its ideological power-house. On a clean, orderly, tastefully landscaped campus stands an assemblage of soaring buildings (much concrete, more glass), some stark and severe, most incorporating classical Islamic embellishments that don't quite come off. The overall effect is of an ultra-modern factory complex – perhaps pharmaceutical? Here young Gazans are programmed to be 'correctly' Islamic and each building's design caters for segregation. Males and females enter the campus by different gates, enter the library and other facilities by different doors, relax in rigidly demarcated areas of the litter-free, well-watered grounds where lawns are green, flowering hedges delight the eye and herb-beds delight the nose. A bilingual guide-booklet explains:

> IUG is keen to offer the best environment for students by including green places and parks which will surely make a comfortable atmosphere that encourages students to spend the most of his time at the Campus.

Off campus, there's an ever-present danger: young men and women might talk to one another as they do at Birzeit and An-Najah universities on the West Bank. However, on my several visits to IUG the students invariably looked cheerful and busy. In surroundings so utterly unlike the rest of the Strip they may well feel this is their share of that 'normal' world seen daily on TV and YouTube. The abnormality of IUG, by twenty-first-century standards, they seem not to resent. I asked Anwar about this. Dryly he replied, 'For most of them, the programming works.'

When the PLO denounced President Sadat's peace treaty with Israel a vengeful Egypt closed its universities to Palestinians, prompting the Muslim Brotherhood to found IUG in 1978. At first it was under PLO control, then came an urgent need to seek funds from abroad – through the Mujamma. This meant a not-so-gradual assertion of Islamic influences; Mujamma student groups ousted the nationalist/PLO candidates in student council elections, often using violence or the threat of violence. Thereafter the quickening pace of religious revivalism, throughout the OPT, debilitated Palestine's liberation movement. In January 1980 the Islamists, having lost an election to the Palestine Red Crescent Society (PRCS) council, were further enraged at the suggestion that the secular/nationalist al-Azhar college might be expanded to rival IUG. A long-bearded mob set out to burn the PRCS office and library in Gaza City, pausing en route to wreck alcohol-selling cafés and video shops. Meanwhile, Israeli soldiers sat watching the mayhem from parked jeeps. When Gaza's military governor, Brigadier-General Segev, was later challenged about their inactivity he blandly replied, 'Our enemy today is the PLO.'

At that date the Muslim Brotherhood's goal was to wean Palestinians off secularism in their daily lives and off nationalism in their political thinking. By the beginning of the First Intifada it was firmly in control of IUG and all Gaza's cinemas and purveyors of alcohol had been closed.

IUG's ten faculties provide 55 undergraduate programmes, 40 postgraduate programmes and eleven higher diplomas. Sara Roy has described it as 'arguably the most visible expression of social penetration through institutional means'. She points out that by now it has educated thousands of religious leaders for Gaza and (until the blockade) the West Bank and hundreds of civilian leaders for most sectors of Palestinian life. Yet for all its brave face (listing international honours won by professors and links with foreign universities) it must limit coming generations if they hear the same message from home, mosque and university. The founders of Mujamma/Hamas, who all studied abroad, were better equipped to confront European and American antagonists and make the most of foreign friends. One postgraduate male student told me, 'You're wrong about independent thinking, it's not correct Islam. We're not allowed to argue with parents or teachers.'

IUG's security is much tighter than the Department of Foreign Affairs' – one doesn't stroll in casually, as to an Oxford college. Two armed men guard each narrow entrance and on my first visit Deeb had to escort me. When I paused on the pavement to hide my white locks beneath a *hijab* borrowed from his wife the bushy-bearded sentries glowered at the brazen infidel. Uncovered, I (aged eighty!) would have been refused admission.

On Sunday 28 December 2008 Israel marked IUG's significance by totally destroying the Science Labs building and the Engineering and Technology building. Within moments, 74 research centres, containing a wide range of complex and delicate appliances and apparatuses, lay beneath hundreds of tons of concrete and metal. Nothing could be salvaged. Prince Torkey Ben Abdul Aziz and the Islamic Bank for Development had invested US$15 million in this equipment. The academic careers of a majority of IUG's 20,000 students had also been wrecked or at best severely disrupted. I can think of no better recruitment ploy for the Qassam Brigades, Islamic Jihad et al. Nine other buildings were partially destroyed but have been more or less restored.

When Deeb as a male could go no further Suhair appeared, an English-speaking member of the administrative staff whose beauty was equalled by her self-assurance. She wore a special badge authorising her to enter male territory and led me to the vast crater where once had stood the multi-storeyed victims of Israel's fanatical (and ultimately self-destructive) aggression. No trace of rubble remains; all has been reincarnated in scores of camp homes. The photographs taken next day are painful to look upon, even for an outsider.

Suhair gave me a leisurely conducted tour of the campus, starting with a 1,000-seat conference hall where – the guide-booklet tells us – 'IUG conducted Graduation Ceremonies annually to complete the happiness of students among their family and parents. About 29,000 students have been graduated since 30 years of establishment.' This building is perfectly suited to adaptation as theatre, concert hall, debating chamber – all forbidden activities.

Dr Moheer, Dean of the new Medical School, entertained me generously in his large, expensively furnished office on the top floor of a rather pretentious edifice. Finishing touches were being put to enormous rooms – reminding me of nuclear power plant control centres – where international video conferences would be held and other esoteric cyberspace capers could take place to outwit the blockade. (Or so I was told.) Hi-tech lecture halls and sophisticated labs were about to go into action. In some corridors high quality furniture was being unpacked and giveaway sand trickled out of those crates. For the unpacking of one small parcel two elderly, excited professors came panting upstairs. Only they could do this job. Expectantly we waited, until a boring little machine appeared – for the medical genetics department, price US$58,000.

To me this exuberant spending, within a cat's spit of extreme poverty and overcrowding, felt inappropriate. The medical school's fancy design seemed shockingly wasteful; given such extravagance, is it not hard to beg convincingly for more funding? I reckoned the electronic pencil-sharpeners summed it all up – one attached to the edge of each desk. *Too* Gulf State . . . ! On the other hand, if oil-sodden princes and bankers have so many surplus dollars why not spread them around by employing armies of construction workers and buying incalculable quantities of construction materials – even if the end product does look excessive to someone who thinks in tens rather than millions.

The campus's purdah quarter has a conventual tinge because of all the *hijabs* and *jilbabs*. Even the traditional Palestinian flowing gown (the *thobe*, often exquisitely embroidered) doesn't satisfy Shari'a fashion demands. Instead, women students must wear the *jilbab*, an ankle-length coat of uniform design, high-necked and long-sleeved, fitting closely around the wrist. The approved *jilbab* is black; just occasionally a rebellious young woman ventures out in milk-chocolate brown which makes quite a loud statement. Many poor students receive clothing vouchers, donated by one of IUG's oily patrons and only valid for the purchase of *jilbabs* and *hijabs*. As someone abnormally heat-prone, I found it personally uncomfortable merely to see these unfortunate women going about the streets in temperatures up to 38°C. All those with whom I commiserated assured me they were used to it, didn't suffer; yet I noticed that indoors, when their homes were male-free, they wore the infidel summer garments one saw hanging in all markets – including tank-tops and very short shorts. The wide availability of such fashions must mean a high percentage of Gazan women appreciate them.

Suhair made much of the fact that 62 per cent of IUG students are women. (A common statistic in Islamic universities elsewhere.) Was this not proof of equality? Similarly , Dr al-Zahar – looking smug – told me his wife had been a teacher before the IDF broke her back, and their first daughter was an engineer, the second a teacher of English, the third an accountancy student. I was not impressed. The Islamist emphasis on equality of educational opportunities, and women's freedom to practise in the professions, can confuse the issue for newcomers – and soon one realises it is meant to do just that.

Rather meanly, I asked Suhair why IUG segregates its students. Promptly she replied that an Englishwoman (name forgotten) has *proved* (sic) that 'coeducation is bad because girls are more intelligent than boys and when they learn together boys resent this and disrupt the girls' work'.

'That may be,' I replied, 'but it's still a pity they can't relax together when not learning.' Whereupon Suhair changed the subject, informing me that IUG takes no fees from handicapped students and 'all coming from poor families get free books and materials. Also the government tries to help us. We've internship arrangements with the Department of Industry for engineering students and with Finance for accountancy students. But that help is very little. Most of our graduates, with good qualifications, have nowhere to go.'

Before I left Suhair agreed to meet me at the entrance, to escort me past the sentries, whenever I returned to spend time in the library.

That evening I read through the IUG guide-booklet and learned that 'the Library Services hold over 100,000 printed items, and vast quantities of materials in many other electronic formats'. Also –

IUG launched a new satellite TV channel named 'Al-Ketab' which aims at promoting values, spreading good morals and participating in solving the problems that face the Arabic and Islamic communities focusing on the Palestinian community. Through this channel, IUG hopes to expand the educational process from its geographical limits to reach out to every house in the world, in addition to broadcasting some other varieties.

And then there's the Business and Technology Incubator (BTI).

BTI aims to offer professional business services to Palestinian entrepreneurs who have mature concepts for unique and innovative IT related products assessed to have strong market potential. BTI will design, develop, implement and promote those initiatives that will support the development of entrepreneurial business ventures with high growth potential by providing them with an integrated package of world-class business development services that will nurture and support the commercialization of ideas and enhance the development and growth of dynamic enterprises.

What sort of unhinged person will hatch out in this incubator?

Subsequently I spent long sessions alone in IUG's library, the most agreeable building on the campus. Like An-Najah's newish library in Nablus, it is short of books because too much was spent on the building. (Some West Bank UNRWA schools are short of teachers and equipment for the same reason.) There was little new stock; at the time most volumes dated from the 1990s or before. Beside the few 'English' shelves, I met Jannath, taking notes for an essay on Jane Austen. Afterwards we walked together down the long corridor to the women's entrance and I began yet another 'Women's Rights' debate. Jannath fumbled around my argument that the Islamists' 'Gazan traditions/local custom' smokescreen deserves to be mocked. The grandmothers of contemporary students – and their mothers as teenagers – were free to go bareheaded and bare-armed, wearing short skirts, if they so wished; the fact that many preferred customary garb is beside the point.

'But now,' said Jannath, 'traditions and customs have changed!'

'Quite so,' said I. 'Changed by whom? And why?'

Jannath laughed, then invited me to visit her in Jabalya on the following Friday morning. She wrote her address on something interesting – the top flap of a cigarette packet. Could it be that she was a secret smoker?

*   *   *

On 15 January 2009, during Operation Cast Lead, I had taken a minibus taxi from Ramallah back to Nablus and on the way we heard al-Jazeera radio reporting attacks on four Gaza City hospitals. When I looked around at my fellow-passengers' faces they variously showed anger, disgust, contempt and what can only be described as incredulous horror. One man recalled that in the Lebanon, in

2006, some of Israel's worst war crimes were committed on the eve of their withdrawal. And he recognised that Cast Lead must end before President Obama's imminent inauguration.

One of those four targets was the deservedly famed and honoured al-Wafa Medical Rehabilitation Hospital which in 1979 began as a nursing home for the destitute aged left without family. By 1995 it had become the Strip's first and only in-patient rehabilitation centre, dealing with head and spinal cord injuries and other neurological afflictions. It collaborated with Israel's Tel Hashomer Hospital and with a number of relevant Norwegian NGOs; IUG trained its physiotherapists. In 2008 it was at last able to expand – just in time for the IDF to target it with eight artillery shells which completely destroyed the men's ward and did so much damage all patients had to be discharged. Since my arrival in Gaza I had heard al-Wafa mentioned a dozen times, with gratitude and affection, by the most disadvantaged people on my visiting list. And now I had been given an introduction to its Director, Dr Khamis Elessi.

As an ISI (Islamic Social Institution) al-Wafa naturally has links with Hamas; over the years some of its management team and probably many of its staff will have been members or sympathisers. This however does not affect their professionalism. Al-Wafa's record proves that it is not swayed by political or religious leanings. It exists to do the best it can, with the limited resources at its disposal, for all Gazans who need its expertise. In an immensely valuable book (*Hamas and Civil Society in Gaza*) published shortly after my return from Gaza, Sara Roy writes: 'Hamas's social support structure played a key role in building up popular support for the organization [but] this was not the same as mobilizing people into an activist constituency based on the political ideology of Hamas.' Here is reliable confirmation of my own (necessarily superficial) impression of how things are on the Strip. The West Bank, too, had shown me conflicting currents: gratitude for an ISI like the Nablus clinic where my damaged hip was X-rayed, coexisting with resentment of increasingly Islamic influences on the socio-political scene.

Tragically, such subtleties are beyond official Israel's grasp. During Cast Lead, a senior Israeli government representative told the *New York Times*:

> The operation's central aim is to destroy both aspects of Hamas – its resistance or military wing and its *dawa*, or social wing . . . In a war, its instruments of political and social control are as legitimate a target as its rocket caches.

Back-up came from Reserve Major-General Amiran Levin:

> What we have to do is act systematically with the aim of punishing all the organizations that are firing the rockets and mortars, as well as the civilians who are enabling them to fire and hide.

(In case you've forgotten – between 2001 and 2011 rockets from Gaza killed 22 Israelis and one immigrant labourer.)

No wonder the *Goldstone Report* described Cast Lead as 'a deliberately disproportionate attack designed to punish, humiliate and terrorize a civilian population'.

The Israelis' sustained imposition of all-out collective punishment is by any standards a very frightening phenomenon. For decades they have been attacking defenceless populations through curfews, closures, sieges, house demolitions, olive-grove bulldozings, well poisonings, shootings, bombings, torture and indefinite imprisonment without trial. One of my Gazan friends proposed that this Israeli obsession, this conviction that collective punishment is the way forward, may well be a hideous hangover from the Holocaust when Jews were collectively punished for being Jews. The logic behind this proposal escaped me. But then my friend argued, 'We're not talking about *logic!* We're talking about something very deep and dark and twisted. Something so sick the international community is afraid to go near it.'

Several years ago, the same comparison was drawn by Richard Falk, UN Special Rapporteur in the OPT, a Princeton international law authority and himself a Jew. He said, 'Is it an irresponsible overstatement to associate the treatment of Palestinians with this criminalised Nazi record of collective atrocity? I think not.'

Perhaps this grim analogy no longer shocks because Zionist criminality is becoming ever more strident and arrogant. Now a retiring head of Israel's security forces feels free to brag on TV that 'Our successful operations have made political assassinations internationally acceptable.'

In my *serveece* to al-Wafa a retired professor of English sat beside me and insisted on paying my fare. His brain-damaged grandson lay comatose in the Rehabilitation Centre; a wall had fallen on him as he sought to salvage stones from a recently shelled house. The professor's specialty was George Bernard Shaw but I soon steered him off *John Bull's Other Island* and onto the Strip. He blamed 'Protestant sentimentality about biblical places' for the Balfour Declaration. And he, too, spoke of Zionism's 'humiliation campaign' against Palestinians as having Nazi roots. 'It's how they were treated in the '30s.'

Habitually I arrive too early (a perverse form of unpunctuality) and at 8.30 a young doctor, seeing me on an outside bench, invited me into a small stuffy room off the hallway. Here several young men sat around discussing case notes, drinking tea and eating home-made chocolate cookies from a huge box in the centre of the table. It was someone's birthday, an occasion not traditionally celebrated in the Arab world but now adopted. They were a friendly bunch, apart from one physiotherapist whose very long, very thick black beard must have taken a lot of maintenance. I had come to associate disapproving stares with that sort of beard.

The only English-speaker told me about donated wheelchairs seized from the 2010 Flotilla and taken to an Ashdod warehouse where they were cunningly vandalised – rendered almost useless –

before being delivered to the ICRC at Erez. One's first reaction is to disbelieve such stories ('must be propaganda!') but the Zionist exercise of wanton cruelty, which I had so often witnessed on the West Bank, made this story only too credible.

To greet me, Dr Khamis Elessi stood up behind his makeshift desk: a small man, balding, round-faced, soft-spoken, kind-eyed. He comes of a notable Gaza family and one soon senses a *noblesse oblige* attitude (not very common among Palestinians) to the Strip's least privileged. No money had been wasted on this rather cramped, utilitarian Director's office.

Dr Elessi opened the conversation by deploring all violence, whatever its source or motive. A tediously trite statement, you might think – yet it's contestable in Occupied Palestine where there are plausible arguments in favour of violence as an assertion of people's right to freedom. Indisputably, as Dr Elessi said, 'All forms of retaliation must increase suffering and bitterness.' Yet he could understand, as I cannot, the sort of martyr's mother who rejoices because her son has 'given himself' for the cause and is now being rewarded by Allah – while his community is being collectively punished by the IDF. Dr Elessi also conceded that to an extent attacks on Israelis, military or civilian, do boost communal morale in territories with a 60-year backlog of impotent rage. 'Which means,' he said, 'the Occupier is corrupting the Occupied.' I remembered then Anwar literally shuddering as he described an Islamic Jihad street party spontaneously organised to celebrate a 'successful' suicide bombing in Israel – 'like you see in normal countries when the local team wins'.

Dr Elessi agreed with me that the world should not be allowed to forget a fact now hidden behind stacks of Israeli *hasbara*. On 23 December 2008 Hamas offered to renew for at least ten years the truce violated by Israel on 4 November. Their condition was that Israel would fulfil the two original clauses of the ceasefire: a complete stop to hostilities *and* lifting the blockade of Gaza.

Zionists genuinely interested in a 'Peace Process' would have discussed this offer; Hamas has a deserved reputation for sticking to agreements and had jailed some of its own militants for breaking the previous ceasefire. However, Cast Lead had been planned soon after the IDF's shaming Lebanese experience in 2006. 'And it was timed,' said Dr Elessi, 'to reward warmongers in the Knesset [February 2009] election.' I now learned that the no-expenses-spared planning included a Gaza City mock-up beside a remote training camp in the Negev. Nothing Hamas said or did could have prevented Cast Lead, which had very little to do with deterring home-made rockets – or even Iran-made missiles. It was a continuation of the Nakba by other means.

The barrenness of youngsters' lives in the Strip's most deprived areas – such as that around al-Wafa – greatly distressed Dr Elessi. Many more football clubs were needed – but where to kick? He told me then about al-Jazeera Sports Club for the disabled, started by himself and a few colleagues. Before the blockade locked them in, its members had won several medals in international competitions – achievements which gave a tremendous boost not only to the competitors' families and friends but to their whole community. Now, with the Rafah Gate open again, the club could begin to plan and fundraise for further endeavours in foreign stadia. But would Rafah remain open? And even if it did, would the Egyptians facilitate the exit and re-entry of disabled Palestinians and their escorts? Deeb had put it rather well – 'Gaza's future is a forest of question marks.'

While showing me around (discreetly: one doesn't want the severely disabled to feel like tourist fodder) Dr Elessi introduced me to several of the staff and what I glimpsed of their relationships with the patients set off good vibes, confirming my observations while visiting other clinics with Nita. Al-Wafa's rehabilitation work is unofficially extended beyond the physical. The Director only mentioned the bombing en passant; rebuilding was almost completed, one had to live in the present, not brood over the past or despair of the future. As he escorted me to the nearest taxi route, along a pavement seething with small children, he admitted to finding the Zionists' demographic fears quite rational. Already the Palestinians, if united in a show of non-violent strength, could end the Occupation and move the problem onto another plane. 'Binationalism?' I suggested. But Dr Elessi pretended not to hear. People in his position can't step forward as political leaders. Al-Wafa is there for everyone imprisoned on the Strip who is misfortunate enough to need it.

In the taxi I thought about that 'if' . . . *If* the Palestinians could unite – a possibility made ever less possible by energetic schemers. And the very next afternoon afforded a disturbing example of such scheming.

At al-Wafa I drank tea with an exhausted-looking nurse who habitually works overtime for no extra pay (so said one of her patients). She had urged me to visit her cousin, Director of the Ministry of Health's Central Drug Store which was reporting 'zero stock levels' for many essential medications. Nita came too and we crossed an empty car park to a hastily rebuilt (after bombing) warehouse – surprisingly open and unguarded. 'There's not much to guard,' Nita reminded me.

In a dingy office, lined with shelves of files, the Director and four of his colleagues were gloomily conferring. When Nita introduced me he stood and bowed slightly (no hand-shaking) – a compact, grey-haired, clean-shaven man, his expression compounded of tiredness, irritation, sadness and a determination to be cheerful. In response to his formulaic 'How are you?' I replied, 'Depressed because Gaza is suffering so much.' He laughed. 'Sit down! Sit down and be happy! You must be happy because Gaza is liberated! We are free – here no Israeli soldiers or settlers like on West Bank – be happy with us!'

Nita said something to stop this Hamas patter and at once the

Director stood up again to lead us down a long grey corridor, smelling of damp concrete, to an enormous, almost empty storeroom. This is the distribution centre for all the Ministry of Health's medications for the Strip's 13 hospitals and 54 primary health care clinics. Here the Director let us see the depth of his own depression. This crisis began in January 2011 and the store was now short of 180 types of crucially important medications. Gazans suffer from the range of diseases one would expect in any malnourished population of 1.6 million – plus complicated IDF-induced injuries and illnesses. Every day news came of needless deaths. Tunnel-derived medicines were costly and often dangerously unreliable. The varieties that might occasionally come in otherwise were even more costly and no more reliable. Substitute medicines were gaining in popularity – their effects usually dire and quite often fatal. For some reason the sight of all those empty shelves touched me more than the standard 'Appeal' photographs of starving children.

Israel was not directly to blame for this collective punishment. The missing donated medications had long since arrived in Ramallah where the PA, living up (or down) to its 'quisling' label, was withholding them from Hamas-governed Gaza. In Jerusalem in December 2010, I had heard Mahmoud Abbas's security services being praised for their merciless manoeuvrings to demoralise and discredit Hamas' administration and Hamas' West Bank supporters. The PA police had probably impressed the CIA by arresting six faculty members at An-Najah university, all voluntary workers for an ISI, therefore accused of 'assisting a front for Hamas'. More serious because even more divisive, 1,000 schoolteachers had lost their jobs – some Hamas members, some related to individuals suspected of Hamas leanings, some who refused to promote Fatah. One of my Nablus friends belonged to that last category and I knew he disliked Fatah and Hamas equally. But he still lost his job.

Nita admitted that being collectively punished by fellow-Palestinians was the unkindest cut of all.

*   *   *

At IUG Dr Moheer had described other health-care impediments. Because of an acute shortage of specialists, many complicated cases need to go elsewhere but most are unable to leave the Strip. For the lucky few, it can take a long time (sometimes too long) to find a suitable Israeli (or other) hospital willing to accept them and to arrange payment through the Ministry of Health – or a private benefactor, if such is available.

There is also a shortage of experts to maintain equipment and the lack of one tiny, irreplaceable part can leave a $50,000 machine crippled. The irregular electricity supply ruins sensitive machines, when suddenly the power drops below or shoots above the required voltage. (In my flat, dependent on the family generator, I had noticed that this often happens.) I suggested seeking voluntary experts from among the Palestinians' many foreign friends (ISM-like people) but according to Dr Moheer 'commercial confidentiality' rules this out. Each firm's cherished know-how must at all times be protected, even at the cost of patients' lives. Another complication: many of the firms' own experts won't travel to Gaza, either for ideological or fear reasons. Alternatively, they may be so expensive to import it makes more sense to buy new machines with guarantees covering one or two years.

Bureaucracy and corruption (or both combined) present major problems. To minimise their effects the rich donor (individual or group) arranges for the manufacturer – preferably with a branch in Israel – to send the gift directly to the Gaza hospital after the manufacturer (not the donor) has done all the tortuous paperwork in Israel. The donor pays by sending money straight to the manufacturer's bank account. 'In this way,' explained Dr Moheer, 'we keep it absolutely transparent. These manufacturers are big multinationals so no one can suspect them of dishonesty.' It seems Dr Moheer has a lot to learn – I hope not the hard way.

*   *   *

A *serveece* set me down in the middle of Jabalya town early on a Friday morning when the streets were quiet and all the shops shut; the ramshackle drabness and littered gutters seemed peculiarly depressing without the usual jostling throngs and noisy tangle of motor/equine/hand-cart traffic. Jannath had given 'Jabalya camp' as her address, which was misleading. When I showed it to a few astonished-looking men, wearing white mosque gowns and prayer caps, they directed me this way and that (by gesture: no one spoke English) – until finally a ragged, friendly youth led me through a maze of laneways to a long, high mud wall overhung by the mature trees within: fig, palm, lemon, flame-of-the-forest. The refugees' dwellings had grown up around an imposing two-storey mansion built in the dying days of the Ottoman Empire by Jannath's great-grandfather. My guide pulled hard on an old-fashioned bell rope and as we heard a metallic clanging he smiled at me and waved and hurried away. I had learned that in such circumstances, when help has been spontaneously offered, a tip can cause offence – however ragged one's helper.

A small shy boy opened the gate as Jannath came sauntering across a parched lawn – bare-headed and wearing tight lime-green slacks and a low-cut cherry-red blouse. She introduced the boy as Mahmoud, a cousin, one of twelve family members now living in a house with ample space for forty. We sat on a wide verandah, enjoying the strong breeze coming from the sea across open ground, the property of a neighbour who was 'keeping it undeveloped as an investment'. Meanwhile food was being grown there: lettuce, fennel, spinach. On the far side a few skeletal dwellings marked the site of a March 2008 IDF attack on Jabalya.

At the end of February 2008 a forty-seven-year-old resident of

Sderot in Israel was killed by a home-made rocket and, for the first time, other Qassam Brigades missiles reached Ashkelon where they did little or no damage. A week or so later the IDF killed 61 Jabalya camp residents in one day – among them two of Jannath's cousins (Mahmoud's sisters) and their mother. Tzipi Livni, then Israel's Foreign Minister, found it easy to explain this mass slaughter of (mainly) civilians. 'Everybody needs to understand that Israeli citizens are being terrorized by rockets coming from Gaza Strip. This is something we cannot live with.'

Two years later Jannath and her sister Ayshah (aged respectively twenty-two and twenty-three) unwillingly migrated from their UAE birthplace to settle in Gaza. Their father ('managing a big business in Abu Dhabi') had been widowed in 2006 and remarried in 2007, his new wife not much older than his daughters. In that purdah quarter the atmosphere soon soured – though Jannath said their stepmother had a good relationship with the five brothers, all younger than the girls. In January 2010 the sisters were despatched to Gaza to live with their grandfather in the ancestral home, study at IUG and get married. Now all was well. Their previously unknown extended family had welcomed them enthusiastically and they were allowed more personal freedom on the Strip than in the paternal home.

At that moment Ayshah joined us, wearing shorts and T-shirt, keen to show off a month-old infant in an expensive carry-cot. She had married a second cousin soon after their arrival, a young man who was making his mark at IUG as a 'researching agronomist'. When I complimented both on their fluent English Ayshah explained, 'Abu Dhabi is bilingual – has to be, with most of the population foreign!'

Jannath looked at me and suddenly seemed embarrassed. 'We should apologise for the university's booklet in such *bad* English! It makes me angry and when I see Internationals laughing over our mistakes it makes me sad. So much money comes from Saudi, they could hire a qualified translator. It's damaging our reputation. If bad English is OK, maybe we're not so smart as we say about other things?'

Then the bell rang. Mahmoud hurried to the door and shouted 'Ahmed!' – so the sisters had to scurry inside before the visitor could be admitted. Ahmed was a tall, bony young man with lingering acne and a slight squint. He shook hands and greeted me in halting English, then sat down and helped himself to tea. When the women returned, wearing colourful hijabs and all-enveloping plain cotton gowns, he was explained as Jannath's first cousin and fiancé. Before marriage he must never see her hair uncovered or her curves discernible. I provocatively recalled Mrs Halaweh's reminiscences of swimming parties on Gaza beach. Everyone looked shocked and after a moment Ahmed, frowning, pointed out that in Mandate and Egyptian times British customs prevailed and the Holy Koran was not properly interpreted. Now correct interpretations guide Gazan life. I persisted, remarking that West Bank women are less controlled than Gazan women. By now Ahmed looked indignant. On the West Bank, he sternly reminded me, there is a Jewish influence and also many more Internationals and some weak people want to copy their behaviour and harm is done too in some mosques where the Holy Koran is not interpreted by correct imams.

Soon Ahmed went indoors to pay his respects to their mutual grandfather and Jannath said, 'I'm happy, I worried a bit coming here, about would I like him. It's fine, he's a nice kind person, I'm very happy.'

Ayshah said, 'Some of our age group get the idea, from outside, about girls choosing husbands. A few years ago I was confused, thinking maybe I should be more independent. But really I know I couldn't, I'd be afraid to make a mistake!'

The baby woke, whimpered once and was taken under the maternal gown. Both sisters made banal remarks about Israel and the blockade but neither was interested in any form of activism, or speculation about future possibilities. As we chatted on in a desultory way I wondered if they were unaware of the risk involved in all these cousinly matings or if they had been warned but preferred to ignore the risk. The day before, at the Al-Nasser Paediatric Hospital, I had learned that from the Palestinians' high con-sanguinity rates come abnormal levels of (among other afflictions) IEM – Inborn Error of Metabolism. Out of the hospital's 18 cases of this rare condition (causing skeletal deformities and mental retardation) 17 were the children of cousin marriages. In three of the Gazan families I visited regularly, IEM cases were sadly obvious – relatively mild cases, yet a source of much parental anxiety. In one family, not only were the parents first cousins – both came of consanguineous marriages. And this is not as unusual as one might hope. The young paediatrician with whom I talked wanted a thorough study done of the Strip's incidence of IEM, as preliminary to a major anti-consanguinity campaign. In general her advice to parents was rejected, seen as 'Western' interference with an ancient custom that had served the Palestinians well by reinforcing clans' assets. She herself had become estranged from her own parents – the unhappy consequence of a refusal to marry a first cousin.

I was saying goodbye to the sisters when Ahmed reappeared and escorted me, as is the custom, to the nearest taxi route. This gesture provoked a mixed reaction: appreciation of the courtesy, resentment of the implied dependency or vulnerability of women. Life among the Palestinians was taking its toll. A decade ago the appreciation would have been unmixed.

Two *serveece* rides took me to Yara's family home, where I was expected at noon.

*   *   *

I first met Yara in a sub-office of the Palestinian Working Woman Society for Development (PWWSD), a group severely handicapped by its title: even the initialism is a tongue-twister. It was established in 1981, inspired by a damp squib – the Arab Charter on Human Rights – which banned all discrimination against women but was not put into force because at that date only Iraq would ratify it. I was shown the figures which PWWSD helps to gather for the Palestinian Central Bureau of Statistics. In 2006 50 per cent of Gazan women and 69 per cent of West Bank women suffered psychological violence. For physical violence the figures were 25 per cent and 26 per cent . When I objected that 'psychological violence' is too vague a term Yara replied sharply, 'You know it when you live with it. Here it often means forced marriages.' Events since 2006 have impeded the statisticians.

Yara was tall and too thin: not beautiful but with an arresting face, strong and mobile, showing volatile emotions as a landscape changes under swift clouds. She spoke fluent English, self-taught with BBC World Service assistance, and worked for PWWSD as a part-time volunteer. Her 'earning job', as she called it, was demanding: no sinecure. Her hobby was wood-carving, 'to prove I'm a feminist'. She refused to shake hands with Muslim men – 'Let them feel what it's like when women are up against mysophobia!'

I had to ask, 'What's mysophobia?' When Yara replied, 'A morbid fear of defilement' I at once remembered my first day in Gaza. Mehat had introduced me to a reliable money-changer, a charming old man who graciously apologised for not shaking hands. He asked Mehat to explain that since marrying fifty-five years ago he had never touched any woman but his wife. In Mehat's view, this was an edifying boast. Yara said, 'Some people see it as a neurosis needing treatment.'

For her mother's sake Yara wore the *hijab*. 'I'd take a chance – she has nightmares about acid in my face. A blinded disfigured daughter!' But she wouldn't wear the *thobe*, never mind the *jilbab*. 'What's wrong with trouser-suits? They show no skin, I'm covered to the ankles and wrists!'

173

Aged twenty-six, Yara had married at nineteen, been divorced at twenty-five. She saw her three sons once a week, on Fridays, and invited me to meet them in her parental home. At first she seemed to me stoically resigned to her situation – a sad one, but not uncommon.

*   *   *

Finding Gazan addresses is not easy for the non-Arabic-speaker. I tried my luck in a huxter shop where two youths sat on crates sharing a tin of Coke and talking to the elderly owner, still wearing his mosque gown and cap. He eyed me with disfavour – then, on seeing the well-known family name, ordered a youth to guide me to my destination half a mile away. En route we attempted conversation but got no further than an exchange of names. All UNRWA school pupils learn English – in theory . . .

From the street Yara's home was invisible behind a high concrete wall. When she opened the wicket gate I got quite a shock – this was not the Yara who had taken me into the most deprived recesses of Shatti and Jabalya camps on a round of morale-boosting visits to the widowed mothers of disabled children. In six days she seemed to have lost her poise and vitality, to have become uncertain and frightened.

The long three-storey house overlooked a wide, bleak concrete forecourt unrelieved by any fleck of green. 'We built in 1997,' said Yara, 'and it's three flats. My two oldest married brothers live here. But the planning was silly – too ambitious. Money dried up and inside it's mostly unfinished.'

A long flight of shallow, semi-circular steps (crumbling at the edges) led directly into an enormous high-ceilinged salon that felt unused. The gaudy Chinese carpet didn't match the two four-person sofas; ten ornate dining-chairs were symmetrically placed against the walls, equidistant from a central row of glass coffee tables; holy texts decorated two walls. Yara apologised for the three non-functioning ceiling fans and opened a big window opposite the door. From upstairs came a cacophony of small quarrelsome children. 'My mother is feeding the boys,' explained Yara. Her father appeared then, returning from the mosque; tall and heavily built, he avoided my eye and greeted me gruffly while passing through the salon. 'He doesn't like independent women,' observed his daughter.

Over the next few hours I heard the full story. When Yara was allowed to meet her twenty-nine-year-old fiancé, a week before the wedding, she instantly disliked him and begged her father not to force the marriage through. He told her not to behave like a spoiled child. To break an agreement with an important business partner, to cancel an elaborate wedding party – merely to cater for Yara's whim – unthinkable! He reminded her of her eldest sister's awful fate. Having spurned her father's choice, she eloped with a university lecturer and found herself the divorced mother of twins in less than a year. *And* the scoundrel had to be taken to court to secure maintenance of their babies. Whenever Yara's mother tentatively supported her daughters 'she was punished'. I didn't ask what form that punishment took.

Two weeks after the wedding Yara ran home, craving mercy. She exerted every sort of pressure, including a mock suicide attempt, in an effort to escape, to be allowed to live at home. But that too was unthinkable – the *shame* of it! Within forty-eight hours she had been returned to captivity. For a Palestinian woman there was no Third Way; she must live either with her parents or husband.

The next seven years were tolerable only because Yara was allowed to study at IUG, an alleviation made possible by her mother's caring for the children as they came.

'All the time,' said Yara, 'I hated him more every hour. Slowly I learned how to show my hate in ways that humiliated him. Last year I escaped but the price is high. He won't let me have the boys. Shari'a law says mother should have boys until they're seven and girls until nine. Have you noticed Shari'a is kept for when it suits men? Here is a big house, enough money, everything easy for me to have them. And they hate their stepmother! Next month her first baby comes and she must take care or they'll kill it!'

By then I had seen enough of those very disturbed children (aged six, five and three and a half) not to scoff at this prediction. Yelling and screaming, they tumbled wildly around the salon, dragging sofa cushions across the floor, jumping from chair to chair, thumping the glass tables to make them reverberate. They were aggressive, rude and angry. Plainly it had been a bad idea for Yara to have a foreign friend intruding on their precious half-day with Mamma.

Yara's youngest sister, Jindiya, joined us briefly – a worryingly overweight seventeen-year-old who might have looked better in a *thobe* than in tight shorts and a tank-top. She spoke no English but was intensely curious about me and my family and my strange way of life. Yara's interpreting for her provoked the boys to slap their mother's face, pull her ears and kick her shins. Jindiya was betrothed to the youngest brother of Yara's ex-husband and seemed happy with the engagement though she hadn't yet met him.

I asked Yara, 'Why hasn't she met him? You all live within a few miles of each other!'

'It's my father,' came the reply. 'He likes the oldest customs.'

I felt helplessly sorry for Yara, who couldn't cope – alternately she cuddled and kissed her sons with a desperate sort of urgency, then shrilly snapped at them. Once her eldest brother came to the doorway and shouted a protest about the furniture being damaged. He closely resembled his father in build and aura. The boys couldn't play outside because he objected to their noisiness. 'He hates children,' said Yara, 'even his own and he has seven of them.'

When inviting me, Yara had mentioned how much her English-speaking mother enjoyed talking with foreigners. But now it transpired that her husband had said it was not necessary for her to meet me. I began to feel what might be described as emotional claustrophobia. Glancing at my watch, I murmured about having to move on. 'No!' exclaimed Yara. 'I've a big new problem, we must talk when alone!'

There was a fixed routine; at 5.00 pm a taxi came to fetch the boys. Under no circumstances could their time with Mamma be extended. Now Yara rang for another taxi to take us both to 'a quiet place'. I noticed how her hands trembled as she struggled to put sandals on wriggling boys – no longer screaming but sobbing piteously. Jindiya reappeared, to help drag the trio to the wicket and push them into the taxi. I hurried ahead and sat in the other taxi. As Jindiya persuaded the older ones to stay in their seats Yakob clung so fiercely to Yara that she stood immobilised by the wicket, ashen with grief, until the driver came to prise her son away from the maternal legs and carry him, kicking convulsively, to join his brothers.

I could think of nothing to say as the boys' taxi sped away and Yara sat beside me on the back seat. At once she lit a (forbidden) cigarette and addressed the driver in English. 'You haven't seen this!' For the first time since my arrival on the teetotal Strip I longed, in a visceral way, for a stiff drink.

Then Yara admitted, 'Last Friday I made an excuse not to see them. Each week it's worse – maybe best if they never see me? Children forget quickly . . . '

The driver intervened. 'You're wrong! That's cruel! Being left trying to forget a mother destroys kids!' This young man, Yara later explained, was an Eng. Lit. graduate who drove a taxi for lack of more appropriate work.

Our 'quiet place' was a large, circular palm-thatched restaurant-café, set back a little from the Strip's main road, surrounded by palm trees and even at sunset on a Friday almost empty. One-third had been curtained off with loosely woven coconut fibres –

a token purdah space, not providing enough seclusion for the strictest. A few elderly men puffed at their hookahs or played backgammon; on the women's side we were alone. 'Here I can go on smoking', said Yara. 'I started after the divorce and nicotine tranquillises me.'

There was no smell of food and no waiter appeared. 'They keep it open for big parties,' Yara explained. 'It was popular when new in the '90s – people had more money. We came here as a family for ice-creams – parents and six children, my father and brothers always on the other side. They could have sat with us, it was allowed, but everything had to be *rigid!*'

Away from the family environment, Yara was regaining some of her vitality. But then as she revealed that new problem, tears flowed. It all took a long time to clarify and there were several détours down dismal alleyways of family history.

In brief: since the divorce a year ago Father had often talked of remarriage as inevitable though Yara had been resolute – '*Never* again!' The day after our last meeting she had been told, 'It's all arranged.' One of her father's closest business associates had a 45-year-old son who married late (by Palestinian standards) and now, five years after the wedding, his wife's barrenness had been medically confirmed. Divorce was not being considered; their cousinly union had been a success, they were devoted to one another and the wife understood that a second wife was essential. A man *must* have children! (Oddly enough, I had encountered a similar case when living in Hebron Old City.) Yara knew the barren wife (six years her senior) but didn't know her well enough to be certain she could share with her a husband and a home. For Father this was Allah being kind: a divorced daughter with three children is not a valuable asset. Yet here was a win-win situation, in Father's own terminology – an excellent husband for a low-value daughter and a chance to please an important business partner.

Yara, red-eyed, looked at me reproachfully and said, 'Foreigners don't understand it can be so much harder for women in business families though they've more money. Also they've more marriage problems, as goods for bargaining.'

Father had made it plain that if Yara resisted she could not go on living with her parents, nor could she live alone, that would be impossible, so there was no alternative to remarriage. He had come to a decision. She should be grateful that such a suitable man was prepared to overlook things.

'But he's bluffing!' I said. 'When you make it plain you're determined to stay single, living at home, earning for yourself, doing your own thing – he's helpless! He can't put you out on the street!'

Tears trickled again. 'He can torture me,' Yara half-whispered. 'Remember you wondered about psychological violence? Our men know how to do it!'

That silenced me for moments. Then I asked, 'What are your options? Emigration if you could get out? And surely you could now, through Rafah? You have skills and training to earn your own living, rent a flat somewhere and be *yourself*.'

Yara gazed sadly down at her hands. 'Do I have a *self*, the way you mean? There's the Canadian option. My favourite brother, the one like me, got away to Canada in '05. He married what he calls an Anglo-Canadian. She converted to Islam and says she's OK about children growing up Muslim – no more than two children and she'll never live in a Muslim country. That seems a fair compromise. I guess she's not believing in Islam but pretending to make Omar happy!'

I wanted to say, 'Isn't your feminism coming unstuck? Why should the woman be doing the pretending on such a crucial matter to make the man happy?' However, given Yara's fragile state that would not have been kind. Instead I asked, 'What does Omar advise?'

'I Skyped him twice this week and he says I should settle in Canada, it's easy with my qualifications. He's not able to imagine how I'd feel never seeing my sons again. What do you advise?'

With three children in the equation, I dared not put a finger on the scales. Undoubtedly life in Canada, with a congenial brother in situ to provide support, would be best for Yara. But was the taxi-driver right? On the other hand, could a mother so tantalisingly inaccessible do enough for her sons to justify wrecking her own life? We talked on for another hour, inconclusively, and I remembered a passage in Ghada Karmi's remarkable autobiography, *In Search of Fatima*. The author, born in Palestine but reared and educated in England, had in many ways been 'Westernised' by the age of nineteen. Yet as a young woman she couldn't oppose her father's decision that she should become a doctor.

> . . . I knew with resignation that, as an Arab daughter, I had no choice but to obey . . . Defying my father in the context of our traditional Arab family was something I could not have contemplated. Despite all my intellectual pretensions to having adopted a liberal, non-authoritarian European paradigm, when it came to confronting my father or opposing his wishes, the cultural imperative prevailed.

As individuals, Ghada's father and Yara's father are not comparable. But the power of the cultural imperative too often prevails, regardless of personalities.

Four months later, I heard that Yara had become a second wife.

* * *

On one of our excursions Nita and I hired Nabeel, a young taxi-driver who had moved to Gaza six months previously from the UAE. There his father had 'found a problem with the government' and returned hastily to the Strip. Nabeel, aged twenty two, would have preferred to remain in his birthplace but was ordered to accompany the family, which included eight younger siblings; his earning power would be needed.

One afternoon we called into that same palm-thatched café, where Nabeel fetched drinks (water and Coke) and a hookah. Nita admitted then that for years she'd longed to try a puff. Twice Nabeel urged her to experiment – declared young women were free to smoke as much as they wished in the Emirates – wondered why the Gazan way of life was so ridiculous.

There followed another futile debate about culture, religion, tradition, customs, family obligations. Nita couldn't conceive of doing something which would upset her parents. (They were kind, loving parents: I'd met them a few times.) Nabeel remarked that as we were the only patrons, they would be unlikely ever to find out. Her mother said smoking was bad for the health. Emphatically I agreed – but then why may men smoke? Is their health not equally important? Nita exclaimed, 'I often think that! But the Holy Koran says women mustn't.' She looked puzzled when I pointed out that tobacco came from the Americas centuries after Mohammed took direction from Allah. I was reminded of Khalil's assertion that not only Muslims but all Jews and Christians were forbidden to drink alcohol. 'The imam said so, in the mosque.' He looked disbelieving when informed that Christ's first miracle was turning water into wine and that Jews drink wine as part of their Sabbath ceremonies – and may have a shot of vodka as an optional extra.

Nabeel questioned Nita about the *jilbab* – why did all the IUG students have to wear black? Apparently because bright colours draw attention to the individual young woman and thus encourage 'competition to be noticed' which is 'against our religion'. Nabeel laughed scornfully. 'This is all Wahhabi stuff!'

I asked about the *niqb* (full face veil) and Nita explained some women (on the Strip an increasing number) choose it because it's more respectful to Allah. A visible woman's face can make her seem more attractive to men – especially 'bad men'. Also it may tempt her to communicate with people outside the family. I asked, 'What exactly do you mean?'

'She could smile at people she shouldn't communicate with, in the market or the street.'

'You mean *smiling* is forbidden? When she buys fruit or eggs and smiles at the trader as she takes her purchase – that's wrong, sinful, against the Koran, offends Allah?'

'Yes', said Nita, 'it's wrong – maybe not sinful, but wrong, we shouldn't do it! But of course most of us do, unless we feel we're being watched by some jihadists.'

'I think this place needs to go for treatment!' said Nabeel.

I agreed. Invariably, people voiced anxiety about my walking alone in the dark; I had regular arguments with *serveeces* reluctant to put me down not directly outside my destination – because of my gender, not my hostage potential. I mentioned this to my companions and wondered, 'When these sex-related fears are cultivated, what does it do to a society? When girls are taught to regard all non-related men as possibly "bad", poised to rape given a chance?'

'Sometimes,' observed Nita, 'the related men are the worst.'

I persisted. 'Isn't this danger-mongering insulting to Muslim males? Or, if they're really so dangerous on the Strip, why not start a movement to civilise them?'

'How?' asked Nita. 'By now you know we've a big problem, females not correctly dressed *are* vulnerable to attack!'

Impatiently I replied, 'So why don't the world's "uncovered" women – the majority – have this problem? Where men are so dangerous, they must have been conditioned to see "incorrectly" dressed women as legitimate prey. That's why I say it's time to recondition them. But yes, you're right – that's much easier said than done!'

Such states of mind, on the part of both predator and prey, are self-perpetuating. For most brain-washed Gazans, reconditioning probably won't take place within the Strip under its present regime.

In entirely trivial and irritating ways (never mind ethical or pseudo-ethical matters) childhood conditioning can be irreversible. Some of my mature US friends would wet their pants on long motor journeys rather than pee by the wayside – yet these are rational beings in all other respects. (Come to think of it, I myself still feel vaguely uncomfortable if a male accompanying me along a pavement walks on the inside – though no one under seventy would understand why.)

*   *   *

I spent half the next day at Rafah Gate, waiting for someone who didn't arrive. Normally vehicles enter Gaza via side-tracks by-passing the main gate, which is opened only for departing vehicles. But that morning one VIP's 4x4 was allowed to use it and we later heard the Person was an EU official on a four-hour visit to Gaza City – 'an insult!' fumed several of my friends.

Two youngish English-speakers approached, offered coffee, asked permission to sit with me. They were an interesting pair though I suspect I wasn't seeing them at their best – and vice versa. The Rafah Gate generates an unquiet atmosphere. Nawaf was a classical guitarist anxiously awaiting his brother, due home after a chemotherapy course in Cairo. His friend was more talkative.

Murad had returned from Sweden three years previously when his father, a former PA security officer, found it necessary to flee to Egypt and dared not come back. Therefore his mother needed her only son at home. Without hesitation he said *au revoir* to his Swedish wife and two-year-old daughter who could not visit Gaza even if they wished to do so. Ever since the three have been bonded by Skype and Murad said, 'It makes an ache in my heart' – he placed a hand on that organ – 'when Miriam says in Swedish "Daddy come home, come home I want you!" ' However, no inner conflict bothered this parent; as an only son he had to put his mother first – not his own preference, he explained, but Palestinian women are conditioned not to be able to cope without a man. So a Swedish woman suffers . . . (Or maybe she doesn't?) Murad couldn't guess when next he might see his wife and child, both displayed to me on his phone in scores of poses.

As a highly qualified hydraulic engineer, Murad lived well in Sweden; in Gaza he drove someone else's taxi while saving up to buy his own. He condemned both Fatah and Hamas as 'power-seekers not caring about ordinary people who only want peace'. (I seemed to be hearing this refrain more and more often.) His wife had introduced him to beer ('Not much, you couldn't afford to get drunk!') but on the Strip he didn't really miss it. However, he resented the Islamists' prohibition régime. He himself loved Gaza but even were it possible he wouldn't want Miriam to grow up on the Strip. At which point Nawaf's brother emerged from a *serveece* – bald and pale – and in the joyous relief of that reunion I was forgotten.

Around Rafah, and other southern Strip districts, it greatly alarmed me to see quite a few pre-puberty girls in adult garb, securely concealed and *hijab*-ed; and in those same areas the *niqb* incidence was higher. Anwar repeatedly lamented that this tightening stranglehold on women's freedom is too easy in a Gaza so isolated – not comparatively open, like the West Bank, to the 'corrupting' influence of Jews and Internationals. Thus, he argued, the blockade reinforces some of the most undesirable elements in Palestinian society: as undesirable, in their very different way, as the PA's quisling elements.

This view was apparently validated by the common riposte to my comparison of Gaza's new hard-linery with the West Bank's relative moderation – Jewish and International presences have corrupted the West Bank. As one academic put it, 'You met weak Muslims in other places, here we know how to stay strong, defending the Holy Koran. You should learn that "Muslim" and "Islamic" are different. Some saying "I'm Muslim" are not Islamic, not respecting our Holy Koran.'

Yet the opposite conclusion to Anwar's may be drawn from *Fundamentalism: A Very Short Introduction* by Malise Ruthven.

The surge of fundamentalist movements . . . we are witnessing in many parts of the world is a response to globalization and, more specifically, to the crises for believers that inevitably follows the recognition that there are ways of living and believing other than those deemed to have been decreed by one's own tradition's version of the deity.

Does this not mean that the isolation of the blockaded Strip should lessen hard-linery?

'Not really,' said Anwar. 'Gaza is a special case. Remember Hamas has been busy physically resisting the Occupation. And maybe will be again, though we hope not. Without the blockade and the Occupation, Hamas' moderates would now have much greater influence.'

Incidentally, Anwar regarded *Fundamentalism* as the most essential guidebook for all visitors to Gaza.

The academic quoted above baffled me. He was an immensely likeable man, an eminent Gazan who had travelled widely in pre-blockade times, being respectfully listened to at international conferences. Yet when the conversation turned to Islam he sounded embarrassingly crude as he raked over all the tedious stuff about women being 'physiologically and emotionally different', therefore needing to be 'protected and respected'. I warned him that life among the Palestinians had belatedly aroused within me those anti-male emotions felt two generations ago by Women's Lib activists. Also I had become a shameless cultural imperialist, no longer willing to tolerate condescending double standards in deference to their being non-European. Example: 'It's for women's protection' when the custom in question is blatantly for the preservation of male control. Indignantly my friend protested, '*Allah* made the rules, it's not men being determined to dominate!' And the rules cannot be modified, must remain as laid down in the seventh century AD.

When I asked if any women were involved in interpreting the sacred texts I was told only men could interpret, very highly trained scholars of whom there are but a few in each generation. Aware of sounding truculent, I demanded, 'Why not allow for the unavoidable, undeniable fact that societies and civilisations ·evolve, change beyond recognition?'

Again my friend repeated, 'No modifications allowed! The word of Allah is not changed by fashions, reforms, revolutions or trends. It's for all time, helping men do what is good and right for society. The Holy Koran protects the family. In the materialistic West, people think themselves separate, not responsible for family and community. The more the West seeks to take over the world, economically and culturally, the more we guard our Holy Koran against those trying to make us imitate others.'

This friend was a keen Hamas supporter, though not a party member. It gave me some satisfaction, when we next met, to show him a 1999 statement from Yahya Musa, speaking as head of a Political Bureau (Hizb al-Khalas) linked to Hamas:

All Islamic parties work under the umbrella of Islam . . . They start from the same point but their differences derive from their interpretation of the Koran and Hadith. The Islam implemented during Mohammed's life is different from the Islam implemented today or should be. Islam should be implemented according to current conditions. Other groups have a more literal interpretation and want to separate out from current reality. This is the difference between the letter of the law and the spirit of the law.

Eight

Seen from the coast road, UNRWA's summer camps for 'refugee' children form blue blots on the beach. Each is enclosed by high walls of plastic sheeting, curving down to meet the wavelets, and there's not a child in sight – but the sounds of hordes having fun are reassuringly loud. Since 2010 these recreation spaces (some hundred yards long by sixty yards wide) have perforce become isolated, with something of a prison ambience as one approaches seeking entrance.

On 23 May 2010 UNRWA's Director, John Ging, took delivery of a communication containing three bullets (for him not a new experience). In part, the letter said:

> We were shocked when we heard about establishing beach locations for girls at the age of puberty and adolescence aiming to attack Muslims' honour and morality. You have to know that we will give away our blood and life but we won't let this happen and will not let you malicious people beat us. So you either leave your plans or wait for your destiny.

This message had been left with an UNRWA guard who was tied up by thirty or so *jihadists*, masked and armed, before they burned down a sports facility being constructed for the summer camps. Who were they? Naturally the answer you got depended on whom you asked. A few weeks later, another camp was comprehensively vandalised.

Anwar suggested as the most obvious suspect one of the Salafists' armed wings, Jund Ansar Allah (Soldiers of the Supporters of God). Before the attacks, they had been circulating leaflets denouncing the employment of women teachers in boys' schools and the sponsoring of North American and European trips for female students.

My Fatah friends had no doubt: 'Definitely Hamas, they're so angry about competition with their own brainwashing holiday camps.'

'Of course it's Salafists,' said my Hamas friends, 'they know Ging wants mixed camps.' Deeb was slightly on the defensive. 'Why would Hamas attack? We're the government, if we want to close a camp we order it to close!' Which made sense, but that sort of logic doesn't always operate on the Strip. However, the relevant Ministry was now providing guards for all beach camps. And their purdah plastic walls meant nobody could be scandalised by the sight of bare-headed little girls making sandcastles, and playing such risqué games as leapfrog and blind man's buff, while 'malicious' supervisors taught females how to swim (fully clothed), and dance and perform acrobatic tricks – and even imitate their brothers by practising breakdancing which in Islamic eyes is a vile perversion.

Because of Gaza's fast-growing refugee population each batch of schoolchildren (aged six to sixteen) can be happy campers for only two weeks of their three-month summer holiday. The adult/child ratio is 15 to 100 and the campers are so happy that discipline is maintained without any hint of authoritarianism. I'd expected these supervisors to be dutiful rather than enthusiastic yet they, too, were obviously enjoying themselves. To me, coming from a society where rebellious adolescent tendencies are cultivated by The Market, these intergenerational relationships seemed extraordinarily harmonious.

My two happy days as a guest at girls' camps showed UNRWA at its best. I arrived as the first busloads were scampering down the sand dunes, being monitored from a dormobile-style police post parked by the roadside. Each girl carried her own picnic and, for security reasons, all had to queue at the one narrow opening in the tarpaulin. For us, confinement to these plastic cages would not induce 'seaside' elation; knowing from where these children come,

I could empathise with their sense of release. Once beyond eye-reach of the male population they discarded their 'correct' street attire, as did most of the adults.

Some groups were organised, others formed spontaneously to dance, sing, play a space-limited version of volleyball or attempt gymnastic feats with improvised equipment – the real thing having gone up in flames. Quite often linguistically ambitious seniors gathered around me to improve their English. Others preferred sitting in circles on the sand, chatting and giggling and experimenting with cosmetics; these trickle through the tunnels and are, according to Yara, of dangerously poor quality. One girl, messily applying mascara, informed me with a wide grin, 'Salafists hate this!'

The adults, as UNRWA staff, were understandably wary of discussing with a stranger anything remotely political. In contrast, several older girls were healthily uninhibited in their criticisms of officialdom. Especially they condemned the strict dress code regulations, announced in July 2009, which allow government schools to expel pupils who refuse to exchange their jeans and shirts/sweaters for IUG-style *jilbabs*. This Salafist-pleasing move was made – Deeb told me – to avoid attacks on the schools or their pupils. Yet to many it looked like another example of the unsettling fuzziness surrounding Hamas *qua* ruling authority. Several girls mocked the Education Ministry for imposing such rules by remote control – countering complaints by blaming individual school heads.

In general these youngsters were an ebullient lot, upholding the Palestinians' hard-earned reputation for resilience. But I remembered Yara's comment that those most in need of such breaks don't get them: can't afford the picnics – or feel self-conscious about threadbare garments – or have been too traumatised by Cast Lead and other horrors to feel secure away from their home corner (too often literally a corner).

*   *   *

At least one of Gaza's clouds has a silver lining; the blockade has driven farmers back to organic agriculture. Since 2007 the chemical fertilisers and pesticides once so popular have not been available and the ancients of my generation, who can remember 'how things were', find themselves in great demand as agricultural advisors. It helps that the Minister of Agriculture, Dr Mohammed al-Agha, is an IUG professor of environmental science. In 2010 the government launched a ten-year programme designed to restore traditional farming methods. This rewarded the hitherto ignored preaching of Gaza's Safe Agriculture Producers' Society whose Director, Abd el-Munem, announced: 'The siege gives us our first opportunity to persuade cultivators that chemical-free growing can work.'

Bader, another of Anwar's numerous grand-nephews, had recently upset his parents by dropping out of university and becoming an apprentice with Palestinian Environmental Friends. He was a most engaging young man, full of hope for the Strip's organic future and choosing not to think about its political future. 'Allah is planning what to do, we must wait to see that plan.' He described himself as 'training to be a dung consultant' and invited me to admire his workplace.

In a pungent palm grove, near fields of raised strawberry beds, Bader proudly led me between mounds of rotting foliage and mature dung collected from farmers all over the area. These fertilisers are applied in alternate layers, having been chopped up by a neat home-made mill not unlike a concrete mixer and designed locally; nothing of the sort would be allowed past Israel's border guards. 'We might develop a nuclear weapon in it!' chuckled Bader. This enterprise is now producing about 600 tons of fertiliser annually at US$100 per ton – less than half the price of the only available Israeli fertiliser, derived from sewage and distrusted by the Ministry of Health.

A short *serveece* ride took us to the central Strip where I was suitably impressed by a fish-cum-vegetable farm; fish-enriched water is delivered by drip irrigation to sandy plots of carrots, tomatoes, rocket and spinach. But for the foreseeable future – Bader sadly explained – Gazan produce will be unable to gain organic certification since the relevant inspectors are excluded from the Strip. When next I met Yara she opined that this absence of inspectors had one advantage; they would certainly object to the use of child labour. And at least four families in her neighbourhood were largely dependent on the admittedly meagre wages earned by their pre-puberty children. 'Poverty isn't just a statistic in Gaza,' said Yara. 'It's for real.'

* * *

I spent memorable evenings in the home of Dr Nasser Abu Shabaan, surgeon in Gaza City's al-Shifa hospital. I had first heard his name during Cast Lead, in Beit Sahour, where Professor Mazin Qumsiyeh was my host. When the IDF began to fire white phosphorus shells into Gaza, Mazin's advice was sought. I remember wandering off to the Shepherds' Field, sick with horror, while he tried to fax al-Shifa. The IDF couldn't deny that war crime. About 200 155-millimetre shells were fired into the Strip, where people subsequently collected the canisters to present as evidence to Amnesty International investigators.

As my base was close to al-Shifa, Nasser picked me up at 6.30 pm when he usually came off duty. (Usually but not always; in any emergency he remained available.) One evening Nita met him briefly and afterwards remarked that he looked more like a film star than a surgeon and should have operated in another sort of theatre. I saw what she meant; Nasser is very tall and well built with classical Arab features. But his old-fashioned graciousness and compassionate temperament might not have been appreciated in Hollywood.

At our first meeting, as we drove to the Shabaan flat in a luxury (by Strip standards) apartment block on the edge of Gaza City, Nasser put his background in a nutshell. The patrilineal great-grandfather was a wealthy merchant operating on the Yemen–Gaza trade route. Grandfather distinguished himself as an Arabic scholar at Alexandria University, fought with the British army during the First World War and died soon after, leaving his widow to raise a large brood on a small income. When Father found work as a minor civil servant in Jerusalem he resolved to put his eldest son through medical school in Cairo. Nasser graduated with honours, quickly achieved FRCS status and spent most of his working life in Saudi Arabia. In 2003 he decided to return home, as the Second Intifada was taking its toll on the Strip. His Saudi monthly salary was US$10,000 and al-Shifa offered only $1,200 for a much longer working day – and, often, night. 'But that was no problem,' said Nasser. 'We'd saved enough.' Now he and his multi-talented and very beautiful wife (Nita might say 'another film star') work with various voluntary projects including developing courses in Primary Trauma Care, established in Gaza by two English doctors, John Beavis and Terence English.

As Nasser remarked, his family history well illustrates the reverse-globalisation of our time. It was easy for great-grandfather to trade personally with the Yemen – sometimes accompanying his camel caravans to and fro, not merely doing financial deals by computer. For his grandfather it was easy to study in Alexandria, and nothing hindered his father from becoming a cog in the Mandatory machine in Jerusalem while maintaining important links with Sa'na, Cairo, Alexandria and Gaza. Now, despite air travel, middle-eastern political borders curtail most people's movements.

In an elegant fifth-floor drawing-room one window's venetian blind was half-closed to shut out Cast Lead's nearby devastation. Mrs Shabaan's English was as fluent as her husband's and we talked of many things while far in the background two adored grandchildren were being high-spirited in a civilised way and their willowy mother (inches taller than her husband) was preparing supper. I learned then that among the generality of Muslims the pill and condoms are approved contraceptives and hysterectomies are allowed for medical reasons but the very notion of vasectomy made both my host and hostess flinch. After all, marriage's main objective is to provide men with children – preferably sons. To voluntarily make oneself sterile – well, that's a twisted denial of Allah's plan for humankind. Such aberrations inspire Muslims to try to shield their communities from Western influences.

Not until the younger generations had left for home did Nasser talk about Cast Lead; during those three weeks he rarely got more than one hour's sleep at a stretch.

When a white phosphorus shell hit the Halima farmhouse, at Siyafa village, the father and four of his nine children were killed, his wife and the other children grievously burned. Their neighbours, terrified by this uncontrollable mass incineration of human bodies, fled across the fields. The survivors were brought to al-Shifa and Nasser described the bewildered frustration of his team, who at first didn't know what they were dealing with. 'We had never before seen anything like these burns. They reached down to bone and muscle and continued to smoke for hours and that smoke had a sickening stench.' Finally, Nasser and a colleague 'took out a piece of foreign matter' and the colleague identified it as white phosphorus. That was the first of dozens of similar cases.

The IDF routinely used these munitions. On contact with air, white phosphorus ignites and continues to burn at 816°C until completely starved of oxygen – hence the smoking wounds, before Nasser and his team learned how to cope. Each air-bursting artillery shell spreads 116 burning wedges over a radius of, on average, 125 metres from blast point. The IDF deliberately fired phosphorus into densely populated areas. Among its public targets were al-Quds hospital, the Red Crescent headquarters, UNRWA's main Gaza City compound and an UNRWA school in Beit Lahia where more than 1600 'displaced persons' (bombed out of their homes) were sheltering.

Khoza'a village was declared a 'closed military zone' before being attacked. Six people died at once, enveloped in flames; more than a score were deeply burned and permission to evacuate them was refused. A Red Crescent ambulance, defying this ban, attracted more white phosphorus. Gazan paramedics can have no masks effective against this smoke. Its victims may fall unconscious for three or four hours, then seem to recover and be sent home – only to return soon, in agony, their extensively burnt lungs not responsive to treatment. In many cases, as the body gradually absorbs the white phosphorus chemical, potentially fatal damage is caused to all the major organs. Perhaps Ehud Olmert, the then Israeli Prime Minister, had this in mind when he warned: 'Rockets from Gaza will bring a severe and disproportionate response.'

Nasser also treated scores of injuries inflicted by other 'innovative' weapons. Some patients, apparently merely in shock when admitted, with not a mark to be seen on their bodies, began to deteriorate within hours – and within a few more hours were dead. Post-mortems revealed internal injuries consistent with the use of thermobaric weapons which Nasser showed me, close up and in colour, on his computer. This 'portfolio' included melted brains, shredded lungs, cooked livers, exploded kidneys. Do arms manu-facturers and their politician customers ever look at such pictures? Do they ever think about children or parents gazing at bodies unidentifiable as their children or parents – mangled beyond recognition as human beings . . . And why did the Quartet not demand an end to war crimes during those hideous three weeks? Instead, the *Goldstone Report* has been 'managed' to Israel's satis-faction, proving yet again – to quote Richard Falk – that 'The United Nations shows neither the capacity nor the will to implement its own resolutions.'

The current drugs shortage had compelled Nasser to postpone

or cancel numerous operations and many more patients urgently needed to leave the Strip. In May 2011, 92 per cent of applicants for permits to seek medical treatments elsewhere were successful – a considerable improvement on the 2010 monthly average. However, Israel habitually uses slow-motion bureaucracy to torture the gravely ill and their families. The granting of the original permit can still leave patients immobilised at the Erez crossing amidst a tangle of red tape and quite a few die while this is being unknotted. The Shabaans were particularly concerned about the number of IDF-maimed (far in excess of al-Wafa's capacity) for whom so little can be done on the Strip. In many cases, advanced medical technology could make a life-changing difference were those victims free to travel. No wonder most Gazans want foreign campaigners to emphasise their demand for *freedom* rather than material 'aid'. Incidentally, I relished Nasser's only half-joking comment that Hamas' insistence on its democratic right to rule on the Strip had helped the tiresomely named 'Arab Spring'.

Then Nasser gave me the good news. Dialysis patients' timetables had recently been adjusted to make the most of the machines still in working order. And at the beginning of June the Health Ministry had reluctantly authorised the reuse of some 'disposables'. As a lay person I refrained from comment but my (rather prominent) Green bit reckoned this 'emergency measure' might be no bad thing. Octogenarians can remember hospital equipment being routinely sterilised before 'disposables' came on stream to generate indecent profits for their manufacturers. Alas! there will soon be no one left to bear witness to those days when we were comparatively free of The Market.

*　　*　　*

M— had suggested (by mobile) our meeting on the beach, under the awning of a makeshift café, soon after sunrise. As he approached (elderly, tallish, neatly bearded, still wearing his prayer-gown) I

195

noticed two soberly dressed youths seating themselves half-behind the café trestle-table; they were out of earshot but could keep the surrounding beach – as yet almost deserted – under surveillance.

M— was an old friend of Said Siam, the first Hamas Minister for the Interior, who had topped the poll in Gaza in January 2006. Back in the '90s, M— told me, while resentment of Oslo was deepening and the Second Intifada brewing, Said had *de facto* resigned himself to the existence of the State of Israel and was developing his political thinking in accordance with that difficult readjustment. (No comparable adjustments were ever made on the Zionist side.) M— added, 'I say *de facto* because he couldn't bring himself to put it in simple Arabic. He conveyed it clearly without being explicit. To me that seemed a mistake and I told him so. But he had a tangled constituency to consider.'

Like Dr al-Zahar, Said didn't last long in the cabinet once attempts began to regain Western funding (lost after the election). On my first (2008) visit to Israel I had heard him included in lists of hardliners who were feared and hated. 'Hardliner' is in this context an ambiguous term. It can mean an Islamist fanatic, or a Palestinian who has no scruples about killing Israeli civilians because Israeli soldiers kill (with impunity) so many Palestinian civilians of both sexes and all ages. Or it can, as in Said's case, mean a Palestinian who greatly upsets Zionists because his realistic grasp of the current political situation and its historical background is frequently and clearly articulated. Mr Siam (a schoolteacher by profession) saw that the indispensable keystone for peace-building is Zionism's recognition of the injustices done to a people who, as human beings, have certain basic rights. And this, as M— pointed out, is precisely what the famous Olga Appeal, discussed below, argued a few years later.

Said Siam had long been in the IDF assassins' sights and after a few near misses a targeted bombing 'eliminated' him towards the end of Cast Lead. Israel's long-term policy of political assassinations has incidentally drawn attention to Hamas' high quota of talented leaders. As M— shrewdly observed, Zionists fear Hamas' collective brain-power much more than its rocket stockpile. He invited me to imagine peace negotiations in which all Hamas' murdered leaders were sitting opposite the best and the brightest from Zionism's governing class, everyone peace-seeking in earnest and the convener a neutral, if such exists. Given the quality of the Zionist case, and the sort of military/political hybrids who come to power in Israel, the Palestinians couldn't fail to win every round.

M— referred scathingly to those official visitors to Gaza (like the VIP I saw zooming through at Rafah) who spend their few hours on the Strip meeting UNRWA representatives and NGO staff but never any member of the democratically elected government. We mustn't talk to 'terrorists', our Washington bosses would never forgive that . . . Gaza's present Prime Minster is Ismail Haniyeh, an Arabic literature scholar and a level-headed leader who has always belonged to Hamas' political wing and narrowly escaped an assassin on 6 September 2003. Immediately after the election he announced that 'Hamas will formulate its own peace plan, with a long-term truce with Israel at its centre'. By long-term, M— said, Ismail meant 10 or 15 years – preferably 15, by the end of which period, it was hoped, mindsets all round might have shifted. The international media paid little attention to this statement ('never trust a terrorist!') but *Ha'aretz* had a cheerful headline: 'Hamas Appoints Moderates as PM, Speaker of PLC' (17 February). Exactly one week later *Ynet* reported that Avi Dichter, former Shin Bet chief, Ariel Sharon's main advisor and now Minister of Internal Security, had proclaimed, 'The Hamas top man Haniyeh is a legitimate assassination target.'

As M— commented, only the peculiarly twisted Zionist mind could use this phrase. According to Chambers, to assassinate is 'to murder by surprise or secret assault; to murder (especially a prominent person) violently, often publicly'. Killing may be legal in self-defence, if one cannot otherwise avoid being killed, but anyone above the mental age of seven can identify 'legitimate assassination' as a contradiction in terms. However, Israel routinely deals with political opponents by murdering them and its boast to have made 'political assassination internationally acceptable' seems justified, given the muted global reaction to such behaviour.

M— saw a close connection between Zionism's contempt for the law (international or domestic) and Israel's refusal to provide that 'keystone' Said had spoken of by accepting responsibility for past or present crimes. Which took us back to the Olga Appeal.

In 2004, at Givat Olga overlooking the Mediterranean, a large group of Israeli scholars and activists (supported from a distance by hundreds of their colleagues, including Professor Baruch Kimmerling and Meron Benvenisti, former Vice-Mayor of Jerusalem) met for a three-week discussion, mainly in Hebrew, about changing the political discourse in Israel. The initiators were: Anat Biletzki, Andre Draznin, Haim Hanegbi, Yehudith Harel, Oren Medicks and Michael (Mikado) Warschawski. They were not, they emphasised, launching another political party or movement or lobby. Their aim was:

> to initiate a genuine public discussion about the Israeli dead-end in which we live and the profound changes needed in order break out of it. Every Israeli knows that this is not a matter of political trifles, but a matter of deep concern for the fate of the peoples of this country . . . The State of Israel was supposed to be a democracy; it has set up a colonial structure combining unmistakable elements of apartheid with the arbitrariness of brutal military occupation . . . We are united in a critique of Zionism, based as it is on refusal to acknowledge the indigenous people of this country and on denial of their rights, on dispossession of their lands, and on adoption of separation as a fundamental principle and way of life. Adding insult to injury,

Israel persists in its refusal to bear any responsibility for its deeds, from the expulsion of the majority of Palestinians from their homeland more than half a century ago, to the present erection of ghetto walls around the remaining Palestinians in the towns and villages of the West Bank . . . We believe that peace and reconciliation are contingent upon Israel's recognition of its responsibility for the injustices done to the indigenous people and on its willingness to redress them . . . We seek coexistence of the peoples of this country, based on mutual recognition, equal partnership and implementation of historical justice.

By this stage we had moved to M—'s home, in one of the less insalubrious corners of Shatti camp, and were sitting in front of a sluggish table fan being sustained by Egyptian shiny biscuits and many little glasses of mint tea.

I told M— about my first impressions of Israel, before my sojourns in the OPT. While waiting to depart from Ben-Gurion airport I wrote in my diary: 'This country is unreal. It can't survive in its present form as a Jewish pseudo-democracy.' My gut-reaction was confined to my diary; after a brief visit it seemed much too presumptuous to be voiced, even among friends. That was in December 2008. By June 2011 my spontaneous choice of the word 'unreal', in a scribbled diary entry, seemed fully justified on one deep level – far removed from 'economic development'.

During November 2008 I had repeatedly encountered Zionism's evasion of reality – its refusal to accept responsibility for 'the Problem', its chilling depiction of Palestinians as sub-humans. For more than sixty years Israel's governments have been deftly manipulating their kaleidoscopic population, conditioning people to think of themselves as under permanent threat from malicious forces plotting to obliterate their country. This explains my initial perception of Israel as an artificial creation, founded on self-deceit and bolstered by the success of world-deceiving propaganda. It seems all the ingredients of the Problem have been poured by Zionism into a misshapen mould – then turned out and presented to a gullible public as 'the real situation'. Whereupon most of the Western world, prone to what Tony Judt diagnoses as post-Holocaust 'self-blackmailing', tries to deal fairly with this malformed mass of 'history'. And always the spectre of 'anti-Semitic' accusations hovers over the scene, prompting official visitors – if inclined to protest against the Occupation, the settlements, the Apartheid Wall – to preface their timid criticisms by expressing a sympathetic understanding of Israel's 'security concerns'. Yet those concerns would not exist were Zionism to take the Olga gathering's advice and 'redress the continued injustice inflicted on the Palestinians, generation after generation'. Olga continues: 'Only thus shall we Israeli Jews stop being plagued by the past's demons and make ourselves at home in our common homeland . . . If we approach the Palestinians with an open mind and a willing spirit, we shall find in them what we bring with us.'

On al-Jazeera, in December 2011, Teymoor Nabili talked with Yehuda Bauer, the Hebrew University's esteemed Holocaust scholar, who was introduced with the observation that Israel is 'a region where there are as many versions of history as there are people telling them'. To an extent this is true of every region and every history. However, al-Jazeera seemed to be conniving here with those who like to present the Problem as one in which each side has a valid argument – or both sides are equally intransigent. Yet certain basic facts, such as those confronted in the Olga document, are not dependent on any historian's interpretation or analysis. They stand alone, needing no explanation – only recognition.

M— was the third Gazan to tell me of his past support for suicide bombers and his present conviction that their missions had been a mistake. In the two other cases no remorse was felt; those jihadists regretted the Israeli lives lost only when it became obvious that most Palestinians condemned mass-assassinations – though they might lack the courage to say so aloud. Moreover, the missions had been counterproductive on the international political stage, losing popular support for 'the cause' and not being destructive or dramatic enough to scare governments.

M—'s case was different. I felt honoured and very moved when, during our second meeting, he described his 'conversion'. Suddenly the slaughtering of civilians had looked like an unIslamic crime. 'It happened after the war on Gaza. All our dead and wounded made me think "No! Humans should not do this to one another!" I'm an old man, I don't know why something changed inside me *then* . . . We've all seen many corpses, killed by Israelis or other Palestinians. When our missions were successful I never got excited and happy, I never liked this way of war. But we needed action at the time and what else to do? I'm careful now, not letting martyrs' families see I'm changed. They need respect, to feel sons, brothers, husbands will always be honoured.'

Latterly M— had become a closet binationalist, inspired by Ehud Olmert's prognosis at the end of the futile 2007 Annapolis 'peace' talks. Then Israel's Prime Minister spurred on the BDS movement by saying, 'If the day comes when the two-state solution collapses, and we face a South African-style struggle for equal voting rights . . . as soon as that happens, the State of Israel is finished.' Already Zionists recognise binationalism as a serious threat to their Jewish state. The argument that a two-state solution would leave Israel's borders indefensible has carried much weight for many years with Zionism's supporters. But in the twenty-first century, could even AIPAC justify arguing against the establishment of a one-person-one-vote secular democracy? However, as M— saw it, binationalism's main opponents will not be Israelis but those US Zionists. 'They don't have to live with our conflict,' he said. 'We and the Israelis both want peace. Zionism only offers more conflict.'

We agreed that there is a comforting inevitability about

binationalism – and here again the Zionists are fleeing from reality. Stridently they complain about anti-Semites scheming to 'delegitimise' Israel – though the 'delegitimising' has been achieved by their own flouting of international law ever since the State's foundation. We also agreed, while saying goodbye, that neither of us is likely to live long enough to see binationalism in action – despite M— being my junior by fifteen years.

*　　*　　*

I sometimes looked for a secluded corner in a café to transcribe a conversation while the exact words remained fresh in my mind. Thus I occasionally came upon young couples, on their own before my intrusion, who momentarily looked guilty and scared. Then, identifying me as an International, they would relax, smile, invite me to join them. By sitting together, drinking tea, they were breaking that 2009 law which forbids schoolgirls to wear jeans and which also bans women from riding pillion on motorbikes, having their hair cut by a male hairdresser and dancing in public with a male. Anyone detected misbehaving so flagrantly would be auto-matically fined by the Internal Security Agency. This is not the sort of 'independent state' the Palestinians want. Nor is it the sort of regime Hamas would impose were it not so scared of the Salafists. And the longer the blockade, the stronger that minority gets . . .

One such encounter took place in the gloomy upstairs room of a large run-down café (all its confectionary display cases empty) on Omar al-Mukhtar Street, overlooking the palm-lined Square of the Unknown Soldier. The young woman, Aida, was an English teacher at an UNRWA school, her friend hopes soon to be earning a living as a photojournalist – not an easy profession to follow on the Strip. He spoke no English and seemed quite put out because this left the female in a position of power . . . Soon it was time for him to go and when we were on our own Aida immediately reprimanded me for being 'naked'. 'The Holy Koran,' she sternly asserted, 'orders every woman to keep every one of her hairs covered.' We talked on for an hour or more. Aida longed to marry the photographer but for both 'other arrangements are made'. Had it been possible to leave Gaza they would have eloped: or so they told one another. Among the Palestinians, and especially among the Gazans, one often comes upon these unexpected conjunctions: 'every hair covered – elopement considered'. Before we parted Aida gave me her grandfather's name and mobile number and suggested I visit him in Jabalya town because 'he likes foreign books and the people who write them'.

Much as I detest mobile phones I have to concede that they do simplify life on the overpopulated Strip where it can take a very long time to locate an address. When I showed the *serveece* driver what Aida had scribbled in my notebook he conversed animatedly with her grandfather, Abdel, and mere moments late we found Abdel and his nephew Salem waiting for me on a crowded pavement in the heart of Jabalya town.

Grandad was small and pot-bellied with a short grey beard, a high domed forehead, deep-set grey-green eyes, fluent English and an oblique sense of humour. Salem was tall, thin, intense and at first rather shy. They led me through a maze of sunless passageways to a warped, unpainted door suited to a slum dwelling. It gave access to a narrow, unroofed corridor from which an outside stone stairway, long and steep, led to the spacious home where Abdel was born in 1947. His parents had married (aged fourteen and eighteen) in 1938, during the war on Zionism. The family was poor ('new poor') and times were hard when so many refugees were driven onto the Strip; Abdel had eleven siblings but six died young. His own nine children were thriving and already he and Mariam had fifteen grandchildren. Mariam was young enough to be my daughter – a bulky woman who can't ever have been beautiful but made up for that by being gracious and quick-witted and radiating a special sort of matronly charm based on contentment. I had to lie to her about my meeting with Aida; it had taken place in the UNRWA school, not in a café.

In two pleasing respects, Abdel was slightly unusual. Although Mariam spoke no English he ensured her full participation in our conversation, translating every word. Also, he was as eager to listen as to talk and seemed genuinely interested in my view of things. Aida had been right about her grandad: he did like foreign writers.

The four of us sat in a wide breezy window embrasure and Abdel drew my attention to the bomb-damaged balcony, its new delicately wrought bars made from scavenged steel rods. 'Gaza is the world's recycling capital!' boasted Abdel. Below us lay an oblong of land, two acres or so, uglified by a central bomb crater but still supporting a few olive, lemon and apricot trees and two bedraggled banana plants. Enclosing this space were several other eighteenth-century three-storey houses, all occupied by members of Abdel's clan. Here I learned two new words – *muwataneen* (a native Gazan) and *mehajera* (a refugee).

On one cousin's roof a yellow Fatah flag fluttered but I soon realised that Abdel's branch of this clan lived above the fray. Another branch, however, stubbornly supported an old plan, no longer much discussed, to transfer at least half of Gaza's *mehajera* population to the West Bank. Some of Jabalya camp stands on clan land, leased to UNRWA. Abdel was firmly pro-*mehajera*. In his view, throughout the Strip, Palestinian disunity had yet again made bad worse. An undeniable truth. In Shatti camp I heard many bitter criticisms of the PA's Oslo-era decision to build a luxury hotel on nearby government land that should have been used to ease Shatti's appalling congestion.

When I arrived an anaemic twenty-year-old (Hoda, Salem's daughter) was wearing a sleeveless blouse and shorts and cuddling the first great-grandchild, an enchanting eight-month-old-girl with a mass of raven curls and hyacinth-blue eyes. Then came a warning shout: two male cousins were arriving. The baby was dumped in Grandma's lap and Hoda hastened away to don a loose, calf-length, printed cotton prayer-gown incorporating a *hijab*, the garment women wear when praying at home (as they mostly do). This comfortable hot-weather attire can no longer be worn out of doors – say the Salafists – because it might blow around, showing too much. Towards noon Salem and the cousins excused themselves: it was prayer time. As they went Abdel smiled at his wife, then said to me, 'Younger folk are more devout than us – or should I say "we"?'

Uncountable small children were all the time darting to and fro, most looking rather anaemic yet none lacking energy. A triple bed, strewn with lavishly embroidered cushions, took up half the floor space and on it a ginger-and-white kitten slept soundly when not being played with, roughly though affectionately, by a six-year-old boy suffering from an eye defect. One lid drooped uncontrollably and Abdel was struggling to get him to an Israeli hospital for corrective treatment. Mariam observed that it was inherited; there were several other cases within the clan. One might have expected this highly educated family to be wary of consanguinity – but no. As Abdel tried to clarify who I was meeting, or was about to meet, he mentioned one cousinly marriage after another. For Aida (the mating she hoped somehow to avoid) a second cousin had been chosen.

Over the next pot of coffee Suzanne joined us, Mariam and Abdel's first-born, the forty-year-old mother of Aida and eight others though her husband had been in a wheelchair (a botched spinal operation) since adolescence. (This couple had been greatly helped, Aida told me at our next meeting, by the al-Wafa workshop on sexuality for patients with spinal injuries.) Suzanne was holding Sawsan by the hand, an eight-year-old daughter, scared-looking and white-faced with elfin features. She had been severely traumatised when the family home was smashed to rubble by one massive bomb. The whole family was sheltering then in an

UNRWA school and none was injured. But the youngest, aged five and a half at the time, had been unhinged by the loss, within moments, of their home and all their possessions including hens, a donkey, a cat. The donkey was always hired out during the ploughing season and those few extra shekels had made what Abdel called 'a Micawberish difference'.

Suzanne angrily compared the international media coverage then being given to the captured Gilad Schalit's five-year imprisonment without visitors and the ignoring of almost 8,000 Palestinians imprisoned without visitors in Israeli jails. (Only one jail is in the OPT, where West Bank relatives can occasionally visit.) Two of Suzanne's brothers-in-law (her husband's sisters' husbands) had been in Israeli jails for more than three years – without a visit. None of their family or friends could get a permit to leave Gaza. During an IDF incursion into Rafah town both had been arrested in their homes, detained for 95 days in an interrogation (torture) centre, then tried and sentenced by military courts but never treated as POWs. The IDF had vandalised several Rafah homes that night, kicking TVs, computers, fridges, ripping upholstery, smashing kitchenware, scattering food all over floors before urinating on it. Throughout the West Bank I had heard many similar stories and in some cases seen the 'morning-after' evidence as families wept over destroyed possessions they couldn't possibly afford to replace.

Abdel said, 'The IDF is a very sick institution. Maybe we shouldn't blame individual kids. They're taken out of the school-room, processed in a dehumanising machine, injected with fear and loathing of Palestinians. I hear people say, in another way *they're* victims.'

Salem, by now back from the mosque, said, 'Maybe all armies do this sort of thing but we notice it more where all are clamped together, in our Holy Land.'

Suzanne, sitting with Sawsan on her knee, was uninhibited about arguing with Father. She, too, spoke excellent English. 'Those kids *choose* to be processed! They could do jail for a month or pay a fine. And the officers who send them out to hunt us and persecute us, they're no kids! And the politicians who reward the officers with big jobs when they retire – are they kids? If they're all sick, they're sick the way Hitler was and no one makes excuses for him!'

At that moment some mischievous local jinn decided to provide the foreign writer with raw material and, as lunch was being served, a very loud thump shook the floor and made everyone jump. (Except me: I don't react to sudden loud noises, which probably means there's something radically wrong with my central nervous system.) Salem hurried to the little annex bathroom, added in the 1950s and jutting over the garden. He couldn't open the door: half the ceiling had collapsed. I recalled then my visit to the cartography department, in Gaza City's labyrinthine municipality building, where I was told that most structures on the Strip, however outwardly unaffected, have in fact been weakened by Cast Lead and are liable to show the strain as time passes.

That thump made poor little Sawsan scream in terror and cling frantically to Suzanne as though she were trying to return to the safety of the womb. When at last she had been soothed, all fourteen of us settled down on the inner room floor to eat from piled communal platters. Then Salem voiced a widely held suspicion – Cast Lead's air attack had been so extreme because the US-donated GBU-39 bombs, weighing 250 pounds and reputed to be 'smart', needed testing in 2008 and were not quite suitable for 'humanitarian interventions' in such places as Kosovo and Libya.

I had long since given up trying to sort out relationships within such extended Palestinian families, a task greatly complicated by generational overlap, given so many early marriages in families of ten and twelve – leading to anomalies like a three-year-old being uncle to a twenty-year old.

Our luncheon party had an unusually high incidence of English speakers: Abdel, Salem, Suzanne and two young men (Mariam's nephews, I think) who were doing 'Teach Yourself English' computer courses and looking forward with determined optimism to the day of their escape from the Strip. Abdel failed to foster their optimism by focusing on the birthrates disparity. 'As a Zionist state, Israel must fade away. It's the dying kick of European colonialism. Zionists still hope they can do like Europeans in North America – demoralise us, drive us into reservations, make us dance for tourists. Or work for slave wages in their friends' business parks.'

Salem intervened. 'Islam protects us – they can't turn Palestinians into alcoholic slaves! We're sure to win, with Allah behind us. That's why we listen when our imams praise many children. Most governments back Israel, our hope's in numbers.'

'Demographics will solve it,' agreed Abdel. 'We'll outbreed them in Israel as well as the Territories. That's why they offer low rents and taxes to bring Diaspora Jews here. Anything to keep numbers up! Those Oldies will soon die but Zionists hope children and grandchildren will visit and think, "This is where we want to live!"' He paused and looked at the two young men. 'Demographics go slowly! For now we must be patient, accepting our destiny.' To which Mariam added, 'Ownership of Palestine has changed many times over the millennia and the Zionists will follow the Crusaders!' (Give me a shekel for every time I've heard that 'Crusader' analogy and I'll be a rich woman.)

When I complimented Abdel on his English he laughed and said, 'I finished my education over there – golden stone, not red brick!' He lamented having almost no access to new publications but now he and Salem were planning to overcome the effect of the blockade through some antics in cyberspace way beyond my comprehension.

My mentioning binationalism brought the reaction I had come to expect in such company: a reluctance seriously to consider it. Zionism's perceived invincibility creates this blockage – *not* Palestine's obduracy in the struggle for independence. My companions had no nationalistic aspirations left; they saw the two-state solution for what it is. They also scorned 'President' Abbas's application for UN recognition of Palestinian statehood, at that date a fresh bone of contention. Abdel wondered, 'How can you have statehood without a state?' This ploy was soon to be exposed by Guy Goodwin-Gill, Senior Research Fellow at All Souls, as a bit of legal/constitutional nonsense. But damaging nonsense, leading the politically naïve Palestinian masses down yet another garden path. We marvelled then at a startling phenomenon: on this 'statehood' issue each of us was completely in agreement with Benjamin Netanyahu, the Obama administration, AIPAC and the Quartet.

'Here's something useful,' said Abdel. 'All this makes for so much public confusion people have to stop pretending there's a Peace Process. With that charade out of the way, maybe there's more space for thinking about binationalism.'

'Or even talking about it', I said. But obviously no one present was an eager proponent of the idea. They all lacked Anwar's missionary zeal, his rare long-distance vision and – most important – his temperamental optimism, the sort that frees the imagination, enabling it to leap into a pragmatically inconceivable future. (M— is in another category, not openly campaigning.)

While escorting me to the *serveece* route Abdel said something he might not have said in Mariam's presence. 'I can't forgive those Salafist kids getting high on rocketry. Two days ago they hit Sderot, firing from open ground near here. Now we all wait for the collective punishment – could be a few shells right through this house!'

*   *   *

At sunset I arrived home to a kitchen floor flooded with red-brown blood. The giant fridge had run out of gas and in the family's deep-freeze section many kilos of ox liver – a precious hoard – had been thawing all day. Poor Nermeen wouldn't risk re-freezing meat in very hot weather and was desolate. It seemed small consolation that the only other hoard – large jars of lemon juice for winter use – could take re-freezing.

While Amal set about cleaning up the mess – an arduous, unpleasant task – her husband Khalil sat cross-legged on the living-room sofa bewailing his boring life. After the pre-dawn prayer he goes for a run and a swim, then is lounging around at home with his computer for the rest of the day, apart from three more visits to the mosque. Keeping in touch with Allah is very important for solving problems. He went to school in Saudi Arabia, then studied at Gaza's al-Azhar University – Saudi universities are reserved for Saudis. Until the Hamas takeover he served as a junior officer in the PA security forces. Despite his seventeen years' residence on the Strip, he has only one real friend, one man he totally trusts – the rest are acquaintances.

Listening to Amal mopping and scrubbing, I felt more and more exasperated. Finally I stood up and said, 'I think Amal could do with some help.' Khalil was shocked. 'No, no! This is not work for guests!' Nastily I snapped, 'But why not work for husbands?' Khalil laughed, seemed in no way discomfited. When I entered the kitchen and firmly took mop in hand he stood by the doorway for a moment, then went downstairs to visit his parents.

Increasingly I regretted not being able to talk with Amal. Whenever I saw Khalil taking off for his run and swim, leaving her to cope with the daily chores in their stifling flat, I wondered how she would fare if ever they emigrated to a European country. She too, I suspected, would like to run and swim. As things were she couldn't even walk around the corner to the bakery and the grocery store, or go to the market; Khalil was happy to see to those chores. He was among the several young men with whom I regularly had circular and occasionally heated arguments.

However, as far as my limited observations went, most young

Gazan women – even postgraduates on the way to their third degree – seemed resigned to their fate and robotically referred me to the Holy Koran, Mohammed, the Sura. Mujamma influences have been around for a long time. In contrast, the covert 'liberated', of both sexes, pleaded with me to write honestly about Palestinian Women's Rights. Here they were echoing some of my Palestinian friends on the West Bank and in Israel who complained about the tendency of foreign pro-Palestinians to fudge this issue – being so conscious of the Zionist propaganda mill. According to one woman professor at Birzeit University, such fudging not only impedes the work of local campaigners but emboldens their Islamist critics abroad who sense the foreigners' hesitation to denounce home-made cruelties as strongly as the IDF's.

Deeb could be very touchy about Women's Rights and the 2009 regulations. These, he tried to persuade me, were merely reinforcing 'family rules and customs'. He became almost angry when I suggested Iranian influences on IUG's ethos. Impossible! There could be no Iranian input because of the religious divide – 'Here *all* are Sunni!' But might not a shared anti-US sentiment bridge that divide? I teased him that before the Battle of Lepanto newly Protestant England backed the Spanish/Venetian/Papal alliance. Yet the most he would concede was a certain Saudi Arabian Wahhabi fervour on the Strip – discouraged by Hamas.

Many consider the grotesquely named 'honour killings' as the most disturbing feature of 'backward' Islamic societies. These are the murders of girls or women who have 'shamed' their menfolk by breaking a rule regulating relations between the sexes. For minor transgressions (like Aida's meeting with her photographer friend) an unmarried woman may be severely beaten and/or imprisoned within the home for an indefinite period. For the ultimate disgrace – pregnancy out of wedlock – death is so socially acceptable a punishment that such killings are not included in crime statistics. On the West Bank, in March 2009, I was reliably informed that during the previous year 32 such murders had been committed within the OPT. And of course not all cases are known; it can happen that a young woman or her baby or both simply disappear. In the Hebron area I heard of two cases of a mother being helped to escape into Israel – despite having no permit – leaving her baby behind with a married sister. In both cases the 'shamed' father sought out and murdered his own grandchild.

This is not hearsay. I met one of the grandfathers (who had three regularly beaten wives) and his eldest son spoke in my presence of the action that 'restored honour' to the family. My interpreter, a friend and PWWSD member, found it hard to believe that Roman Catholic Ireland, until comparatively recently, was scarcely less censorious of illegitimacy. Although the murder of an erring daughter was not condoned, she could expect total rejection by the family. Therefore some panic-stricken women did murder their own babies. The profound shame associated with illegitimacy made possible Ireland's notorious nun-run Magdalen Laundries. Within those institutions, subsidised by both Church and State, hundreds of the most vulnerable unmarried mothers were incarcerated for life – their only 'crime' a teenage pregnancy, their daily labour unpaid.

It cheered and astonished me to learn, from Yara, of Gaza's al-Rahma Association, an ISI founded in 1993 by Dr al-Zahar's brother, Ahmad, and a few of his friends – to care for babies delicately described as 'infants of unknown parentage'. The average intake is one baby per month. Some are brought from a hospital within hours of birth, others are handed in by an anonymous female who is never asked to identify herself, some materialise in the time-honoured way: left on the doorstep in a cardboard carton, wrapped in rags. Al-Rahma at once names the child, then applies to the Ministry of Social Affairs for a birth certificate, the parents' names to be filled in following adoption. This standard certificate gives no indication of the child's parentage being unknown. Al-Rahma keeps a list of dependable potential parents, usually but not always childless couples. Four bureaucratic hoops have to be jumped through before legal custody is established and this can take a few months. Traditionally, the baby is felt to be a family member once suckled by the adoptive mother or a paternal aunt. Thereafter the child cannot marry a 'sibling' and can inherit in accordance with Islamic laws. Children not placed with a family, perhaps because in some way handicapped, remain at al-Rahma to the age of sixteen. All their health and educational needs are cared for and the ISI, acting *in loco parentis*, arranges a suitable marriage.

Equally (or more) remarkable are the ISIs established to look after the wives and children of men who have been executed for collaborating with the IDF. Naturally such families are ostracised and present a much bigger problem, numerically and psychologically, than illegitimate babies. Yara boasted that only in Gaza were associations set up to do everything possible to ease those misfortunates back into their communities by encouraging participation in ISI-sponsored activities – perhaps football for the boys, sewing classes for the girls. Up to the age of sixteen each child receives a monthly allowance of about $30, supplemented if necessary by food rations, clothes and school requirements. If destitute, the families of martyrs, and prisoners held in Israeli jails, are also helped. Many ISIs organise kindergartens for the poorest – often within a mosque; the classes of 40 or so running from 8.00–11.00 am.

Sara Roy begins her enthralling study of Gaza's Islamist social sector by noting the methods used to cripple it. On 23 January 1995 President Clinton's Executive Order 12947 pronounced Hamas to be a 'foreign terrorist entity' and post-9/11 the US Department of Treasury froze the assets of all US-based Muslim charities. Best known was the Holy Land Foundation for Relief and Development (HLF). In September 2001 President George

W. Bush declared: 'Money raised by the HLF is used by Hamas to recruit suicide bombers and to support their families. Our action today is another step in the war on terrorism.'

The story took a turn for the worse when the PA's unelected Prime Minister, Salam Fayyad (formerly employed by the World Bank and the IMF and Washington's favourite Palestinian) supported the calls to blacklist the Strip's largest Islamic charity, al-Salah Association. Its accounts were duly frozen – accounts through which outside donors sent 80 per cent of al-Salah's funding. This blacklisting was devastating as those US donations were desperately needed because of the Israeli and US-led international blockade.

I was in Israel on 24 November 2008 when five HLF leaders were charged in US courts with providing monies 'in support to Hamas and its goal of creating an Islamic Palestinian state by eliminating the State of Israel through violent *jihad*'. None of the five was accused of *directly* funding terrorism but of illegally contributing to Hamas through its social welfare structures. Some of my Israeli friends opined that all five deserved the death penalty. Six months later the HLF CEO, and its Chairman, were each sentenced to 65 years; another worker went down for 20 years, two more for 15 years.

In June 2010 the US Supreme Court ruled against non-violent activism by criminalising any 'material support' to groups labelled 'terrorist' by the US. 'Material support' includes organising demos in support of human rights and the peaceful resolution of conflicts, distributing related literature, advocating discussions with Gaza's democratically elected government and (most heinous of all) 'having direct contact with terrorists'. The Court explained that such activities 'strengthen the image of the group and thereby legitimize it'. David D. Cole, in *Advocacy is not a Gun*, commented: 'For the first time ever, the Supreme Court has ruled that the First Amendment permits the criminalization of pure speech advocating lawful, non-violent activity.'

Sara Roy writes:

Scholars such as myself could be imprisoned for up to fifteen years for conducting research of the kind presented in this book . . . The equation of Islamist social institutions with violence and the belief that the work of these institutions is merely a guise for promoting terrorism . . . remains deeply embedded and uncritically embraced at many levels of American society including the Supreme Court.

Were I to seek another visa to visit the US it would probably be refused. Every day for a month I had 'direct contact with terrorists' and I'm very happy to strengthen Hamas' image when the opportunity arises to do so honestly. This arrogant US insistence on everyone else accepting their definition of a 'terrorist' leaves some foreign NGOs in an anomalous position – wishing to help Gazans with professional detachment but fearing to tread on US corns.

I decided, before leaving the Strip, to pay my respects to Save the Children Fund (SCF), with whom I worked, almost fifty years ago, in a Tibetan refugee camp in Dharamsala. An inconspicuous notice pointed to their spacious house, in a large, shrub-filled garden in affluent Rimal. The security guard who unlocked the street door went out as I came in and because the hall door was obviously unused I descended a slope to the rear, passing the wide windows of several unfurnished rooms. Then, in a small hallway with a bare reception desk, I was greeted effusively but cagily by a tall, slim, forty-ish man, a fluent English-speaker. He said he couldn't give me permission to mention SCF in my book – that would have to come from someone higher up, in London. Rather testily I replied that I live in a free society where authors don't need such 'permissions'. A smiling young woman, standing by the desk, nodded at me approvingly while her boss looked taken aback. He refused to provide any information about SCF's work on the Strip (I had come upon no trace of it) though most NGOs welcome the publicity that may accrue when writers take an interest in their projects. The Director had learned his English with the British Council – long since closed – and he regretted the younger generation's 'Amereng'. (Is this word a Gazan invention? I have heard it nowhere else.) When I asked how the medication crisis impinged on SCF's activities, and if 'Miles of Smiles' was likely to help, he said he knew nothing about that motor convoy, then approaching through Egypt. It would deliver everything to the Ministry of Health and as SCF belonged to the 'international community' it didn't deal with 'this administration'. Plainly the poor fellow was longing for me to stop asking awkward questions and go away. I wanted to talk to the young woman who seemed eager to talk to me. But her boss ruled that out by firmly conducting me to the street. One wonders why SCF hangs in there, when so hampered by deference to US edicts.

At the other end of the scale is Medical Aid for Palestinians (MAP), described by its last President, Chris Patton, as 'a tremendously important charity both because of the huge good that it does on the ground and its role as an advocate of better treatment of Palestinians'. It's a piquant thought that in the eyes of the US Supreme Court that role criminalises this British NGO.

Early one morning Fikr Shaltoot, Director of MAP's Gaza office, came to collect me – bareheaded and driving her own tiny elderly car. At first I assumed her to be one of the Strip's few Christians (I saw only one other Gazan woman driver: Mrs Shabaan). But no: Fikr was born in a refugee camp and schooled by UNRWA before graduating from a US university. She then felt a compulsion to be back with her own people – though on her own terms, hence the bare head and self-driving. She is a small, compact woman, radiating energy, competence and compassion. I took to her at once but unluckily we met on the eve of her departure for England (a fundraising trip) so we could talk only briefly in MAP's simple office which needed no apparent security.

According to Fikr, few Gazans go hungry but most are by now subsisting on a high-carb diet, unable to afford many fruits or vegetables and rarely eating meat. The mothers of young families are notably malnourished: 70 per cent anaemic, says the latest survey. Many share their own rations with growing children and sometimes with working husbands. (As though the mothers of six or nine children are not working!) MAP runs a long-term programme to provide the most needy with vitamin and mineral supplements. As the 'international community' collaborates ever more closely with the US to restrict ISI health services, MAP's input becomes ever more urgently needed. Its teams operate not only throughout the OPT but in the Lebanon's twelve refugee camps where 280,000 Palestinians have no government support and very few rights – a too-often-forgotten consequence of the Nakba. In all, some 425,000 refugees are registered with UNRWA in Lebanon but no Palestinian is allowed to work as a doctor, dentist, lawyer, engineer or accountant.

Islam is relatively flexible about contraception though there's always a vocal minority protesting that condoms and the pill are invitations to promiscuity – 'just look at the West's filthiness!' However, leaving sexual morals aside, this is a politically hazardous area at the centre of a demographic battleground. Some discreetly promoted family planning is possible (four or five children instead of ten or twelve) but the ideal twenty-first-century two-child family is unmentionable. On the West Bank one notices considerable hostility to any foreign NGO suspected of colluding with Israel to lower the Palestinian birthrate. On the Strip those suspicions seem even stronger though the NGOs are fewer.

To me this issue looked not entirely political – 'let's outbreed the Zionists!' Palestinians love children. Of course there have always been dysfunctional families and their numbers are increasing under the multiple strains of Occupation, a problem I consider in my account of the West Bank. That said, even under the most trying

217

conditions, in the grimly congested camps and the semi-destitute villages where farmers can't safely farm, one sees parents and siblings *enjoying* the largeness of their families. On my melancholy last visit to Anwar we discussed this. As my wise old friend saw it, in a society as disrupted, deprived and insecure as the post-Nakba Palestinians', children are the main source of comfort, pride, security and independence. He said, 'People denied all the normal freedoms feel their children protect them against disintegration and guarantee survival – family, clan and communal survival. Within a big household they have a sense of being safe – even though they know they're not, under the Occupation. Am I explaining well? Can you imagine what I'm saying?'

I assured Anwar that I could well imagine it, despite being myself an only child and the mother of an only child. His words expressed the emotions I had intuited while visiting families all over the Strip.

I met Yara for a farewell coffee at the al fresco beach café and we speculated about Hamas' attitude to foreign NGOs. They are, after all, introducing their Gazan clients to certain non-Islamic ways of being, however tactfully they may trim their sails to the prevailing wind. Yara argued that Hamas people who seem cynical about the workings of some foreign NGOs are not being irrationally xenophobic. Immediately after Cast Lead one of Gaza's medical elite was invited to lead a team of expats collecting data on permanently damaged children. Before the survey was emailed to the NGO's European head office, all references to the maiming caused by the US-manufactured white phosphorus shells had been deleted – behind the Gazan doctor's back.

Yara was twitchy that afternoon. According to rumour, another attempt had just been made to assassinate Ismail Haniyeh. Although never confirmed, this rumour served to keep people on edge – and, in some circles, mutually suspicious. Not all Gazans appreciated their Prime Minister's willingness to talk constructively to Fatah and the Zionists and anyone else who might develop a genuine interest in peace with justice. Yara said she was braced for Ismail Haniyeh to be assassinated in the near future. 'Netanyahu is eating his nails with the thought Europe will stop calling him a terrorist and come to meet him!'

I remembered then Noam Chomsky's reference, as Cast Lead was ending, to the Israelis' 'desperate fear of diplomacy'. Days before that attack began Ephraim Halevy, Mossad's Director (rtd.), told the cabinet of Hamas' willingness to accept a two-state solution within the 1967 borders. This must have confirmed the Zionists' belief in Cast Lead as the only sensible way forward. As Norman Finkelstein put it, 'Israel had to fend off the latest threat posed by Palestinian moderation and eliminate Hamas as a legitimate negotiating partner.' In fact, by then, Hamas had missed the two-state bus. Those '67 borders are no longer relevant and, as I said to Yara, the next bus leaves for the Land of Canaan.

On my farewell visit to the unusually resilient town of Beit Hanoun I found Ismail and his family in jubilant mood. The day before, building materials for a communal clinic, sponsored by the Palestine Medical Relief Society and the German Medico International, had begun to get through at the Kerem Shalom crossing. Ismail's three excited little boys invited me onto the donkey-cart and we trotted off to a guarded warehouse gate and there gazed admiringly through the bars at 6 tonnes of iron rods, 40 tons of cement and 117 tonnes of gravel in colossal white plastic containers – as big as some of the rooms in Gaza's camps. Looking at them, I remembered the expensive sacks of gravel coming up the tunnel shafts. How many sacks in 117 tonnes? During the five years since construction materials were last allowed into the Strip, only the relatively rich have been able to build new houses or restore old ones; which is why so many homeless Gazans venture into the buffer zone, risking their lives to collect rubble.

Back at my friends' house (sixteen family members, three small rooms), the boys unharnessed the donkey while Ismail described the ordeals – bureaucratic and security – involved in this movement of basic goods. As an ISI volunteer social worker, he took a professional interest in the new clinic. The project was announced in August 2010 when international reactions to the nine Flotilla murders made Israel feel some minor concessions to Gaza might be politic. The Struggle of the Documents took six months, ending in February 2011. Firstly, four affidavits guaranteeing the clinic's sponsors' authenticity; secondly, a permit to build, though Hamas forms the elected government of Gaza; thirdly, a permit to purchase materials in Ramallah; fourthly, a permit to transport goods from the West Bank to Gaza via Israel. All this required precise coordination between the Ramallah office of the PA's US-appointed Prime Minister, Salam Fayyad, and the UN office for the Coordination of Humanitarian Affairs. And more (*much* more!) coordination is needed between the UN Coordinators and the IDF captains at the Kerem Shalom crossing. Most officers refuse to communicate with the Palestinian representatives of those responsible for taking delivery of the loads and making sure they are used only for the purposes specified. Nor are such representatives allowed into the hyper-secure terminal where loads are transferred from vehicle to vehicle. Here everybody's papers are checked and double-checked by policemen operating computers and mobiles. Ismail said the mass of documents generated itself needs fork-lifting. Moreover, throughout these super-stressful months merchants' invoices and Travel Authority faxes and lawyer's affidavits had a strange way of getting lost so that the process of replacing them had to start again from square one – or even square zero, when there were suggestions that the lost papers had been 'tampered with' or submitted to the wrong office in the first place.

The materials were bought in Ramallah, trucked to the West Bank border at Betunia, then transferred to Palestinian-owned vehicles with Israeli number plates for the short journey to Kerem

Shalom's high-security cargo bay; not until its Israeli gate has been closed does the Gaza gate open. Then the Strip's fork-lift team enter to transfer the loads to Israeli-approved West Bank Palestinian lorries which drive a few hundred yards to another high-security cargo bay – there to unload and reload again onto Gazan lorries hired by the Ramallah firm which sold the materials.

At that point I asked Ismail to repeat himself; I found it hard to credit what he had been telling me. But it was true, I wasn't misunderstanding. This crazed procedure is essential, claim the Israelis, to prevent 'bogus traders selling gravel and cement on the local market' or 'terrorists constructing bunkers to fire rockets into Israel'. We debated the real motive. Ismail's wife (a physics lecturer at IUG) observed that thousands of rockets have been, and may continue to be fired into Israel without bunkers. Very obviously, such a process ensures that an adequate supply of building materials will never get through to the blockaded Strip. So is all this a natural extension of Zionism's long-term plan to break the Palestinians' spirit and drive them, en masse, into exile? Or have the Zionists become paranoid enough really to believe such procedures are essential for their own safety? We concluded, 'It's probably a bit of everything.'

Ismail was not alone in his conviction that the Zionists' addiction to collective punishment is a symptom of collective madness. I heard many other Palestinians making the same diagnosis. He looked back over exactly five years, to the killing of two Israeli soldiers and the capture of another at Kerem Shalom army post. In retaliation, Operation Summer Rain was quickly launched to punish all Gazans. When the Strip's only power plant was attacked, 750,000 people were left without electricity. In two months 240 people were killed, including 48 children. Similarly, the abduction of two Israeli soldiers on the Lebanese border led in 2006 to mass slaughter and the destruction of much of Lebanon's infrastructure. Even were one thinking exclusively of Israel's security, these are totally irrational reactions. They serve only to *inflict suffering*. Ismail said, 'Israelis are sick people, you can see it in their eyes.' His wife added, 'They know their country is not real, can't go on like now, they're in permanent hysteria.' We agreed that the real threat comes from within, from the falsity of the notion of Israel as a 'Jewish and democratic homeland'. Religion-based states are known as theocracies.

During Summer Rain the IDF advised some 20,000 Beit Hanounians to leave their homes as these were likely to be bombed. Ismail was among those who then stood on the roofs of suspected militants' homes to deter the F-16s. This town also covered itself in glory on 3 November 2006 when the IDF cornered several militants in a mosque. Hundreds of women, including Ismail's mother and three sisters, hurried through the streets at sunrise to confront the troops. Two women were killed and dozens injured when the IDF opened fire. In the confusion the militants all escaped, disguised as women. My Fatah friends had told me this story to illustrate how unscrupulously Hamas exploits its faithful followers. Ismail told exactly the same story to illustrate how loyal and courageous are Palestinian militants of both sexes.

As Ismail walked me to the *serveece* route, along narrow alleyways between unstable shacks cobbled together from rubble, he too reflected that the longer the blockade continues, the greater the risk to Israel's security as militant 'wings' grow stronger and angrier and run out of Hamas' control.

Nine

I had come to Gaza with one bag, I was leaving with two; a Gazan
friend living in Ireland and unable to return to the Strip needed
garments from home. On arrival my bag had been full of gifts for
Gazans, now it was full of gifts from Gazans; even the blockade
cannot cancel out Palestinian generosity. Saying goodbye was easier
here than on the West Bank; if the Gate remains open I can revisit
the Strip. But the Israelis have blacklisted those who signed on for
Freedom Flotilla II – which means exclusion from the West Bank
for at least ten years and by 2021 I'm likely to be either dead or
dotty.

Several friends wished to help me through the Gate, then discovered that only travellers are allowed into Rafah's departure zone.
This let me off a hook; otherwise, how to choose which friend(s)?
And how to prevent a potentially awkward Fatah/Hamas convergence?

When I asked kind Deeb to ring Abdallah in Cairo I thought I
was countering my overoptimistic nature by giving 11.00 am as
our meeting time. I would surely be in Egypt long before then;
leaving the Strip, Deeb had assured me, is much simpler than
entering.

At the Shifa *serveece* terminal I paused to say goodbye to two of
the dozen donkeys who arrive there early every morning, drawing
loads of vegetables, fruits, eggs; their flat carts serve as stalls. I
pitied them as they stood all day fully exposed to the sun, never
unharnessed because where could they be tethered? With two I
had a special relationship; their heads rose when I called from a
distance and they enjoyed between-the-ear massages. These social
occasions greatly entertained the *serveece* drivers.

223

By 7.50 I was outside Rafah's Departure Hall. On the way to the Gate everybody must pass through this building which, from outside, rather resembles a cattle-shed on a Soviet collective farm. I dragged my bags up its steep steps, then decided to linger briefly, observing the scene. Most of the 400 or so would-be-travellers seemed to have spent the night *in situ* and there was a querulous undertone to their noisiness. I could see only one free chair, beside an old man wearing the flowing white robes and traditional turban of a pilgrim to Mecca. At the far end of this high, well-lit hall a counter separates officialdom from its prey. Here Gazans who have registered a departure date with the Department of Transport (at least a month before) must present their papers. Behind the counter three doors lead to inner layers of bureaucracy. Proceedings are scheduled to begin at 8.00 am but not until 8.15 did seven men saunter into view, being greeted by angry shouts. Three were neatly uniformed youngsters (their uniforms anonymous), four were slightly older policemen. Despite the restless and increasingly vocal crowd they didn't at once start work but spent the next twenty minutes chatting, joking, smoking, drinking tea, texting – all the time wandering in and out of those doors. Within this traveller, irritation and impatience were already beginning to accumulate – not yet on my own behalf but because Gazans suffer enough at the hands of the Israelis without also being tormented by their own.

When at last the three youngsters went on duty a crowd surged towards the counter and the police maintained order – more or less – while papers were being sent to an inner office in fat bundles. As these reappeared, a distorting public address system summoned the lucky owners. I couldn't possibly have heard 'Dervla Murphy', as pronounced by a Palestinian, above the din of an excited, frustrated, argumentative crowd – always four or five people standing by the counter, angrily disputing an official verdict. Luckily, as an International, I didn't have to jump through this hoop; Deeb had

instructed me to deal with the office (a converted container) by
Gate 1.

I showed my passport to two policemen, indicating that I must
leave the Hall – whereupon they shouted at me truculently, as
though I were trying to jump the queue. They and all their
colleagues were obviously ignorant of the rules as Deeb had
explained them. I must stay in the Hall until my passport had
been checked, though no one here was authorised to check it. Our
confrontation attracted some attention and now another robed
and turbaned pilgrim, an English-speaker, reprimanded the police.
They argued on, glaring at me with unearned animosity, until my
rescuer shouted at them, his tone contemptuous. He then carried
my bags down the steps and pointed across an already hot expanse
of desert to the distant Gate.

As I hauled my bags through deep sand, with some difficulty, an
agreeable young Egyptian offered assistance and advice. His badge
identified him as a Haj guide, free to operate on both sides of the
gates. I must sit in the café near the office and be patient. When all
the day's pilgrims had got through, the Egyptian border control
would signal their readiness to deal with Internationals. Then someone would lead me through the Gate, after my passport had been
processed by the office staff. I didn't like that word 'processed'; it
suggested a procedure much more long-drawn-out than 'stamped'.

The crowded 'café' – a patch of fine, pale gold sand under a
canvas awning – was furnished with scores of low plastic tables and
chairs and provisioned by two barrows selling chai, coffee, Nescafé-
with-tinned-milk, juices, water and sundry vile comestibles. Thirty
yards away rose Gate 1, wide and high; beyond, visible between its
bars, lay that odd no man's land instituted by EUBAM. Beside the
Gate, agitated people clustered around the Office, jostling for
a turn on the high step; below it one could not see or have a
reasonable exchange with those within.

As I looked around for a seat Dalia caught my eye and beckoned me to usurp her ten-year-old daughter's chair. Fairuz sat happily on mamma's lap and told me she wanted to learn a lot more English. Her twenty-year-old sister held a sleeping baby, the first grandchild. At the next table, talking to male friends, sat father and one of four teenage sons. In public even the most united Gazan families tend to segregate themselves.

The Zeidans were beginning their fourth day of waiting; on the previous Thursday, Wednesday and Tuesday they had sat in this café from 8.00 am to 6.00 pm. They were on their way to Ismailia to spend a month with Dalia's sister from whom they had been cut off for six years. Fairuz (who had transferred to my lap the better to learn English) now announced that this would be her last waiting day. Noticeably, none of the many children in this misfortunate crowd had the standard (for us) supply of books, games and art materials. Yet most seemed cheerfully resigned to their Rafah experience: evidently they had inner resources undeveloped by our over-entertained young.

I then discovered that Gazans, having been processed in the Hall, had to be reprocessesed here. 'Why?' I asked. Dalia shrugged and smiled and offered no explanation. But she urged me to present my passport at the Office without delay, not to wait as the young Haj guide had advised. 'If there's trouble,' said she, 'it's good to know sooner.'

I looked at my watch: 10.40 – almost time for Abdallah to be parking outside Gate 2. Anxiety set in as I joined the crowd around the small barred window through which documents were pushed to and fro. Only one at a time could stand on the little step and queuing didn't feature. Briefly I hesitated on the edge of the crowd: someone might take pity on the aged International. Over-optimism in action . . . Entering the fray, I elbowed my way onto the step with Arabic imprecations assaulting my ears. Momentarily the Office was empty; it contained two easy chairs with torn upholstery, one badly dented metal filing cabinet (*c.*1950), and one landline phone (*c.*1960) on a small table. Until the power went off a mobile fan whirred in a corner.

The three officials returned together: Ali and his assistants, none uniformed. Ali was small, slight, thirty-ish, with a short beard, heavy brows, thin lips, a narrow face, hard eyes – a man who might not find 'honour killing' too difficult. Without greeting me he added my passport to a pile, then took another pile for the consideration of some more important official in a sprawling building overlooking no man's land. One of his mates barked at me, gesturing eloquently – 'Off the step!' I compromised, moving down and to one side while clinging to a window bar. Having handed over my passport, I was reluctant to lose sight of those in charge. Now I was being severely heat-punished; it was near noon in mid-summer at sea level and only the café offered shade.

One man was always on the move, taking papers and passports to and from that distant office. Meanwhile the Gate was being repeatedly opened for departing vehicles, usually Mecca-bound coaches towing enormous UN-blue trailers piled high. Another man made many phone calls, sometimes speaking simultaneously to his mobile and the landline. In between, he filled in countless forms, using a dainty, tiny Arabic script that ill-matched his hairy thick-fingered hands. Only Ali – I noticed later – made entries in a stout leather-bound ledger, perhaps a Mandate left-over.

I was obsessively watching the time. When Ali returned after 18 minutes I begged him to attend next to my passport. He spoke no English but Dalia had despatched her son, Tarek, to interpret. Ali scrutinised my document closely, scowling while turning the pages as though they were smeared with shit – which to him they were, showing all those Ben-Gurion entry stamps. When challenged, I pointed out that one can't study the Palestinians' problems without entering Israel. Peevishly he demanded, 'Why interested in Palestinians?' I told him, but afterwards Tarek and I agreed that the idea of 'writing a book' was not within his grasp.

Returning my passport, Ali stated flatly that I could not leave on 2 July. Because of those Israeli stamps I must go back to Gaza City and get a special permit for Tuesday 5 July. At first I didn't take this seriously, merely felt exasperated by his stupidity. I emphasised that two weeks previously a Department of Foreign Affairs VIP (named) had personally registered me for this 2 July crossing. 'But where is your registration document?' demanded Ali. 'This you must have, talk about registration is not enough!'

Mr S— had assured me that I needed no written permit once registered on his computer. Feeling presciently uneasy about this, I had twice repeated my request for 'a piece of paper' – only to be told, 'There's no need to make a problem, you're in the computer.' Slightly irritably I'd replied, 'I'm not making a problem, I'm trying to avoid one' – and now I was trapped by officials who did not yet live in cyberspace.

I then played my trump – Mr S—'s card, giving his office and personal mobile numbers. My instruction was to ring him should a problem arise – the problem he had guaranteed I wouldn't have . . . 'Ring Mr S—!' I said. 'He'll confirm that *he* registered my 2 July crossing. You can talk to him personally, then you can listen to me talking to him.' Not all trumps are winning cards. As Ali rejected this suggestion, Tarek and I could see how much he was enjoying having the bit between his teeth.

It was now 12.25. I asked Tarek to look for the Haj guide, who should be able to get an apologetic message to Abdallah; but he had gone off duty and not yet been replaced. Then I remembered how easily Deeb, working out of Foreign Affairs, had got through to Cairo. Within moments Tarek got through to Deeb who tried hard, but unsuccessfully, to contact Abdallah. Back at the café, Dalia said soothingly, 'Don't worry about him, we're in the Middle East, he's used to waiting!' On such occasions my punctuality gene can cause needless tension.

All the Zeidans now rallied around. On cell phone lines most

Palestinians are baffled by my Irish brogue so Mr Zeidan called Mr S——, who was immediately available, to everyone's surprise. The message for Dervla was, 'Give me five minutes, then go back to the office.' I took the 'five minutes' to be hyperbolic – a face-saving device of sorts – and for half an hour tried to relax. In similar situations elsewhere, a bribe-hunt might be assumed. Not here, I was warned – not in Hamas territory. Certainly at Gate 2, in Egypt, and perhaps in PA-run Ramallah – but never under that little green Hamas flag.

We scoffed at the nonsense of Arab countries rejecting Israeli-stamped passports, another example of State hypocrisy since so few Arab governments have ever genuinely tried to help Palestinians. Their cause is used only as a stick to beat Israel when that suits a particular government during a particular crisis.

The Zeidans had reason to hope their time was nigh so we sat close to the Office and swapped Rafah Gate tear-jerkers. At Anwar's house I had met a man in a despairing rage. His brother was to visit Cairo briefly toward the end of June, coming from Australia. He couldn't enter Gaza because of the permit time-lag. These brothers hadn't met for seven years but on 10 June Anwar's friend was told he couldn't leave the Strip before 12 August.

With clear-cut ten-year-old logic Fairuz wondered why not employ more officials at both sides of the border? Her brother voiced a majority opinion: the US was leaning on Egypt to keep pressure on the Gazans even while taking credit for opening the Gate. But who, really, was mostly to blame? I couldn't have a view on this, being ignorant of Gazan domestic politics and how things were being reshaped (or not?) in the new Egypt. Yet I was very aware by then of the huge significance of Rafah in all the games being played by everyone.

Suddenly shouts of 'Zeidan! Zeidan!' came from different directions and four adolescent porters converged on my friends as they scrambled hither and thither gathering items of luggage. As one side of the Gate slid back they shouted over their shoulders, 'Good luck!' I rejoiced for them while mourning the loss of my interpreter.

Rumour had it that 503 travellers were on the Egyptians' 2 July list. Perhaps a number with some arcane Pharaonic significance, an al-Azhar (Gaza) professor facetiously suggested. Seeing me bereft of the Zeidans, he had approached to offer tea and sympathy – and practical support, when it was time to confront Ali again. The crowd around the Office had shrunk but my new friend Walid seemed to find its noisiness and latent aggression rather dismaying. It seemed he didn't often leave his ivory tower.

I forced my way onto the step, passing two old women in tears; one had been verbally abused by Ali's thickset mate who thrust her rejected documents at her so roughly she almost fell backwards. When I replaced her at the window Ali enjoyed telling me that Mr S—'s intervention had failed. But now there was a different story; I must return to Gaza City because the Egyptians had cancelled all non-pilgrim 2 July crossings. Walid translated, 'Last Thursday we had a closure and all that list must cross today. Only that list. No one else.'

As my passport was returned, panic loomed. A postponed crossing would involve considerable financial loss. The faithful Abdallah must somehow be paid later on. My Cairo–London flight was booked for Monday 4 July and would be forfeited. On Tuesday 5 July I had a three-hour appointment with an expensive London dentist who imposes a hefty penalty if not given two working days' notice before a broken appointment – and my mobile couldn't reach London and anyway it was Saturday . . . I didn't burden Walid with these sordid details but he recognised my near-panic and advised, 'Ring your Mr S— again. If he contacts the Egyptians, you might get an exception order.' I handed Walid my phone but by then Mr S—'s was switched off and the Department had closed.

Back at the café, I admitted defeat and was about to leave when a spotty youth came hurrying from the Office and said, 'Sit down, please! Sit down and wait!' When Walid questioned him he merely repeated in Arabic, 'Sit down.' Walid himself, having been thwarted by the Thursday closure, would probably get through before Gate 2 closed at 6.00 pm. He then explained why, in his estimation, Mr S . . . being out of reach didn't really matter. It seems my trump card was a dud, and could even be counterproductive. Gate 1's International sufferers might be victims of Department of Transport versus Department of Foreign Affairs faction fighting. Gate 1's staff were Department of Transport employees, described by Walid as a disheartening example of Hamas' stupid, uneducated, fanatical element, the sort of people who shouldn't be given control of a wheelbarrow never mind a hypersensitive international border – a crossing which affects so many Gazans' welfare on so many levels: emotional, medical, educational, economic. Those two departments employed different sorts of people – or so Walid alleged – and as the cake was being cut Transport perceived Foreign Affairs seizing an unfair share. And of course there were clan issues, into which Walid preferred not to go.

As we spoke the Gate slid open to release another Mecca-bound coach. That was the twelfth since my arrival and each carried 54 pilgrims to be processed individually by the Egyptians. Only three Internationals were listed for 2 July so it seemed perverse – in fact downright malicious – to compel us to wait all day though we had arrived before most of the pilgrims. I asked myself, 'Do certain anti-Western officials enjoy punishing us for our past collective crimes? Is it our turn to be dominated, discriminated against, humiliated if possible?' That would be unfair yet understandable. And in everyday life, away from Gaza's place of torment, most Palestinians and Egyptians do treat one courteously and kindly.

At 1.40 pm Walid was called and a few minutes later the other Internationals appeared – striking figures in Gaza, so tall and fair.

Gunnar and Jan were from Sweden and the former, having spent 23 years in the OPT, spoke fluent Arabic. He wasn't even slightly surprised by what I now thought of as a crisis. Together we advanced on the Office where Gunnar stood at the window, flanked by Jan and myself, and made a long speech while presenting our passports to Ali. My spirits rose; by some means I couldn't divine, these Swedes were exercising a benign influence. For a silent moment Ali stared at Gunnar, his thin lips compressed, his jaw rigid with animosity. Then he picked up our passports and took them into no man's land. When I quietly clapped my hands Gunnar cautioned, 'Don't be too joyful, we still have a long way to go!'

For the next 25 minutes we stood close to the step, in the full glare of the sun, watching Ali's mates being nasty to a succession of distressed Gazans.

Then Ali returned our passports and freed us. I felt quite weak with relief as the Gate slid open, just for us, and we hurried towards the minivan link to the EUBAM buildings where a new set of procedures awaited us – this time computerised.

A dozen or so other non-Palestinians (Egyptian and Emirate citizens) were waiting amidst many rows of orange metal chairs facing six computer booths manned by three PA officials. These were polite and smartly uniformed but not at ease with our passports. As they stood arguing about them, passing them from hand to hand, Gunnar recalled being present in November 2005 when Israel formally handed over Rafah crossing to the PA, to be run in harness with Egypt and EUBAM monitors. The PA were allowed to admit only registered Gazans – no other Palestinians, no foreigners. Then in June 2007 Israel ordered total closure.

A tingle of alarm ran through me when the uniformed men returned our passports unprocessed. Looking apologetic, they explained: a new message had come from Gate 2 – only pilgrims could cross that afternoon, all others must return to Gaza City and register for an alternative date. Now near-panic threatened the Swedes, they who had seemed so in control at Gate 1. Gunnar pleaded with the most-braided official: he and Jan were booked to fly from Cairo at noon on the morrow. All three officials expressed sympathy and looked genuinely concerned but had no pull with their counterparts at Gate 2. Jan then rang the Swedes' liaison officer in Gaza City and sought for pressure to be put on the Egyptians by the PA interim administration in Ramallah. I said nothing; I'm good at playing the role of insignificant female.

We moved to the air-conditioned 'Waiting Lounge', a very long, bright room smelling strongly of EU taxpayers' money with facilities for praying and purdah, soft golden-brown armchairs and sofas, glass and wrought-iron coffee tables, several TV sets and walls hung with anaemic watercolours of European beauty spots and (decorous) Picasso prints. The contrast between this space and Gate 1's 'café' had a disturbing political symbolism.

And there sat Walid, also stymied. He looked aggrieved rather than angry and remarked, when I joined him, that our uniformed friends represented the internationally recognised though unelected Palestinian government. Therefore they were natural enemies of the Gate 1 contingent, adding another faction fight to the Rafah equation. In mid-sentence he broke off with a startled exclamation. 'It's you!' – he pointed to the nearest TV set, showing a publicity video for Freedom Flotilla II. In Dublin, on the eve of my departure for Gaza, I had joined the MV *Saoirse* activists for the making of this video and now I was exhorting viewers to 'Stay human! Stay human!' – Vik's trademark phrase, adopted by the Flotilla as its slogan. I detest TV and in my already hyper-stressed state this was too much: a feeling of total unreality overcame me momentarily. But I had to adjust to stardom: that video was replayed every ten minutes during the next hour.

When the liaison officer reported that Ramallah couldn't help I suggested ringing our ambassadors in Cairo but on a Saturday afternoon neither was within reach. Later I discovered that they are friends who may have been sharing a weekend outing as we stood biting our nails at the Gate.

We were looking at one another – who would first admit defeat and summon a taxi? – when hope was rekindled. A notably tall and handsome young PA official, in civvies, had been contacted by Ramallah and *might* be able to get an Egyptian 'exception order' as we were only three Internationals.

The next half-hour was the worst. I paced the room, thinking of the emergency emails I'd have to try to send from Gaza City – if the electricity allowed computers to function. And how to pay Abdallah? Someone could take a verbal message but wouldn't it be daft to give dollar notes to a total stranger? By then the sheer insanity of the day's events had switched off my optimism.

Walid halted my pacing with the good news. Somehow he knew, before our saviour returned, that the exception order had been granted – of course only for Internationals. This made the Swedes and me feel bad but Walid reminded us, 'Gazans don't expect life to be easy. We'll all sleep on these sofas and tomorrow go on waiting.'

As the exception order was handed to the passport officers we chorused our thanks in our best Arabic – though come to think of it, this was scarcely an occasion for gratitude. We should have been dealt with at 8.30 before the pilgrim flow began. Or was Hamas to blame for not letting us through? Impossible to know and anyway it didn't matter now . . .

My passport was first to be stamped and I rushed to the exit; it was 4.20 and Abdallah had been waiting for more than five hours. Outside the door three policemen stopped me – I must return to the Waiting Lounge and 'Sit down please'. Angrily I protested that I had been sitting in that lounge for more than two hours and at Rafah for six and a half hours and my passport had been through two procedures and now I wanted to get into Egypt fast! I was misbehaving – shouting in English at men who understood hardly a word of the language and were not personally to blame for anything, apart from their own aggressive attitudes. Then two of them made to grab my bags and that cowed me into returning – to find myself being upbraided for trying to evade a departure tax of which I knew nothing. In my rush I hadn't seen a small notice beside a closed kiosk – 'Exit Tax: 60 NIS'. Gunnar and Jan beckoned me: we had to wait for the kiosk to open. And then we had to wait for the minivan that would take us to Travel House, the Egyptian processing plant.

'Sit down, please!' Gunnar teased me, patting the metal chair beside his. I didn't see the joke; my sense of humour was in abeyance. 'Let's walk,' I suggested. 'It's a five-minute drive away and none of us has much luggage.' Gunnar shook his head. 'Walking is very forbidden – sit down please and wait!'

Ten minutes later the tax-kiosk clerk came dawdling along, chatting to a friend. Our 60 NIS earned a glossy receipt for US$15, paid to the Ministry of Finance, Palestinian National Authority. The opening of the Rafah Gate could not be allowed to benefit a 'terrorist' organisation.

We returned to our seats, having been assured the minibus was 'on its way', and I wondered what my companions made of all these convolutions. It would have been tactless to ask; INGO workers have to be circumspect in conversation with writers. Then, telepathically, Jan commented that at present chaos was inevitable. Rafah had opened on 28 May, soon after Egypt's announcement that it would open – which gave no one enough time to get their act together.

For admission to Egypt, Gazans had to be PA-vetted; but they couldn't get past Gate 1 to the PA checkpoint without registering their exit date on a Hamas list back in Gaza City. We noted a sad irony in two of the statements made by Egypt's Foreign Minister, Nabil Elarby. He had given his own spin to Rafah's reopening –

'to end the Palestinian division and achieve national reconciliation'. But he also explained – 'rules in effect before the closure shall be reinstated'. Those two statements couldn't jell. Egypt was still deciding how many might cross each day and the nightmare hours (or days) people spent at Gate 1 were a result of a Hamas muscle-flexing exercise. Their supporters undoubtedly got preference on the 'exit date' register and because they controlled this they were, in effect, empowered to imprison Palestinians on the Strip. Yet no marks had been made on our passports by the 'Ali's Office' faction who were physically able to block individuals' movements. Moreover, though they could prevent people from crossing, their allowing someone through was no guarantee that the PA would do likewise. Or that Egypt would admit them: every day scores were being 'returned' from Travel House.

By now Walid and his fellow-rejects had settled down in the Waiting Lounge and we were on our own in the computer hall. Eventually even Gunnar reckoned it was time to stop adapting to the Middle East. He went exploring, in search of our vehicle – only to find that it had been and gone, its driver having failed to find us in the lounge. A uniformed PA man led him back to us and said, 'Sit down please and wait. Soon the car will come again.'

Twelve minutes later a limousine picked us up and as the driver was about to start, three young men gathered around his door, leaning on the bonnet, demanding a lift to Gate 2. They all spoke together and as the argument lengthened we protested, quite vigorously. 'No problem,' said the driver, 'wait five minutes' – at which point I again misbehaved, thumping my fist on the window beside me, not caring at that moment if I broke it. The driver then took fright and accelerated hard, leaving the young men shouting furiously and waving their fists. We sped under the 'Welcome to Palestine' archway, then crawled through three checkpoints where Egyptian soldiers in crumpled uniforms spent time fumbling with our passports and examining our departure tax receipts as though they were likely to be forged.

Since my arrival there had been a development in the long, wide corridor leading to the Travel House concourse. Four mobile booths displayed hand-written bilingual notices – 'Government of Egypt Customs'. Each was equipped with a luggage weighing-scales and two cheerful, friendly customs officers over-keen to justify their existence. They opened and examined every item of everybody's baggage. At one stage I caught Gunnar looking at me rather anxiously, perhaps fearing the enraged old lady would have a stroke and die on the spot.

Hundreds of obviously stressed-out travellers thronged the vast passport control concourse where our final ordeal was a currency crisis. Passports cannot be stamped before the departure tax is paid and only Egyptian pounds (of which we had none) are acceptable and the bank in the corner was firmly locked. It was now 5.20 and a policeman told us it wouldn't open until the morrow. But for the Swedes, I might have spent that night in Travel House. Gunnar disappeared for some ten minutes and returned with a bank clerk. But then our passports had to be taken upstairs and it was 6.40 before I was free to half-run to Gate 2 where I could see Abdallah frantically waving, wreathed in smiles. He was accompanied by his charming eldest son because he had expected quite a long delay . . .

Epilogue

In mid-June we had heard that Freedom Flotilla II hoped soon to be on the high seas. At the end of the month my ISM friend Tom flew from Cairo to join the US vessel, *Audacity of Hope*. Perhaps she was inauspiciously named; yet again the sailor activists were thwarted. Greece and Cyprus had given in to US bullying and saboteurs crippled the Swedish *Juliano* and the Irish MV *Saoirse*.

Working fast, the Flotilla's international supporters (a group whimsically known as 'the Flytilla') proposed a 9 July protest meeting in Bethlehem to publicise the bullying and sabotaging and to challenge Israel's tightening restrictions on foreigners' entry to the West Bank. Meanwhile, Ruth Zakh of the Israeli embassy in Dublin had provided a classic example of the Zionists' much used smear technique. She accused Freedom Flotilla I, which lost nine activists to the IDF, of being 'associated with IHH, an Istanbul-based terrorist organization'. IHH is a Turkish ISI, legally registered as a charity and an energetic advocate of non-violent movements.

I had just arrived home when the *Irish Times* reported an unprecedented Israeli reaction to the 'Flytilla'. Certain European airlines had been given a list of 342 'suspected activists' who would be denied visas at Ben-Gurion airport – the carriers to foot the bill for any passengers on one-way tickets. As a result (according to a smug Israeli police spokesperson), more than 200 people holding tickets for Tel Aviv were not allowed to board their flights. (Perhaps the airlines feared Mossad saboteurs.) Two US women who arrived in the small hours of 8 July were deported instantly, followed later that day by 65 others, from France, Switzerland and Germany. More than one hundred from a variety of countries (including a middle-aged Irishwoman named Dee Murphy: no relation) refused to sign deportation papers and were held for a week in Ben-Gurion's 'detention facility'. Netanyahu denounced them all as 'provocateurs who would reinforce Palestinian pro-Flotilla rallies'. My good Beit Sahour friend, Mazin Qumsiyeh, Professor of Genetics at Yale, noted that this crackdown confirmed the Flotilla movement's effectiveness. He was well satisfied with the publicity given to Israel's gangster-like interference with the legitimate operations of international airlines.

Four months later the MV *Saoirse* – carrying no aid cargo, only passengers – sailed from the Turkish port of Fethiye accompanied by the Canadian *al-Tahrir*. Some 50 nautical miles from Gaza's coast both vessels were boarded by Israel's piratical sailors; they had not entered, and were not planning to enter, Israeli territorial waters. The fourteen Irish citizens were detained for a week before being deported. I have signed on for Freedom Flotilla III.

Middle East Conflict Timeline

1897 First Zionist Congress in Switzerland establishes the World Zionist Organisation to secure a 'home for the Jewish people in Palestine', in response to European, and particularly Russian, anti-Semitism.

1917 Balfour Declaration. In a letter to Lord Rothschild, Britain's Foreign Secretary, Lord Arthur Balfour, announces his 'government's support for the establishment of 'a Jewish national home in Palestine'. The British also make a potentially contradictory promise of independence for an Arab nation covering most of the Arab Middle East in exchange for Arab support against the Ottomans.

1920–48 Mandatory Palestine. In the aftermath of World War I, Britain is awarded a legal commission to administer Palestine, confirmed by League of Nations. Arab discontent with British rule and increasing Jewish immigration leads to clashes between all parties.

1939–45 Some six million Jews are murdered in the Holocaust by Nazi Germany. Hundreds of thousands of Jews are displaced, fleeing Nazi persecution.

1947 Britain announces that she will withdraw from Palestine in 1948 and hands over responsibility to the UN. The UN passes Resolution 181, which recommends dividing the territory into separate Jewish and Palestinian states and is accepted by the Jewish Agency but rejected by the Arab Higher Committee. The plan was never implemented, overtaken by civil war on the ground.

May 1948 The State of Israel is proclaimed in Tel Aviv. British troops withdraw and Palestinians face al-Nakba, the Catastrophe. In a fiercely fought battle for territory, by the end of the year Israel occupies some 75% of what had been the British Mandate. Almost three quarters of a million Palestinian are forced from their homes and settle in refugee camps in Jordan, Gaza, Syria, Lebanon.

1949–67 Gaza is ruled by Egypt, initially under the auspices of the All Palestine Government.

June 1967 During The Six Day War, known as an-Naksah (The Setback) to the Palestinians, Israel doubles its land-holding, taking Gaza and the Sinai peninsula from Egypt, the West Bank and East Jerusalem from Jordan and the Golan Heights from Syria.

1973 Yom Kippur War. To try to regain territory lost in 1967, Egypt and Syria launch attacks against Israel on the festival of Yom Kippur. Three weeks later Israel has reversed all her initial losses.

September 1978 Egypt and Israel sign Camp David accords, leading to the return of the Sinai Peninsula to Egypt in 1982.

1987–93 First Intifada. The Palestinian uprising against the Israeli occupation of Palestinian territory consists largely of non-violent resistance.

1993 Oslo Accords. During secret talks in Norway, the Palestinians recognise Israel's right to exist within her pre-1967 borders, and Israel agrees to gradually cede control of the Palestinian territories to the Palestinians. Yitzhak Rabin and Yasser Arafat shake hands on the White House lawn after signing the Declaration of Principles, but the most difficult issues, such as the status of Jerusalem, and the right of return of Palestinian refugees, are undecided. These prove impossible to resolve in the suggested five-year timeframe.

July 2000 Camp David Peace Summit. In the seven years since the Oslo accords, continued Palestinian suicide bombings and the expansion of Israeli settlements in the West Bank and Gaza undermine the peace process. This attempt to address outstanding issues, initiated by President Clinton, is unable to break the deadlock.

2000–05 The Second Intifada is characterised by an intensification of suicide bombings by Palestinians in Israel, and of targeted Israeli assassinations of Palestinian militants, as well as Israeli air strikes and incursions into Palestinian areas of self-rule. Israel begins to build a wall dividing the West Bank.

2005 Israeli withdraws troops and settlers from Gaza.

January 2006 Hamas, an Islamist party whose charter then denied Israel's right to exist, wins a majority in the Palestinian parliamentary elections and forms a government, but Israel, the US and the EU refuse to negotiate with it.

March 2007 Hamas and Fatah form a national unity government, headed by Hamas' Ismail Haniya. Israel still refuses to negotiate, calling Hamas a terrorist organisation. Behind the scenes, Israel, Egypt and the US conspire with Fatah to isolate, weaken and topple Hamas.

June 2007 Battle of Gaza. As trust between Hamas and Fatah breaks down, Hamas seizes power in Gaza, ousting Fatah officials.

2007 Blockade of Gaza. Israel and Egypt seal most border crossings. Israel maintains that this is to prevent Hamas obtaining weapons with which to attack Israel. Egypt maintains that recognizing Hamas by opening the border would undermine the Palestinian National Authority and drive a permanent wedge between the Palestinian factions.

December 2008–January 2009 Gaza War. The Israel Defence Forces' Operation Cast Lead begins on December 27th, ostensibly to stop rocket fire into Israel. A ceasefire was agreed on January 18th, after the death of at least 1300 Palestinians and 13 Israelis, four of the latter from friendly fire. The UN Goldstone Report, released in September 2009, accuses both sides of war crimes.

May 31st 2010 Israeli commandos board ships of the Gaza Freedom Flotilla in international waters, killing nine passengers, some at point blank range. The boats are attempting to deliver aid and building materials through the blockade.

June 2010 International pressure forces Israel to lessen the restrictions on importing goods into Gaza, but a 2011 UN Office for the Coordination of Humanitarian Affairs assessment concluded that this had not resulted in a significant improvement in people's livelihoods in Gaza.

May 28th 2011 The Rafah Gate reopens in the wake of the overthrow of Mubarak in Egypt.

Glossary

al-Qassam   the military wing of Hamas, created in 1992

al-Shatat   Palestinians living outside Israel and the OPT

Dayton Brigade
                US-trained Palestinian forces operating on the West Bank

Eretz Israel   all the territory of Ottoman Palestine (Greater Israel)

Galabiya (Ar.) a loose, collarless floor-length robe worn by men and originating in Egypt

Goldstone Enquiry
                Commission set up by the UN to investigate Israeli and Palestinian war crimes during Operation Cast Lead

Gush Emunim a political movement, no longer officially in existence, committed to establishing Jewish settlements in the West Bank, Gaza and the Golan Heights

Hasbara (Heb.) propaganda

Hijab (Ar.)   a headscarf worn in front of men and in public to cover a woman's hair

International   a foreigner (usually an unpaid volunteer) living in the Occupied Palestinian Territories (OPT) and supporting Palestinians in various non-violent ways

Intifada   a period of intensified Palestinian struggle against occupation. The First Intifada ran between 1987–93, the Second from 2000–5

Islamic Jihad   a small Palestinian armed organisation, formed in 1979 to fight for the sovereignty of Palestine and freedom from Israel

Jilbab (Ar.)	an ankle-length, long-sleeved overgarment worn by women
Mizrahi	a Jew whose family migrated to Israel from an Arab country
Nakba	the 1947–8 uprooting of the Palestinians from their homeland
Naksa Day	anniversary of Israel's seizure, in June 1967, of the West Bank from Jordan, the Sinai from Egypt and the Golan Heights from Syria.
Olga Appeal	call for political reform issued by a gathering of Israeli scholars and activists in 2004
Oslo Accords	Agreements signed in 1993 and 1995 between the PLO and Israel
Salafist	Muslims who emphasise their rigid adherence to seventh-century Islam
Samoud (Ar.)	fortitude (sometimes defined as a mix of courage, obstinacy and pride)
Tánaiste	Irish deputy prime minister
Thobe (Ar.)	an ankle-length robe with small collar, worn by men and originating in Arabia

Abbreviations

ADL	Anti-Defamation League
AIPAC	American Israel Public Affairs Committee
AMA	Access and Movement Arrangement
BDS	Boycott, Divestment and Sanctions campaign
EUBAM	European Union Border Assistance Mission
HLF	Holy Land Foundation
ICRC	International Committee of the Red Cross
IDF	Israel Defence Forces
IEM	Inborn Error of Metabolism
ISI	Islamic Social Institutions
ISM	International Support Movement
IUG	Islamic University of Gaza
JNF	Jewish National Fund
OPT	Occupied Palestinian Territories
PA	Palestinian Authority, renamed PNA – the Palestinian National Authority
PFLP	Popular Front for the Liberation of Palestine
PLC	Palestinian Legislative Council
PLO	Palestine Liberation Organisation
PWWSD	Palestinian Working Woman Society for Development
SCF	Save the Children Fund
UNRWA	United Nations Relief and Works Agency for Palestine Refugees in the Near East

Bibliography

Abunimah, Ali, *One Country: a Bold Proposal to End the Israeli–Palestinian Impasse* (Henry Holt 2006)

Aloni, Udi et al., *What Does a Jew Want? On Binationalism and Other Specters* (Columbia University Press 2011)

Arrigoni, Vittorio, *Gaza: Stay Human* (Kube Publishing 2010)

Cook, Jonathan, *Israel and the Clash of Civilisations* (Pluto Press 2008)

Davis, Uri, *Apartheid Israel: Possibilities for the Struggle Within* (Zed Books 2003)

Hass, Amira, *Drinking the Sea at Gaza: Days and Nights in a Land Under Siege* (Henry Holt 1999)

Hilal, Jamil, ed., *Where Now for Palestine? The Demise of the Two-State Solution* (Zed Books 2007)

Karmi, Ghada, *In Search of Fatima* (Verso 2002)

Kemp, Martin, 'Dehumanization, Guilt and Large Group Dynamics, with Reference to the West, Israel and the Palestinians', *British Journal of Psychotherapy* (2011) 27 (4)

Levy, Gideon, *The Punishment of Gaza* (Verso 2010)

Lock, Sharyn and Irving, Sarah, *Gaza Beneath the Bombs* (Pluto Press 2010)

Milton-Edwards, Beverley and Farrell, Stephen, *Hamas: The Islamic Resistance Movement* (Polity Press 2010)

Morris, Benny, *Righteous Victims: A History of the Zionist–Arab conflict, 1881–2001* (Vintage Books 1999)

Nimni, Ephraim, ed., *The Challenge of Post-Zionism: Alternatives to Israeli Fundamentalist Politics* (Zed Books 2003)

Pappé, Ilan, *The Ethnic Cleansing of Palestine* (Oneworld Publications 2006)

Qumsiyeh, Mazin B., *Sharing the Land of Canaan: Human Rights and the Israeli–Palestinian Struggle* (Pluto Press 2004)

Reinhart, Tanya, *The Road Map to Nowhere* (Verso 2006)

Roy, Sara, *Hamas and Civil Society in Gaza: Engaging the Islamist Social Sector* (Princeton University Press 2011)

Ruthven, Malise, *Fundamentalism: A Very Short Introduction* (OUP 2007)

Said, Edward W., *Peace and its Discontents: Essays on Palestine in the Middle East Peace Process* (Vintage Books 1995)

Sandercock, Josie et al., *Peace Under Fire* (Verso 2004)

Shlaim, Avi, *The Iron Wall: Israel and the Arab World* (Penguin 2000)

Index

Note: Dervla Murphy's friends, contacts and helpers have been
gathered under the heading 'contacts'.

About the Author

Dervla Murphy is Ireland's pre-eminent travel writer. Her first book, *Full Tilt*, an account of a journey by bicycle from Ireland to India, was published in 1965. Since then she has travelled in Asia, Africa, Europe and the Americas, publishing over twenty other titles. These range from an account of trekking with her five-year-old daughter in the Indus valley in winter to  trekking with her granddaughters in a sun-soaked Cuba. In between, there have been travels in Northern Ireland during the 1970s, a volume against nuclear power, a consideration of race relations in England during the 1980s and a highly acclaimed autobiography, *Wheels Within Wheels*.

Now in her eighties and with a brand new hip, she continues to travel and remains passionate about politics, conservation and beer.

ELAND

61 Exmouth Market, London EC1R 4QL
Email: info@travelbooks.co.uk

Eland was started thirty years ago to revive great travel books which had fallen out of print. Although the list soon diversified into biography and fiction, all the titles are chosen for their interest in spirit of place. One of our readers explained that for him reading an Eland is like listening to an experienced anthropologist at the bar – she's let her hair down and is telling all the stories that were just too good to go in to the textbook.

Eland books are for travellers, and for those who are content to travel in their own minds. They open out our understanding of other cultures, interpret the unknown and reveal different environments, as well as celebrating the humour and occasional horrors of travel. We take immense trouble to select only the most readable books and many readers collect the entire series of one hundred titles.

Extracts from each and every one of our books can be read on our website, at www.travelbooks.co.uk. If you would like a free copy of our catalogue, please order it from the website, email us or send a postcard.